The Essentials of Trading

Founded in 1807, John Wiley & Sons is the oldest independent publishing company in the United States. With offices in North America, Europe, Australia, and Asia, Wiley is globally committed to developing and marketing print and electronic products and services for our customers' professional and personal knowledge and understanding.

The Wiley Trading series features books by traders who have survived the market's ever changing temperament and have prospered—some by reinventing systems, others by getting back to basics. Whether a novice trader, professional, or somewhere in between, these books will provide the advice and strategies needed to prosper today and well into the future.

For a list of available titles, visit our web site at www.WileyFinance.com.

The Essentials of Trading

From the Basics to Building
a Winning Strategy

JOHN FORMAN

WILEY

John Wiley & Sons, Inc.

Published by John Wiley & Sons, Inc., Hoboken, New Jersey.
Published simultaneously in Canada.

For general information on our other products and services or for technical support, please contact our Customer Care Department within the United States at (800) 762-2974, outside the United States at (317) 572-3993 or fax (317) 572-4002.

Wiley also publishes its books in a variety of electronic formats. Some content that appears in print may not be available in electronic books. For more information about Wiley products, visit our web site at www.wiley.com.

Library of Congress Cataloging-in-Publication Data:

Forman, John, 1969–
  The essentials of trading : from the basics to building a winning strategy / John Forman.
      p.   cm.—(Wiley trading series)
    Includes index.
    ISBN-13: 978-0-471-79063-1 (cloth)
    ISBN-10: 0-471-79063-X
    1. Securities. 2. Speculation. 3. Investment analysis. I. Title. II. Series.
  HG4521.F6157 2006
  332.64—dc22

                                                                2005034031

Printed in the United States of America.

10   9   8   7   6   5   4   3   2   1

Contents

Foreword

As a psychologist who has worked with many professional and casual traders, I have received numerous requests for reading material appropriate for those just beginning their journey through the trading world. With the publication of *The Essentials of Trading: From the Basics to Building a Winning Strategy*, John Forman has addressed this need most admirably. Intrepid souls considering the pursuit of the markets as a vocation or avocation will find in these pages a lucid, engaging, real-world account of what trading is all about.

John is the Content Editor for the popular Trade2Win web site, an online community of traders. His familiarity with trading and traders, born of this and his own direct market experience, is evident in his text. As an author myself, I know how difficult it can be to write an introductory work that avoids the twin perils of talking down to readers versus writing over their heads. John navigates this path effectively, taking readers first through the basics of placing trades and understanding how markets work and then progressing to the development of trading plans, the implementation of risk management, and the building of trading systems. His incorporation of exercises and use of examples brings topics to life, maintaining the interest of even the most hyperactive traders.

When I was writing my book *The Psychology of Trading*, I posed the questions: What is the core skill involved in trading? What separates successful traders from their many, less-successful counterparts? The answer I came up with—and that the intervening years of experience have validated for me—is that the essence of trading is *pattern recognition*. Experienced traders become keen observers of bids and offers, flows of volume, and price shifts that are the hallmarks of auction markets. Over time, they become sensitized to repetitions of these patterns and learn to identify these as they are occurring.

Research in psychology refers to this process of pattern acquisition as *implicit learning.* It is how little children learn to speak grammatically even though they cannot enunciate the formal rules of grammar. Most successful traders cannot verbalize their expertise in a way that would allow another person to immediately duplicate their success, and yet it is clear that these traders do hold knowledge at an implicit level. *They know more than they know they know.* Though the end product of this knowledge seems like an intuitive hunch, it is actually a sophisticated form of understanding that results from a high level of immersion in a field of study.

Investigations across a variety of performance domains, from chess playing to athletics, suggest that years of structured, deliberative practice are needed to achieve expertise. This is why surgeons require years of study, why Olympic athletes prepare for events with years of daily practice, and why fighter pilots spend long hours on simulators before they take to the skies. Of course, not all of us who pursue trading will seek comparable levels of expertise. My experience, however, suggests that even more modest levels of trading success, such as annual profitability, require substantial investments of time and effort in implicit learning. You will need to see thousands of patterns—and their myriad variations—before they begin to feel so familiar that you can pick them out of the chaotic flow of price and volume changes.

Why bother? While trading might seem like an easy way to make a living—click a mouse, place a few trades, and watch the money roll in—the reality is far different. It is not easy to sustain concentration for hour after hour, removing ourselves from social interaction and the basic security that most jobs offer. Markets are forever changing in their trending qualities and their volatility; successful strategies during one set of years often perform abysmally thereafter. Periods of losing money are common, even for the best and the brightest traders, especially at such times of market shifts. With no fixed salary, no fringe benefits, no assurances of success, and very little social recognition, why endure the lengthy learning process demanded by trading?

The answer to this question is complex, and ultimately it is psychological. The majority of people work at jobs where the outcomes of their efforts are determined by teams of individuals and many groups of teams. While this adds a valuable social dimension to the work experience, it distances workers from the concrete success or failure of their labors. I may write software code for a video game or telephony application—and I can certainly take pride in my work—but whether the end product becomes a massive hit or bomb is largely out of my hands. It depends upon the collective efforts of many others, including management, sales, and design professionals.

Trading, like individual sports, strips the layers that normally separate people from outcomes. Every trade has a profit/loss number attached to it.

At the end of the day, traders know exactly how they performed. Average workers in a mediocre business can always reassure themselves that they are doing good work, even as others make a mess of things. There are few such reassurances in trading. You either performed or you didn't: The credit for success and the responsibility for failure will lie squarely on your shoulders.

Those with a passion for trading are attracted to this challenge. They recognize that trading is one of the few activities in which individuals can directly compete with the world's finest talent and take full ownership for success or failure. Traders may be employed by firms, but ultimately they work for themselves. They decide when they will buy, sell, or hold tight. They determine their economic fates. For the passionate ones, such a prospect is more than a vocation or avocation: It is a calling.

If you are one of the ones who feels called to trading, John Forman's text will be an excellent introduction and guide. After reading it, you will not be ready to trade successfully—that, after all, requires the immersion necessary for implicit learning. You will, however, be prepared to begin your training and ready yourself for the challenges that lie ahead. Look hard enough, and you will find qualified mentors and helpful, experienced colleagues at trading firms and in online communities such as Trade2Win. They will help you build upon the knowledge you gain from this book and accelerate your learning curve. You are about to embark upon a journey. May it be profitable—in all respects!

BRETT N. STEENBARGER, PH.D.
www.brettsteenbarger.com

November 2005
Naperville, Illinois

Preface

This book started with the intention of providing university finance and economics students with a practical, real-world resource they could use to learn about trading the financial markets. While structuring the text, I had in mind the length and progression of a standard college semester-long course. In fact, even before I started putting it all into book format, the contents and presentation that follow were successfully applied in a series of university level graduate and undergraduate financial markets and managerial economics courses.

Anyone who has been through a finance curriculum knows that most modern financial coursework is biased toward application in an institutional environment. It does not provide much direct use to the individual in terms of personal investment, risk management, and/or speculative efforts. This text seeks to take a different approach, one that focuses more directly on the individual, but with institutional carryover application of use to those who are, or eventually will become, involved in decision making at that level.

That all said, this book was written for anyone and everyone. While a general knowledge of the financial markets is useful, it is not required. Most of the students with whom I have worked over the past several years had some knowledge of things like the stock market, but they were complete novices to actually trading. For that reason, this book starts at the very beginning, so that no reader—student or otherwise—is forced to play catch-up.

In the course of presenting the basic trading materials, the text touches on some topics that are likely to be new to the reader. I have, throughout, tried to address these concepts in a concise manner. There is not sufficient room here, however, to go into detail on every possible subject put forward, and I have no way of knowing for sure what subjects any given reader will need more information on and what they will not. For that reason, the additional resource of this book's dedicated web site (www.andurilonline.com/book) has been developed to allow readers to research specific topics of interest to them in an up-to-date fashion, which cannot be accomplished by a printed work in these rapidly changing times. It also provides access to the support tools mentioned at various points in the text, as well as to the free companion workbook materials designed to complement this book.

The first portion of this text is Chapters 1 and 2 lays the basic groundwork. The Introduction discusses recent changes in the financial arena and the impact they have had on the individual and their ability to actively participate. The Getting Started section takes the reader through the process of opening a demo trading account for the use of practice (so-called "paper") trading via a hypothetical ("demo") account. The third section, Trading Mechanics, steps through the actual process of executing transactions—making, managing, and monitoring trades.

The second portion of the text is Chapter 3 in which the focus shifts to understanding the markets and how they move. In the lead is Influences on Price, the section in which the various market movers are discussed—answering the question "Why?" Following that, in Price Movement, is a look at the actual way prices move from a quantitative viewpoint, taking a more "How?" approach.

It is in the third section of the book that the heavy lifting gets done, starting with Chapter 4. The concept of the Trading Plan is introduced and defined. Within that overall structure, in Chapter 5, the reader is taken through a discussion of Risk Management and then in Chapter 6 an exploration of the types of Market Analysis. That is carried forward into the Trading System Development and Evaluation process.

The subject matter is finally wrapped up with an exploration of topics that may not be quantifiable in all cases, but nevertheless play an important role in the trading process, to include elements of trading psychology. There are also some recommendations proffered as to courses for further learning and education.

Throughout the book, there are exercises at each stage. They are specifically designed to lead the reader through practical application of the materials and intended to get the reader taking an active role in the learning process. If done in a contentious manner, these Homework assignments will help the reader develop comfort and familiarity with the materials presented.

The overall guiding element of this book is practical application. At the completion of the chapters that follow, the reader should feel quite at home executing trades and monitoring trading positions. In addition, they will have a firm understanding of the decision-making process in which the acts of trading are encapsulated. Finally, the reader should be well positioned to move ahead in the determination of the best trading arena in which to operate, how best to do so from a personal perspective, and how to develop strategies designed to generate profitable trading.

Please note, it is not the author's design to provide a specific method or set of methods to make money in the markets. Rather, it is the intent to provide a base of knowledge and understanding from which the reader may develop trading methods, systems, techniques, and so on best suited to themselves.

The examples used in the pages that follow should not be taken in any way as trading recommendations or as endorsements of any particular trading strategy, method, system, or philosophy.

For additional resources that support this text, refer to the web page set up for you at www.andurilonline.com/book.

Acknowledgements

No significant project can be completed by one individual in a vacuum, this book included. My friends, family, and colleagues were an ever-present source of support and inspiration. The folks at Wiley deserve special thanks, as does Brett Steenbarger, who has been so supportive and helpful through the whole process of developing and publishing this book.

I would also like to most sincerely thank Dr. Gordon Dash for his many years of partnership, with further acknowledgments directed to those University of Rhode Island students who were part of the classes and discussions that motivated the creation of this text. Your questions, comments, and willingness to explore were of immense value to this project.

Heartfelt gratitude goes out to the staff of Trade2Win for their help and encouragement, especially Fran Oliver for his editorial assistance and Paul Gould for his understanding of the impact many, many hours in front of the screen were having on my productivity at the time.

Thanks to my coaching colleague, Diane Short. You may not always understand my motivations in taking on projects like this, but you are always willing to listen when I need to get things off my chest.

I also want to acknowledge the outstanding women of the Brown University volleyball team, past and present. It means more than you'll ever know that you have allowed me to be a part of your life experience. You are a constant source of inspiration and, of course, entertainment. And to all the families who support them, my thanks. You have raised fantastic daughters.

Last, but certainly not least, I would like to acknowledge all those traders out there making a go of it. This book is for you and about you. Keep chasing the dream!

About the Author

John Forman holds a B.S. in Business Administration from the University of Rhode Island and an M.B.A. from the University of Maryland, both with concentrations in finance. He has nearly 20 years' experience trading and investing in a wide array of markets, and a background as a professional analyst covering the foreign exchange, fixed income, and energy markets.

John is currently Content Editor for Trade2Win (www.trade2win.com), a free community web site for active traders around the world. He is also a principal of Anduril Analytics (www.andurilonline.com), a group dedicated to financial markets education and research.

John is author of numerous articles on trading methods and analytic techniques, and has been quoted in major financial periodicals. He is active in financial education, regularly speaking with student groups and working on the development of educational programs and materials, especially at the university level.

Away from the financial markets, John coaches volleyball at the collegiate and youth level, among his other varied interests.

CHAPTER 1

Introduction and Getting Started

I n this chapter we define our topic, discuss recent developments in trading and what they mean for the individual, and get the reader ready for
the practical work that comes in future chapters.

NASDAQ E-MINI Continuous (1,545.00, 1,576.50, 1,499.50, 1,517.00, -28.0000)

INTRODUCTION

This portion of the text draws the reader into the realm of participation in the modern financial markets. There is a bit of history involved to set the stage, but this is hardly the place for an extended lesson on the development of markets and financial intermediation. That can be left for further study. Instead, the focus is on establishing the terminology and setting the parameters by which we operate through the remainder of the text. To that end, let us jump right in.

> *Note:* Throughout this text there are a large number of terms used. Reader knowledge of some terms is assumed, while others are explained in greater or lesser detail. If there is a term used with which you are unfamiliar or for which you would just like more information, a great resource to utilize for definitions and in-depth explanations is the Trade2Win Traderpedia, which can be found at www.trade2win.com/traderpedia.

Definitions

In order to explore trading, one first must define the term and explain the environment in which it occurs. At its core, trading is executing buy and sell transactions in the financial markets. This can be done through an individual account such as those with a stock brokerage firm, or through an institutional operation like that of a bank, investment house, or corporate treasury department. There are a great many financial instruments and markets through which transactions are exchanged on an ever increasingly global scale.

Actually, the aforementioned transactions are often not executed by those whose accounts they are to benefit, but rather through some kind of intermediary. An example is a floor trader at an exchange buying stock on behalf of an individual through a brokerage account. In Chapter 2, we discuss the actual transfer of financial instruments, and the mechanics by which that is accomplished. That is not, however, the intended overall focus of this book. Rather, for the purposes of this text we concentrate on the reasons for and consequences of those transactions.

The working definition of "trading" from which we operate herein is, in general terms, "the purchase and/or sale of financial vehicles for the purposes of pursuing speculative profits." This is not the sole purpose of trading, of course, but for the sake of what we are developing in this text, it provides a comprehensive point of reference for the diversity of trading that actually takes place in the modern markets.

Also, it should be noted that for the purposes of this book, the terms "trading" and "investing" can be considered interchangeable. They are often given slightly different definitions in application, and one could go into a lengthy discourse defining the differences, but at their basic level they function in what amounts to virtually identical fashions. As a result, though we use the term "trading" throughout, the principles discussed are equally applicable to "investing."

If so desired, one can further narrow down the concept of trading. This is often done in terms of time. Day traders are in and out of positions strictly during the span of a trading session (as defined by the market in which they trade), with no overnight positions. So-called swing traders take positions that they expect to hold for one to three trading days. Other traders measure their holding periods in days to weeks, or weeks to months. There is also a group known as scalpers who measure their trades in minutes, looking to take quick, small profits. The time frame in question matters little, however. The same overriding objectives apply, and they are the subject of this text.

Traders also define themselves in other manners. Some do so by the type of analytic method they use. Others base their definition on the market or markets in which they operate. Still others classify themselves by the trading platform or transactional method used. One could, if so desired, have a rather lengthy description of them. For example, the author at times considers himself a "technical S&P futures swing trader," while at other times a "hybrid stock options position trader," and at others a "quantitative spot forex day trader." These varied categories become more clear as we progress.

Financial Markets Readily Available to the Individual Trader

- *Equities:* Stocks and shares representing ownership in companies.
- *Indices:* Composite market indicators that track the movement in a collection of assets or securities such as stocks (Dow, S&P, FTSE), commodities (CRB Index), foreign exchange (Dollar Index), and others.
- *Fixed Income:* Eurocurrency, government debt instruments, corporate bonds, mortgage-backed securities, and other related instruments.
- *Foreign exchange (forex):* Currency exchange rates.
- *Commodities:* Primarily (but not exclusively) tangible goods like metals, energy products, and agricultural goods.

The markets and instruments just mentioned can be traded in a number of fashions via exchanges, over-the-counter (OTC), electronically, or through interbank transactions, and either directly or through the use of derivatives.

There are also a number of growing nontraditional methods for speculating in the markets, such as spread and fixed odd betting.

Modern Trading

Effectively trading the financial markets in some of the shorter-term time frames just mentioned once was quite difficult. The only way the individual trader could get real-time intraday price data was to be at the exchange or in a broker's office watching the ticker. Transaction costs were high, volumes were lower, and bid–offer spreads were wider. This meant that the individual trader had to be well capitalized in order for the cost of trading not to have significant impact on the performance of their portfolio or account. Traders were also limited as to the number of different markets they could play.

Things have changed significantly in that regard. The modern individual trader can access information from across the globe at a moment's notice. He can trade in several different markets simultaneously. She can operate from almost anywhere in the world, executing orders nearly instantly day or night. Transaction costs are a fraction of what they were, and spreads have narrowed sharply across the board. Today's trader has market access that just a few years ago was restricted to only the big institutions and hedge funds. Technology has changed the landscape.

The combination of widespread access and the rapid stock market climb of the late 1990s created a huge interest in trading in general and day trading specifically. The seemingly easy way one could make money in the market drew new traders by the boatload. One could hardly get through a week without hearing about someone who had quit their job to trade full-time. The stories were fantastic. There was money just waiting to be made!

Market Changes

Then came 2000. After Y2K was ushered in, with far less drama than so many predicted, things started to change. The stock market continued to go higher in the early part of the year, but quickly rolled over and started a massive decline. The NASDAQ eventually would lose about 75 percent of its value. Suddenly, it was not so fun or easy to be a trader in stocks. Those who had developed a good, comprehensive strategy were able to survive. Some even thrived. Many, many more watched in shock as their portfolios plummeted in value. Their departure from the market can be seen in Figure 1.2.

Figure 1.2 is a monthly bar chart of the Standard & Poor's (S&P) 500 index futures. Notice how volume (the bottom bar display) actually peaked in 1998, two years before the market topped. See also how average true range (middle plot) peaked in 2001 and has been declining ever since. Average true range (ATR) is a measure of how much actual price movement is taking place (measured in points). Interestingly, the monthly

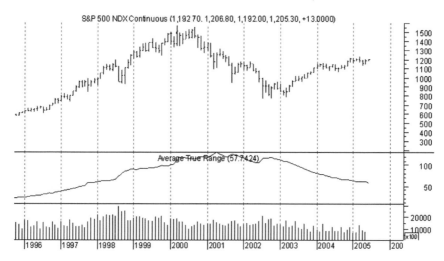

FIGURE 1.2   S&P 500 Futures, 10 Years Continuous
Source: Metastock.

trading ranges (as measured by ATR) seen in late 2004 are very close to what they were in 1998 at the volume peak.

The withdrawal of the individual speculator is a big factor in both the relative decline in volume over the past several years and the narrowing of the ranges seen since the peak in 2001. This is a recurrence of a similar situation that took place in the 1980s and early 1990s. Refer to Figure 1.3.

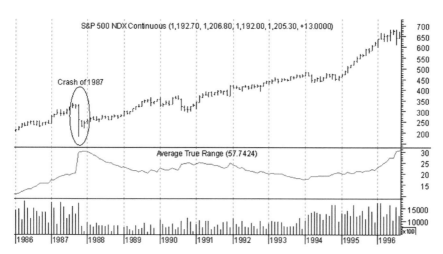

FIGURE 1.3   S&P 500 Futures, 1986–1996
Source: Metastock.

Again we are looking at the S&P 500 index futures, but the time span has been shifted back about 10 years to show the Crash of 1987 and what happened in the subsequent years. Notice how both volume and ATR peaked out at around the time of the crash. Both then dropped significantly thereafter as the trading public withdrew from the markets. It took nearly a decade for volatility and volume to return, even though the market was steadily moving higher almost the whole time. Institutional trading such as that done by mutual funds and pension managers continued, but it took years before the public got over the trauma of the market's decline in 1987 and again became active. It would not be a reach at all to see the same sort of thing happen during the first decade of this millennium.

New Developments

The stock market was the first one to become readily accessible to the average trader. Online trading proliferated quickly in the late 1990s as Internet-based platforms were launched by brokerages both new and old, and trading online contributed to the increased public presence in the stock market. Since then, the online trading universe has continued expanding rapidly. Not only has it become possible to trade stock options and bonds of all kinds through a broker's Internet site or online platform, the individual can now also trade futures and foreign exchange (forex) electronically. In fact, the forex market has probably seen the biggest growth, and has been at the cutting edge of the technology and risk management systems underlying the pricing and execution processes.

Figure 1.4 is comparable to the previous one of the S&P 500, covering about the past 10 years. It depicts the rate of exchange between the U.S. dollar and the Canadian dollar in terms of the number of Canadian dollars it takes to equal one U.S. dollar.

Notice in the graph how volatility, as measured by ATR, has tracked steadily higher in the past decade. There was a period of flatness in the middle of the graph, but at basically the same time stock market volatility was declining, it was on the rise in the foreign exchange. This is at least partly due to the market becoming much more easily accessible to the small trader, and increasingly popular in that market segment.

The forex market is the focus for much of the trading discussion throughout this text. By no means should that be taken to imply that trading in currency exchange rates is any better or worse than trading in any other market. It is merely a reflection of the fact that forex is the biggest (daily volume in the trillions of dollars), most liquid of the global financial markets. More importantly for our purposes, it is one that can readily be traded 24 hours per day. In the education of a trader, forex is quite handy. Unlike other markets that are exchange-based, and therefore have set

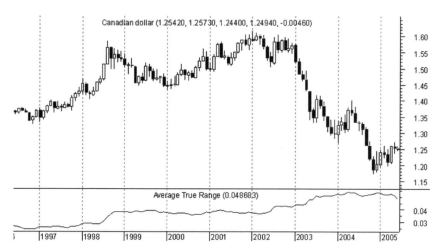

FIGURE 1.4 Canadian Dollar, 1996–2005
Source: Metastock.

hours, forex allows one to practice at whatever time is most convenient. One can also trade long and short with equal ease.

> "The market is inefficient. News is released inefficiently, volume is different across different sessions, and even forex still has the 'trading day' effect, whereby the mere fact that traders are primarily working from the early morning to the early afternoon will change the behavior of prices. Keep that in mind."—Posted on by Phantom_Photon on the Oanda FXMessage board (http://ww2.oanda.com/cgi-bin/msgboard/ultimatebb.cgi).

Efficient and Random Markets

Before continuing, take time to consider the efficient market hypothesis (EMH) and random walk theory (RWT). The EMH posits the idea that at any point in time the price of a given financial instrument reflects all relevant historical or anticipated future information. For the EMH to be true, however, there must be perfect dissemination of information and rational reaction to new data by market participants.

The EMH can be rebutted on both fronts. Taking the information dissemination first, it is essentially impossible. Traders do not all have the same access to news and information. This is partly a function of structural elements (unequal distribution of technology), partly a function of attention (traders are not all looking at the appropriate news vehicles at the same time), and partly a function of the timing of dissemination of news and information (information is not always released via all the necessary vehicles simultaneously). The result is a kind of wave result as traders get, then react to new information at differing times. Sometimes the wave is relatively short. At other times it is long and drawn out. (Using a recent class as an example, some knew that France had rejected the European constitution as soon as the vote results were announced, while others did not know for 24 hours, and still others did not know for 48 hours, all the while the euro was depreciating in reaction.)

As to the rational reaction to new information, one need look no further than to charts of actual trading to refute that idea. Figure 1.5 is a 5-second chart of the euro—U.S. dollar exchange rate (dollars per euro). What you see is the action that took place immediately following the release of important economic data. Notice the speed of the jump. In the span of about 25 seconds following the announcement (8:30), the rate moved from one relatively tight band up to start a new one.

Now you might be thinking that this would tend to support the EMH. The market, after all, is quickly assimilating new data and pricing those in. Take a look at Figure 1.6, though.

What you see in Figure 1.6 is what happened after the rapid market

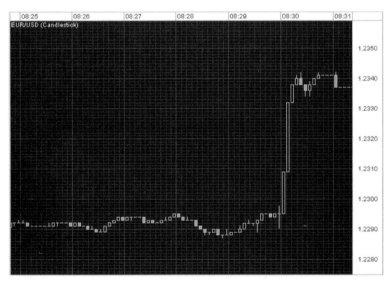

FIGURE 1.5   EUR/USD 10-Second Chart 8:25–8:31
Source: Oanda.

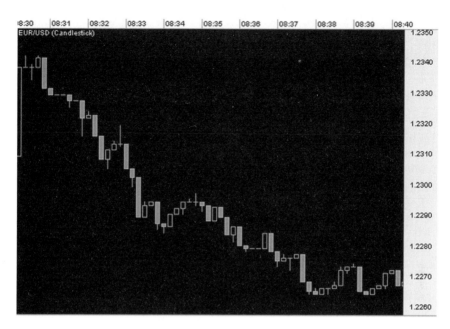

FIGURE 1.6   EUR/USD 10-Second Chart 8:30–8:40
Source: Oanda.

jump. In only a couple of minutes following the initial reaction, the market
moved right back down to where it started, and in fact moved even lower.

What Figures 1.5 and 1.6 demonstrate is the human side of the markets—the sometimes emotional, irrational side. The data released were
clearly not in line with expectations. Traders reacted swiftly, sending the
market higher in a flurry of action. When cooler heads prevailed, however,
things settled down and all of that excitement proved to be irrational.

Shifting to the RWT, the theory is that market movement depends
upon news, and since news is unpredictable, so, too, are the actions of the
markets. While we have seen in the preceding figures that news can be unpredictable, we can also see that price movement comes from more than
just data. As will be seen later in the book, markets are influenced by multiple events and factors.

Although the RWT does not necessarily state this, many observers
equate the appearance of randomness as meaning the markets are random. The argument goes something like this: If you plot some random action, such as the results of a coin toss, the chart that comes about looks a
lot like the chart of a stock or other instrument. Random series often have
patterns akin to those of market action. While that is so, it is a fallacy to
say that just because a thing shares a common appearance to something

random that it is random itself. It does not work that way. One cannot prove randomness, as to do so would require proving the absolute lack of any nonrandom behavior.

Moving Forward

So where does that leave us? Most market participants will generally accept that the markets are mostly efficient, especially the ones with large volume and high participation. At the same time, the best traders can often be heard to comment on how any given trade is subject to the whims of chance, a reflection that there is indeed a random element in the market. The premise of trading as we have defined it, however, is that an individual or institution can find opportunities in the markets providing better than 50/50 odds at success. By exploiting these situations consistently, traders can produce profits over time. The remainder of this text concentrates on the process by which traders attempt to do just that.

This book is not intended to be a "how to make a lot of money in the markets" manual. There will be no presentation of specific trading systems or techniques, except by way of example. Instead, the focus of this text is to first provide a base education on the process of trading the financial markets. The starting point in the next chapter will be execution.

GETTING STARTED

There is a wide array of online trading platforms available to the individual these days. Throughout this text we show examples based on Oanda's FXTrade platform. Please see Figure 1.7. FXTrade is preferred for our purposes here for four important reasons:

1. *Foreign Exchange* FXTrade focuses on forex. We have already commented on how forex is a 24-hour market. That is optimal for the trading student as it allows for practice at any time of the day or night and is not restricted by exchange hours, as is true for many other markets.

2. *Unlimited Duration Demo Accounts* Most trading platforms provide free demo accounts, but they are normally only good for a fixed period of time (like 30 days). FXTrade's demo accounts (called "game" accounts) are open-ended. Once you sign up, it is yours for good, even if you eventually open a real account.

3. *Variable Trade Sizes* FXTrade's platform literally allows trades at any transaction size desired, within margin requirements, of course. That means one could trade 1 unit, or 10 units, or 12,132 units. This is a

FIGURE 1.7 Oanda FXTrade Logo
Source: Oanda.

great feature when it comes to risk management. Other platforms have fixed transaction sizes with minimums of 10,000 units (some 100,000) with trade sizes multiples thereof.

4. *No Lower Limit to Real Account Sizes* Most trading platforms, when one sets up a real-money account, require minimum deposits that can range anywhere from $2,000 to $10,000 (or the equivalent in the account's base currency). FXTrade has no minimum. One can literally start with $1.

A lot of other goodies also go along with the platform, but we address those later. (*Note:* The author has used both demo and live versions of the Oanda FXTrade/FXGame platform for a number of years, and continues to do so, but has no beneficial relationship with Oanda.)

Opening an Account

The reader's first assignment, and first step on the path of trading education, is to open an FXTrade game account. Start by going to the FXTrade web site at http://fxtrade.oanda.com. Look for the Open Demo Account link in the upper left-hand corner of the page. Click that to go to the sign-up page.

The form there is fairly straightforward. Follow the instructions as listed. The one section of the form you will need to decide upon is the Account Currency selection in the Account Details area. FXTrade allows for accounts denominated in U.S. dollars, Australian dollars, euros, British pounds, Japanese yen, and Canadian dollars. Generally, the best course of action is to select your home currency, making things easiest for your personal accounting of gains and losses. For the purposes of this text, we will use a U.S. dollar account.

As tempting as it might be right now, opening a real-money account is not recommended. First, learn how to trade. Then you can take the leap into live trading. There is a whole discussion of that very topic later in this text.

After the online form is completed, there will be a confirmation process before the account becomes active. Just follow the instructions. Once that is done and your registration is complete, log in.

(*Note:* The FXTrade platform is based on a Java applet. You may have some system requirements to meet in order to use it. The FXTrade web site provides a very good support section that should help resolve any such technical issues.)

Now that you are ready to go, let's take a look the FXTrade platform. The screen you will see upon logging in for the first time will look something like what you see in Figure 1.8. If it's all a bit foreign, don't worry. (*Note:* The examples provided below and throughout the remainder of this text were valid at the time of its writing. Oanda could, of course, make modifications to the FXTrade platform at any time. They have made numerous improvements during the author's years trading via their service, and will no doubt continue to do so.)

The platform has four basic sections. Each is addressed specifically

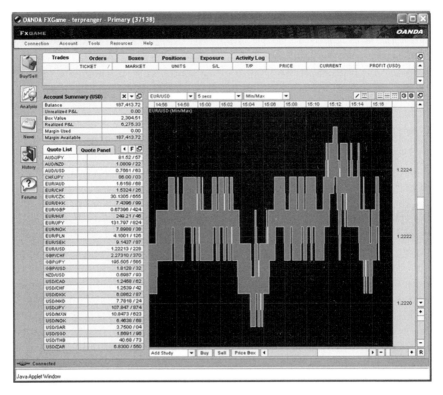

FIGURE 1.8 Oanda FXTrade: Initial Screen
Source: Oanda.

either in this section as we go about preparing to trade, or in the next where we actually start working on making transactions.

Much of what you see on the platform is customizable to your taste and needs. What you see on initial launch is based on the FXTrade default settings. These are easy to change. Many of them can be adjusted through the Tools/User Preferences menu selection, which brings up the box in Figure 1.9.

These are all things that you can modify to your own preferences as you work with the system. Three items we recommend you change:

1. Click the Ignore Weekend Data check box, then the Hide Weekend Data box. For your Weekend Start you can safely use your local equivalent of Friday, 5 P.M. Eastern, and Sunday, 6 P.M. Eastern is a good Weekend End point. Those setting changes will make the graph more readable by eliminating the time when the market really is not trading.
2. Change the Profit Column Format (right-hand column) to Home Currency. Its default setting is PIPs. That means when you are monitoring

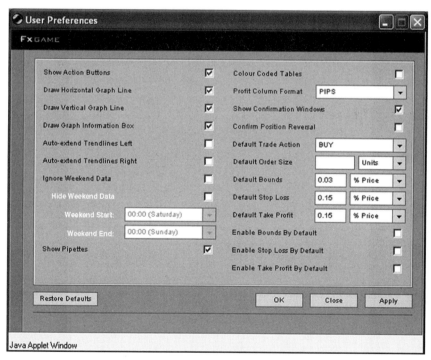

FIGURE 1.9 Oanda FXTrade: User Preferences Screen
Source: Oanda.

an open position, you will see it in real terms rather than as points. That will let you better see your performance in actual account terms.

3. Click the Confirm Position Reversal box. This will give you a notice when a new order would reverse an existing position (long to short or vice versa).

What we end up with is Figure 1.10.

The remainder of the options can be changed later as you start to become more familiar with the platform and establish your trading patterns to suit your needs and/or preferences. For now, you can click OK and we will move onward.

If you would like to change the font size setting for the platform, that can be done through the Tools menu.

There are two other things you will want to consider changing.

4. The graph display. The default is a 5-second graph using the Min/Max format. You will see three drop-downs above the graph with which you can change the currency pair displayed, the time frame used, and

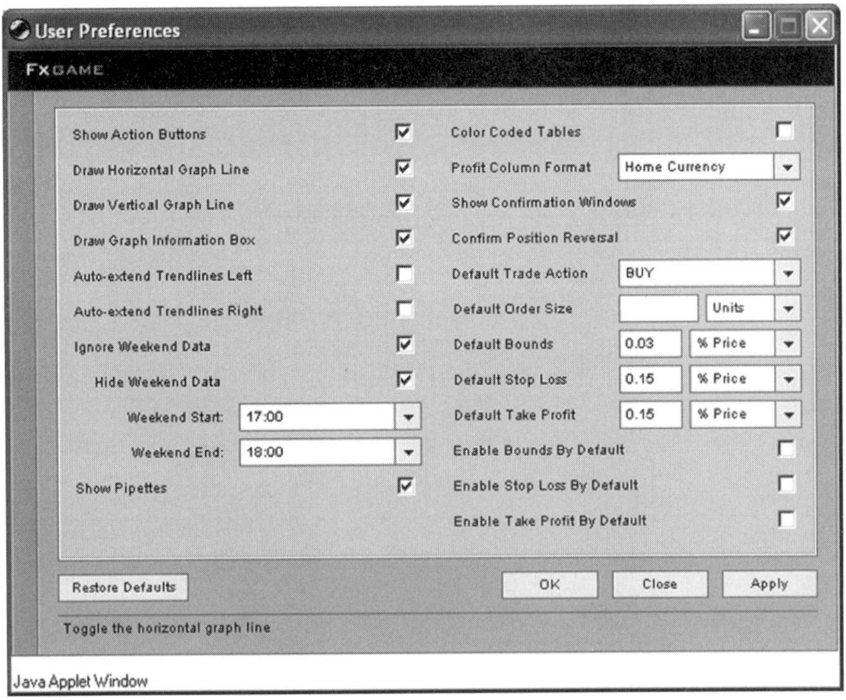

FIGURE 1.10   Oanda FXTrade: User Preferences Screen
Source: Oanda.

graph type. Next to those are buttons to further refine your graph choice in terms of the specific data being displayed and/or to draw lines directly on the chart. On the right-hand side and below the graph to the right are some slider bars and +/− buttons that can be used to alter the scaling of the graph.

You will also notice a drop-down below the graph on the left, which is labeled Add Study. That is for overlaying one of a number of technical indicators on the chart. We address technical analysis and indicators at a later point. (You can open additional chart windows by clicking on the currency pair in the quote list. It will have the same format and settings as the main one.)

5. The currency list determines the currency pairs available in the drop-down above the chart and the ones appearing in the quote area on the left-hand side of the platform. To make your selections, go to the Tools menu again, and pick the Market Selector to get the dialog box shown in Figure 1.11.

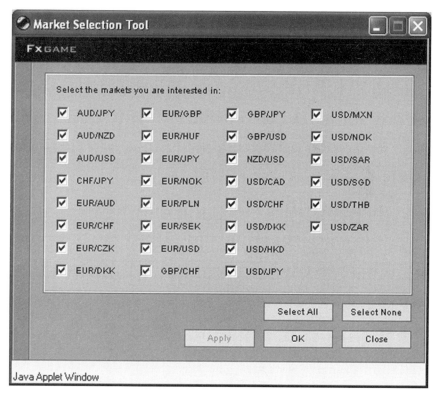

FIGURE 1.11 Oanda FXTrade: Currency Selector Screen
Source: Oanda.

You want the currency pairs selected to be the ones you are going to trade. At a minimum, it is recommended you pick USD/JPY, EUR/USD, GBP/USD, USD/CHF, EUR/JPY, EUR/GBP, EUR/CHF, GBP/JPY, AUD/USD, and USD/CAD. These are the most active and liquid currency pairs. You can select others as well. Just remember that many are more regional in nature, and won't necessarily trade as actively, especially outside their primary time zone. (*Note:* Oanda, from time to time, adds new pairs to this list. In theory, pairs could be removed as well.)

Forex Reference Nomenclature

Each currency has a three letter code. These are the SWIFT or ISO Codes, which are combined in pairs to define the exchange rate between two currencies. The pairs are listed using the base/quote format, for example: EUR/USD. This is the exchange rate between the euro (EUR) and the U.S. dollar (USD) quoted as dollars (quote currency) per euro (base currency). The major currencies (those most heavily traded) are:

EUR: European euro

USD: U.S. dollar

GBP: British pound

CHF: Swiss franc

JPY: Japanese yen

AUD: Australian dollar

(*Note:* A currency pair not including USD (such as EUR/JPY) is generally referred to as a cross-rate or cross.) To find additional codes see: www.oanda.com/products/fxlookup.

Once you have your chart set up to your liking, and all your preferences sorted out, go again to the Tools menu. Then click the Save Current Layout selection. That will assure that the next time you log in you will have the same trading screen settings.

With those selections made, we are ready to more thoroughly explore the trading window.

Starting at the top of the FXTrade screen, you see the following tabs:

Trades: Orders that have been executed and remain open.

Orders: Open orders yet to be executed.

Boxes: Strictly for box option positions. We do not cover that topic at the moment. (Refer to Appendix A.)

Positions: Currently open long and/or short positions. (*Note:* the Trades tab may show multiple executed transactions in a single currency pair—for example; trades buying EUR/USD in sizes of 50,000 and 35,000—while the Positions tab would aggregate those open orders into one line item, in this case long 85,000 EUR/USD.)

Exposure: Currently open net positions in individual currencies, as opposed to pairs. If you had a 10,000 long position in USD/JPY from 125.00 and a 10,000 short position in USD/CAD at 1.2500 the Exposure tab would show a 1,250,000 short position in JPY and a 12,500 long position in CAD with no net position in USD (the two USD positions offset each other).

Activity Log: A history of trades, orders, and interest transactions.

Throughout the course of your trading you will make use of this information on a steady basis. Simply put, it is how you keep track of what is happening in your account. We go into further details on each of these tabs and what they show later on as we progress through the actual steps of trading.

For the time being, do not worry about the buttons on the left-hand side of the screen. Only the top one (Buy/Sell) is important. We deal with that extensively later. The other buttons are for content specific to the FX-Trade system. Feel free to explore them as additional learning tools, though they do not directly relate to trade execution.

The next area of interest on your trading screen is the Account Summary table, as shown in Figure 1.12. Note the "(USD)" to the right of the table's title bar. That indicates the account is denominated in USD, and that the figures in the table are presented in dollar terms. As you noted in your initial registration, FXTrade offers accounts denominated in several other currencies.

Account Summary (USD)	☒ ▼ ⬚
Balance	187,413.72
Unrealized P&L	0.00
Box Value	2,263.19
Realized P&L	6,275.33
Margin Used	0.00
Margin Available	187,413.72

FIGURE 1.12 Oanda FXTrade: Account Summary
Source: Oanda.

The Account Summary table shows several interesting and important items:

Balance: The amount of capital in the account, inclusive of the profits or losses on closed trades to date, plus or minus any interest earned or paid. This does not include the profit or loss on open trades.

Unrealized P&L: The net gain or loss on currently open positions.

Box Value: The current value of open box options positions.

Realized P&L: The net gain or loss on closed positions since the account's inception. (Balance = Deposits − Withdrawals + Realized P&L)

Margin Used: The amount of capital tied up for margin on active positions. Margin is discussed extensively in the next chapter.

Margin Available: Capital available for margin on future newly entered positions. This amount is based not on the Balance, but on your net position (Balance +/− Unrealized P&L).

Obviously, knowing this information is important in gauging the success of your trading methods and planning for future activity.

Below the Account Summary is the current rates table. These numbers are real-time in nature and tradable. As the rates change, those adjustments are reflected in the trading platform. FXTrade uses up and down arrows. You can monitor the activity of the various pairs relatively easily in this kind of table. How much the rates change depends on the activity level in the markets. Busy, high volume days will see more rate moves than slow, lackluster sessions. Further, there are times of the day when market activity is higher than at other times. Please see Figure 1.13.

Be aware that by clicking the arrow next to the *F* you can either display or hide the spread. The spread, as you can see, is the difference between the bid and offer. (*Note:* The screen shot in Figure 1.14 was taken late on a Friday afternoon, which is when weekend spreads take effect. Spreads during normal times are significantly narrower.)

Take note of the two pairs at the bottom—USD/MXN and USD/ZAR. They are the dollar rate of exchange against the Mexican peso and South African rand, respectively. These are regional currencies that do not trade as actively as the majors. That is reflected rather dramatically in the spreads.

If you click on the Quote Panel, you will get the screen shown in Figure 1.15 as an alternative display. Each of the currency pairs is shown with the bid price on top and the offer price below it.

The major currencies pairs (USD/JPY, EUR/USD, GBP/USD, EUR/JPY, EUR/GBP) trade 24 hours a day, across all of the global centers, while

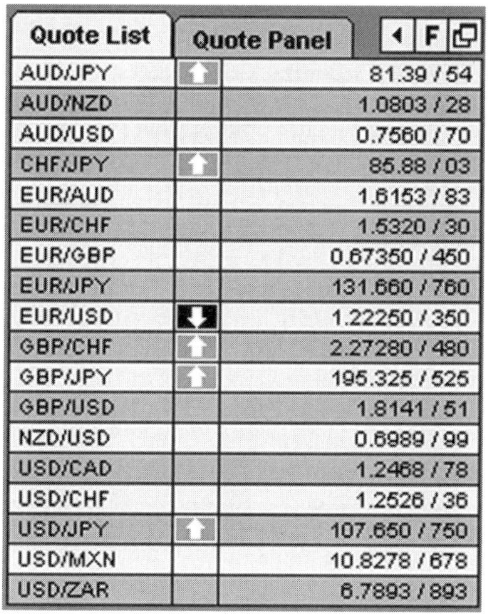

Quote List	Quote Panel	◄ F ⟐
AUD/JPY	⬆	81.39 / 54
AUD/NZD		1.0803 / 28
AUD/USD		0.7560 / 70
CHF/JPY	⬆	85.88 / 03
EUR/AUD		1.6153 / 83
EUR/CHF		1.5320 / 30
EUR/GBP		0.67350 / 450
EUR/JPY		131.660 / 760
EUR/USD	⬍	1.22250 / 350
GBP/CHF	⬆	2.27280 / 480
GBP/JPY	⬆	195.325 / 525
GBP/USD		1.8141 / 51
NZD/USD		0.6989 / 99
USD/CAD		1.2468 / 78
USD/CHF		1.2526 / 36
USD/JPY	⬆	107.650 / 750
USD/MXN		10.8278 / 678
USD/ZAR		6.7893 / 893

FIGURE 1.13 Oanda FXTrade: Price Quotes
Source: Oanda.

Quote List	Quote Panel		► F ⟐
AUD/JPY		81.40 / 55	15
AUD/NZD		1.0803 / 28	25
AUD/USD		0.7560 / 70	10
CHF/JPY		85.87 / 02	15
EUR/AUD		1.6151 / 81	30
EUR/CHF		1.5321 / 31	10
EUR/GBP		0.67340 / 440	10
EUR/JPY	⬆	131.670 / 770	10
EUR/USD		1.22240 / 340	10
GBP/CHF	⬍	2.27310 / 510	20
GBP/JPY		195.345 / 545	20
GBP/USD		1.8141 / 51	10
NZD/USD		0.6989 / 99	10
USD/CAD		1.2468 / 78	10
USD/CHF	⬍	1.2528 / 38	10
USD/JPY		107.660 / 760	10
USD/MXN		10.8283 / 683	400
USD/ZAR		6.7893 / 893	1000

FIGURE 1.14 Oanda FXTrade: Price Quotes
Source: Oanda.

Quote List	Quote Panel		F ⊡
AUD/JPY	AUD/NZD	AUD/USD	CHF/JPY
81.50	1.0828	0.7565	86.05
81.35	1.0803	0.7555	85.90
EUR/AUD	EUR/CHF	EUR/GBP	EUR/JPY
1.8194	1.5329	0.67450	131.780
1.8164	1.5319	0.67350	131.680
EUR/USD	GBP/CHF	GBP/JPY	GBP/USD
1.22360	2.27460	195.555	1.8152
1.22260	2.27260	195.355	1.8142
NZD/USD	USD/CAD	USD/CHF	USD/JPY
0.6999	1.2470	1.2534	107.760
0.6989	1.2460	1.2524	107.660
USD/MXN	USD/ZAR		
10.8683	6.8918		
10.8283	6.7918		

FIGURE 1.15   Oanda FXTrade: Price Quotes
Source: Oanda.

more regional currencies will experience very inactive trading outside their primary time zone. For example, the SGD (Singapore dollar) is quiet most of the time in the U.S. afternoon.

As you watch the rates fluctuate, if you have an active trade on, you will also see real-time changes in your position, and by extension, your account value. More on that later.

Now that we have explored the vehicle through which you will be executing your transactions, we can move on to start learning how to use it.

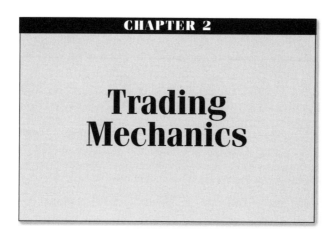

CHAPTER 2

Trading
Mechanics

In this chapter we begin trading. All facets of the basic elements of trade execution and position management and monitoring are introduced and discussed.

THE BASICS

Trading is incredibly easy these days. Click a few buttons on your computer and you can move huge amounts of money around. That is exactly why one must understand what actually happens when trades are executed. It is VERY easy to make a costly mistake. This section of the text lays the groundwork for the actual trade execution, which is discussed later.

Price Quotes

The first thing each trader needs to understand is how to read prices. There are two types. One is traded price. That is what can be found each day in the business section of a newspaper. The *close*, as listed, is the actual price where the last trade of the day was transacted. Likewise, the *high* and *low* are the highest and lowest prices at which trades were made during the course of the trading session, and the *open* is the very first trade of the day. (Most likely you will also see a volume figure, indicating how many units—shares, contracts, options, and so on—were transacted during the session.)

Prices appear to be quite straightforward when viewed in this fashion. When actually trading, however, one deals with indicative price quotes. An indicative quote is a combination of two prices, referred to as the bid–offer or bid–ask. The bid can be thought of as the highest price the market is willing to pay to buy. Think of it like a bid in an auction (which is exactly what it is). The offer or ask is the lowest price at which the market will sell. It can be thought of in terms of how much the market is asking one to pay.

Refer to the FXTrade quote screen shown in Figure 2.2. These are bid–offer rates. The first one in the table is AUD/JPY, the conversion rate between the Australian dollar and the Japanese yen quoted as yen per Aussie dollar.

The first part of the current market price quote is the bid. In this case it's 81.39. The second part, after the "/" is the offer price of 54. To save space, the first part of the quote was left off, so in this example, AUD/JPY is trading at 81.39 bid–81.54 offered.

Something else to take note of is the difference between the two prices. This is referred to as the bid–offer or bid–ask spread. Small, narrow spreads indicate liquid markets. Wide spreads indicate illiquid ones. Refer to the FXTrade quotes just mentioned and notice that AUD/JPY has a spread of 15. It trades pretty actively. If you look near the bottom of the table, though, you will see USD/MXN (U.S. dollar exchange rate against the Mexican peso) with its spread of 400, suggesting a much less actively traded market.

Quote List	Quote Panel	◀ F ⧉
AUD/JPY	⬆	81.39 / 54
AUD/NZD		1.0803 / 28
AUD/USD		0.7560 / 70
CHF/JPY	⬆	85.88 / 03
EUR/AUD		1.6153 / 83
EUR/CHF		1.5320 / 30
EUR/GBP		0.67350 / 450
EUR/JPY		131.660 / 760
EUR/USD	⬆⬇	1.22250 / 350
GBP/CHF	⬆	2.27280 / 480
GBP/JPY	⬆	195.325 / 525
GBP/USD		1.8141 / 51
NZD/USD		0.6989 / 99
USD/CAD		1.2468 / 78
USD/CHF		1.2526 / 36
USD/JPY	⬆	107.650 / 750
USD/MXN		10.8278 / 678
USD/ZAR		6.7893 / 893

FIGURE 2.2 Oanda FXTrade: Price Quotes
Source: Oanda.

Traded versus Indicative Price

All markets trade bid–offer. This is the *indicative price* where trades can be made at the current time. *Traded price*, meanwhile, is where an actual transaction took place, which is generally how exchanges present data, as a collection of transactions.

It is important to recognize the difference. While in active markets there is little variance between the last traded price and the current indicative quote, the same is not true of thinly traded instruments. The options market is a prime example. Many options do not trade actively. As a result, the last traded price can be hugely different from the current bid–offer quote.

It should also be noted that traded prices can make a market seem to have moved without its actually doing so. For example, a stock is indicated at 100-102. If a sell order comes in, it would be executed at the bid of 100. If a buy order then came in, it would be filled at the offer of 102. In terms of traded price, it would look like the market moved from 100 to 102 when it did not actually move at all. This is a very important thing to keep in mind.

This brings up another point, one of terminology.

There are a couple of common terms in the market related to price. They are "pip" and "tick." In use the two terms are fairly interchangeable, though one or the other may be more used in a particular market. Both are essentially defined as the measure of a single price change unit. In the current equity market, stocks change price in cents, so one tick is equal to a penny. Other markets have other units of measure that equate to a tick or pip based on the specifics of the instruments involved. In forex, pip is used more than tick, and it can be one of two things. For exchange rates quoted with two decimal places (as AUD/JPY), a pip is $\frac{1}{100}$ of a point. In the case of those rates quoted with four decimal places (see EUR/USD in Figure 2.2) a pip is $\frac{1}{10,000}$ of a point.

It should be noted that the shrinking of the spreads in the markets has actually led to fractional pips, referred to as "pipettes" in forex. For example, the EUR/USD quote might be $^{1.36055}/_{070}$. That is a spread of 1.5 pips.

That covers price quotes. Let's move on.

Order Types

The next thing a trader needs to understand is what kinds of orders there are. Here is a listing of the various types.

Market Order: An order to be executed immediately. A market order to buy 100 shares of IBM means buy the stock at whatever the current offer price is at the time the trade is executed.

Limit Order: An order executed at a specific price, or better. That means when buying it would be at the limit price or below, while the reverse is true for a sell order. For example, a limit order to sell S&P 500 futures contracts at 1200 means the trade will be executed at or above 1200.

Stop Order (or Stop): A delayed market order of sorts. A stop order is set at a point above (for a buy) or below (for a sell) the current price. It becomes an active market order (see above) when the current price reaches or goes through that level. For example, a sell stop at 205 would be triggered if the market price touches or falls below 205. It is very important to understand that a stop order does not guarantee a fill (trade execution) at that price. It all depends on how prices are acting at the time the order is triggered. In fast moving markets, stop orders can get filled well away from where the stop was set.

Stop Limit Order: A combination of the stop and limit orders. Unlike the simple stop order, which triggers a market order when a certain price is reached, the stop limit order triggers a limit order. As such, the trader will get a fill at or better than the limit order price. This type of order is useful for getting into positions, but can be dangerous for exiting because you cannot guarantee the order gets executed.

These four orders are the most common and frequently used. There are a couple of others that can come in handy as well:

Market-on-Close (MOC) Order: A market order executed at the close of the day. With an order of this type, the trader essentially tells her broker that she wants to buy or sell at approximately the closing price for the day's session. The actual execution price may not be exactly the close, but it should be pretty close.

One-Cancels-Other (OCO): A combination of two orders in which the execution of one cancels out the other. Traders can utilize this sort of order to very good effect in a number of ways.

There are also two modifiers that are applied to an order related to its duration. They are day and good-until-cancelled (GTC). A day order is one that is good only for the current trading session. If it has not been executed when trading closes, the order is cancelled. A GTC order is one that will stay in the market until it's executed. It should be mentioned, however, that not all GTC orders are truly open-ended. Some brokers and trading platforms have fixed limits on how long an order can stay open.

In order to get a final order, the aforementioned order type is combined with one of the two qualifiers. The result is something like

Limit Buy 100 shares of IBM at 102, GTC

This translates to the following:

I want to buy 100 shares of IBM at a price of 102 or better. Please keep my order open until it is filled.

Market orders are day orders by nature.

Leverage and Margin

Leverage is the use of borrowed money (generally from one's broker/dealer) to take on a position that is larger than one would have been able to do with strictly one's own capital. The money the trader is required to deposit as surety for those borrowed funds is referred to as *margin*.

Using a real-world example, think in terms of buying a house. Most home buyers do not pay 100 percent of the price in cash. In most cases the buyer can pay a certain percentage, which is referred to as the down payment, but must borrow the remainder. This is the application of leverage and the down payment can be thought of as margin.

In the markets, leverage and margin are used in one of two fashions. One can put up margin and apply leverage to take control of a collection of assets larger than they would have been able to do otherwise, as in buying a house. Alternatively, the deposit's margin is applied as surety for the future fulfillment of an agreement to exchange assets (forward or futures contract).

An example of how this works in the market can be seen in stocks. One could purchase 100 shares of a $50 stock by putting down only $2,500 on deposit—50 percent margin. Margin requirements vary from market to market in terms of what percentage must be used. In the U.S. equities markets, the trader must put up at least half the money, 50 percent. In other markets it can be a much lower percentage.

In modern trading, the use of leverage is ubiquitous. For anyone entering positions in markets such as forex, and in the futures arena, trading practically requires leverage. Doing otherwise either makes it impossible for lack of funds or ineffective due to very small changes in price.

The use of leverage presents the trader with both opportunity and risk. Leverage allows for larger profits than would be possible otherwise. Using the aforementioned stock example, if the price of the shares rose to $55, a 10 percent increase, the trader would make a 20 percent profit using

Margin: Initial versus Maintenance

Initial Margin is the deposit the trader must put down when initiating a position. Once a position is opened, the trader must keep funds equal to the *maintenance margin* in the account to cover any losses. In many cases, the maintenance margin level is half the initial margin requirement. If the initial margin requirement is 50 percent, maintenance margin might be 25 percent. In the case of a $10,000 trade, for example, where $5000 was put up for initial margin, the trader would have to keep at least $2500 in the account to avoid a margin call. [A margin call is the demand for additional funds to be deposited or the position will be closed.] The requirement varies from market to market.

Keep in mind that margin interest is charged in some markets, but not in others. For example, stock brokers charge interest on margin loans, while futures brokers do not. This is something to be aware of as it can impact trading performance.

leverage ($500/$2,500, transaction cost and interest on the margin loan not included).

Leverage works the same on the downside, though. Were the shares to instead fall $5 per share, the trader would experience a loss of 20 percent. This is why leverage is referred to as a two-edged sword. It works equally well at accelerating gains as it does at hastening losses, so it must be used conscientiously.

With leverage and margin under our belts, we can move on to doing trades.

TRADE EXECUTION

Now that the groundwork has been laid, we can move on to the actual process of executing trades using the FXTrade platform.

The Order Screen

Oanda has conveniently provided several easy ways to place a trade. One can click the Buy/Sell button on the left-hand side of the screen, click either the buy or sell buttons below the graph, or click directly on the graph to use the menu. Any choice will bring up the order screen shown in Figure 2.3.

Order screens vary across platforms, but the basics are consistent. Note at the top that there are two tabs, one for the Market Order, the other for the Limit Order. The Market Order tab is currently the active one in this example. Let's examine what we see.

Action: This is where you indicate whether you are buying or selling.

Currency: The pair to be traded. Note that the first currency listed is the currency to which the Action is referring. In this example the order is to buy EUR/JPY. That means buying EUR and selling an equivalent amount of JPY.

Units: The amount you wish to trade, in whole amounts. Again, this relates to the lead currency in the pair. Our entry of 1,000,000 means we want to buy 1,000,000 EUR and sell the equivalent amount of JPY.

A quick interjection is required at this point. FXTrade allows the user to set the leverage for the account. The default level is 50:1, which means a 2 percent margin requirement for a trade. This can be changed via the menu bar by selecting Tools/Set Margin. The demo account options range

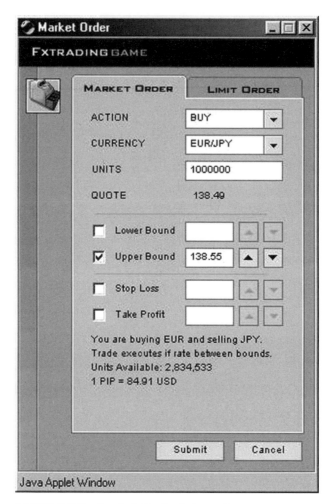

FIGURE 2.3　Oanda FXTrade: Order Ticket
Source: Oanda.

from 10:1 up to 50:1. In a live account one could go up to 100:1. The lower portion of the order screen shows Units Available, which is how large a position can be entered.

Getting back to our trade entry as shown in Figure 2.3.

Quote: The current market rate (price) for the transaction you are entering. This will be the offer (or ask) if you are buying, and the bid if you are selling. Keep in mind that the market is active. If prices change while we try to place an order, it will be reflected in the Quote. In other words, one cannot take their own sweet time entering an order and expect the price to stay the same.

Upper/Lower Bound: If entered, these are the high and low rate points beyond which you do not wish your transaction executed. In our example, we put in an Upper Bound of 138.55, meaning we do not want to buy EUR/JPY at a price higher than 138.55. This is something that can protect you from getting fills (executions) way beyond what you were expecting.

These all relate to the trade currently being entered. There are also a couple of other elements to the trade ticket.

Stop Loss: Here you may enter a stop order price for your trade.

Take Profit: Here you can enter the limit order price at which you would like to close the trade to exit with a gain.

Recall that stop and limit orders were discussed in the previous section of this chapter as were definitions of entry and exit points. For the time being you may ignore these entries on this screen. They will, however, come back into play.

You also note that at the bottom of the order screen, FXTrade actually tells you in words what the trade you are entering will do. You also are told how many units you may trade based on your available margin and the value of each pip based on the Quote and position size.

If we click on the Limit Order tab, we can see a couple of differences (see Figure 2.4).

Notice now that the Quote line allows for input. This lets you to set the price at which you wish to trade. Rather than just buying at the market, we want to buy 1,000,000 EUR/JPY when the offer hits 138.75 (remember that as buyers we buy at the offer or ask price). The trade will be executed automatically when the market reaches our predesignated point. No need for us to do anything further.

The other difference between the Market and Limit order tabs is down near the bottom. See the Duration? That allows you to dictate the time frame during which the trade will be made. In our case, we have said 12 hours. That means if EUR/JPY does not hit 138.75 within the next 12 hours, the order will be canceled. This is a reflection of the 24-hour nature of the forex market where it is difficult to define a "day trade."

(*Note:* FXTrade does not differentiate between stop and limit orders. The limit orders will operate exactly like stops or limits as we previously defined them.)

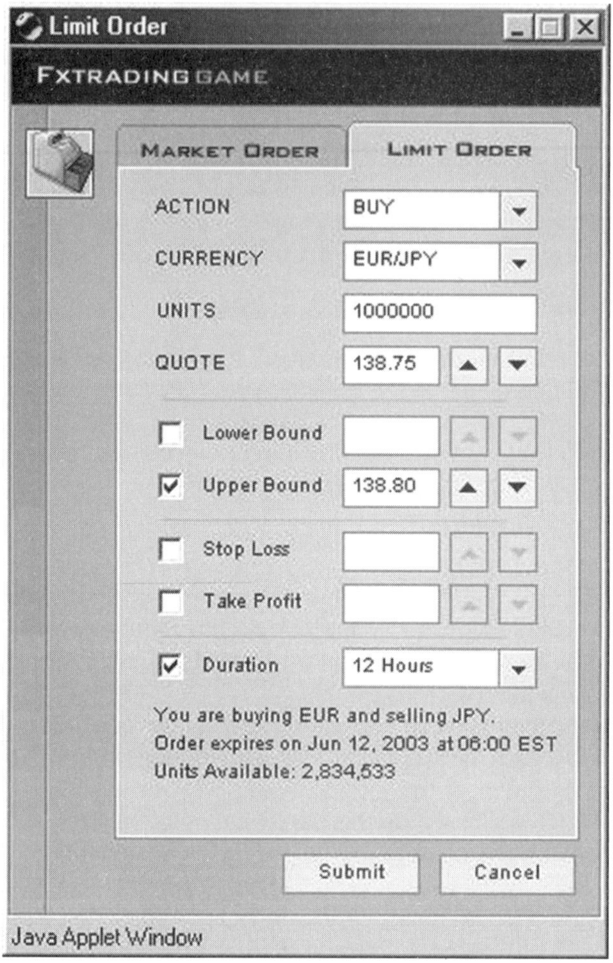

FIGURE 2.4   Oanda FXTrade: Order Ticket
Source: Oanda.

Trade Execution

Now that we know how to enter a trade, it is time to jump in and execute an actual foreign exchange trade. For this example we enter a market order to buy EUR/USD. Figure 2.5 shows our ticket from an actual trade done on an FXTrade game account.

Notice we are putting in an order to buy 1,000,000 EUR/USD. The current market quote is 1.1761 to buy.

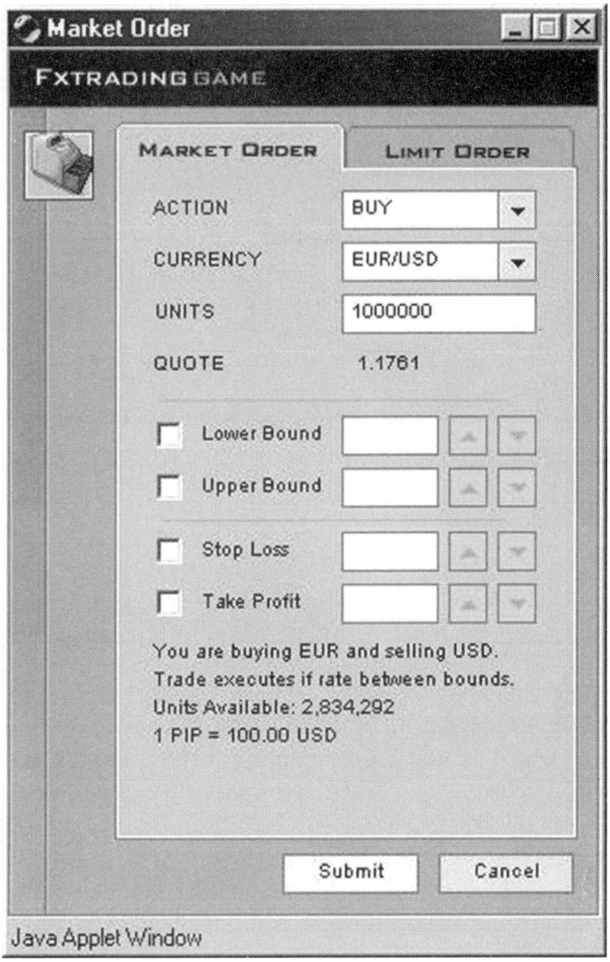

FIGURE 2.5 Oanda FXTrade: Order Ticket
Source: Oanda.

EUR/USD is a very active market, so we got a quick fill. Notice in Figure 2.6, our confirmation, that the order executed at 1.1761 and we used $58,805 in margin (5 percent).

We now have an open long position of 1,000,000 EUR/USD. We can now go through the tabs we only just touched on briefly in the last section. (In the next section we go over exactly what takes place in a foreign exchange trade.)

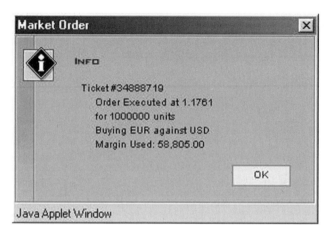

FIGURE 2.6 Oanda FXTrade: Trade Confirmation
Source: Oanda.

Trades: Our purchase of EUR/USD (long, as noted at the far left of Figure 2.7) can be seen with the size (UNITS) and executed rate (PRICE) from our confirmation.

We can also see the current rate (MARKET), in this case the bid as we would sell to get out of the position. On the right is our gain/loss (PROFIT) based on the current market price. Had we entered Stop Loss (S/L) or Take Profit (T/P) rates when we completed our order, those would have appeared in the S/L and T/P columns, respectively. (This is demonstrated shortly.)

Orders: This tab remains empty, as we have no open orders (see Figure 2.8).

Skip *Boxes.*

Positions: Since we have only our one EUR/USD trade on, the information on this tab, as shown in Figure 2.9, is the same as what we see in the **Trades** tab. If we were to have multiple open trades in the

		Trades	Orders	Boxes	Positions	Exposure	Activity Log			
		TICKET /	MARKET	UNITS	S/L	T/P	PRICE	CURRENT	PROFIT (USD)	
Buy/Sell	Long	125295200	EUR/USD	1,000,000			1,20202	1,20207	050,00	

OANDA FXGame - jhforman - Primary (9544000)
FXGAME   OANDA
Connection   Account   Tools   Resources   Help

FIGURE 2.7 Oanda FXTrade: Trades Tab
Source: Oanda.

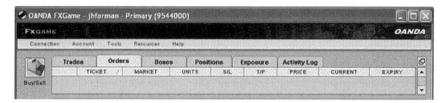

FIGURE 2.8   Oanda FXTrade: Orders Tab
Source: Oanda.

Trades	Orders	Boxes	Positions	Exposure	Activity Log		
	MARKET	/	UNITS	AVG. PRICE	CURRENT	PROFIT (USD)	
Long	EUR/USD		1,000,000	128202	1,28310	1,080.00	

FIGURE 2.9   Oanda FXTrade: Positions Tab
Source: Oanda.

same currency pair, they would be aggregated here and presented with an average entry price.

Exposure: Since we bought 1,000,000 EUR/USD we are long the EUR as seen in the Exposure tab (Figure 2.10). At our purchase rate of 1.1761, that is 1,176,100 USD. Again, this is an aggregate screen. It will display all currency exposures in total so that we can see exactly what our overall exposure to any given currency is at that moment.

Activity Log: You see the record of our trade with all its details listed, as depicted in Figure 2.11. (*Note:* When looking at the Margin Used line of the Account Summary you will notice that value does not necessarily match what is on the confirmation ticket. This is because the value of the position changes. The margin used is based on the current value of the open positions.)

Trades	Orders	Boxes	Positions	Exposure	Activity Log	
			MARKET		/	UNITS
Long			EUR			1,000,000
Short			USD			1,262,020

FIGURE 2.10   Oanda FXTrade: Exposure Tab
Source: Oanda.

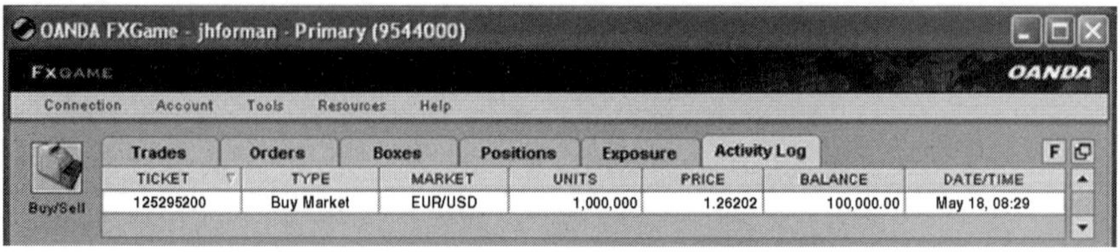

FIGURE 2.11   Oanda FXTrade: Activity Log Tab
Source: Oanda.

Homework

With an understanding of actual trade execution, it is time to get some hands-on experience. Using your FXTrade game account, open and close several positions. Get a feel for how to do it. Observe the price changes, if any, as you actually do the required things to put the trade in. Make sure you understand how the margin requirement is being determined and how the profit/loss calculations are working. It is very important that you are comfortable with all the elements of trading discussed in this section before you move on.

BEHIND THE TRADE

Okay, so we've done a trade, but what does that mean? The financial markets bring together buyers and sellers. Some transactions are very straightforward, as in the stock market. The buyer pays the seller money and receives shares in return. Even when using leverage and margin, the basics of the transaction remain very simple. This is not always the case.

The stock market is what can be referred to as a cash market. That means the buyer gives the seller cash now to receive an asset immediately. It may take a period of time for the actual exchange of the assets to take place (three days in the U.S. stock market), which is referred to as settlement, but the buyer is considered to have taken ownership at the time of the trade.

The forward market is a kind of deferred cash market in that the traders agree to exchange assets at some future time, generally with a set of specific terms (price, date, transaction size, asset quality). An example could be a gold transaction. The agreement could be that Trader A commits to buy 100 ounces of certified gold bullion from Trader B at a price of $400/oz for delivery in three months. Note that when the agreement is made, no exchange of assets takes place. Trader A does not own the gold yet. That will not happen for three months when he gives Trader B $40,000 and takes delivery.

Futures are standardized forward contracts. They trade on exchanges (forward contracts are generally transacted in the over-the-counter market). Each contract has a set size and asset specification (in the case of deliverable assets). The contracts have a specific set of delivery date options. The only variable is the contract price, which is determined in the market through the trading process.

The buyer of stock is considered to be long because ownership generates benefits through price appreciation. When entering into a forward or futures trade, however, no asset changes hands until some future time. Even so, the party who agrees to be the buyer takes on a long position. In the previous example, Trader A will be the buyer. He is therefore considered to be long due to the fact that he will benefit from a rise in the price of gold. If gold were to rise to $410 by the time he has to buy those 100 ounces from Trader B, he could take possession and immediately turn around and sell for a $1,000 profit (100 × $10). Trader B, on the other hand, would be short. Were gold to fall in price to $380, she would benefit in that she could buy the gold in the market and turn right around to deliver it to Trader A under the contract terms and make $2,000 (100 × $20).

Why Forwards and Futures?

The forward market (and by extension the futures market) began as a way for producers and consumers to help hedge and/or preset their costs and revenues.

For example, a corn farmer wants to lock in a fair price for the upcoming crop. That can be done by entering a forward contract to sell the harvested corn. Meanwhile, a cereal producer wants to lock in a good price for the corn it needs to buy for production purposes. It could enter into a forward agreement to buy that corn at some future time.

Market makers and speculators provide liquidity to the markets.

In most cases (all for the individual trader) forward/futures agreements require margin. This is to protect the counterparty against default of the agreement (for futures the exchange is the counterparty).

The options market differs from the forward/futures market in one very meaningful way. Like a forward contract, an option is an agreement to exchange assets at some future time. The difference, however, is that in options one of the parties—the buyer of the option—does not have to fulfill the contract; hence the "option." The option market, however, is a cash market in its own right, though. Options are bought and sold in the same manner as stocks, with the buyer paying the seller for the right to conclude a future transaction or force the seller into a future agreement (forward/futures, for example).

The spot forex market, which is what we are trading via the FXTrade platform, is at its core a forward market with a contract period of two days. In practical application, however, especially when using Oanda, it operates for the individual trader just like a cash market, but with a major wrinkle. When executing a forex trade, there are actually a series of transactions taking place. It is not as simple as trading one currency for another.

Simple Spot Forex Trade

Buy 100,000 EUR/USD.

Borrow 121,000 USD.

(Pay USD Overnight Rate.)

‖

Convert USD to EUR at 1.2100.

‖

Deposit 100,000 EUR.

(Earn EUR Overnight Rate.)

As the diagram shows, the forex transaction is complex. The trade is made in expectation that the rate will move in a positive fashion, causing the currency the trader owns (has on deposit) to appreciate against the one the trader is short (borrowed), producing a profit when the trade is closed by reversing the series of transactions.

In this example, let us look at what happens if the EUR/USD rate were to rise to 1.2200. The 100,000 EUR is converted back into USD at $1.22 per EUR. The result is $122,000. After repaying the $121,000 that was borrowed, the trader is left with $1,000 in profits. This does not, however, take into account the interest paid on the USD loan and the interest earned on the EUR deposit. This is what is referred to as the *carry* for the trade.

Carry can be either positive or negative depending on the differential between the two interest rates. We can check those rates in the FXTrade platform by choosing Resources/Interest Rates from the menu. That brings up the dialog box shown in Figure 2.12.

By selecting EUR and USD (Control-Click to select multiple currencies), we get the table depicted in Figure 2.13.

Remember, interest rates are like everything else in the markets. They work on the bid/ask principle. That means that as borrowers we pay the higher ask rate, and that as lenders/depositors we receive the lower bid rate.

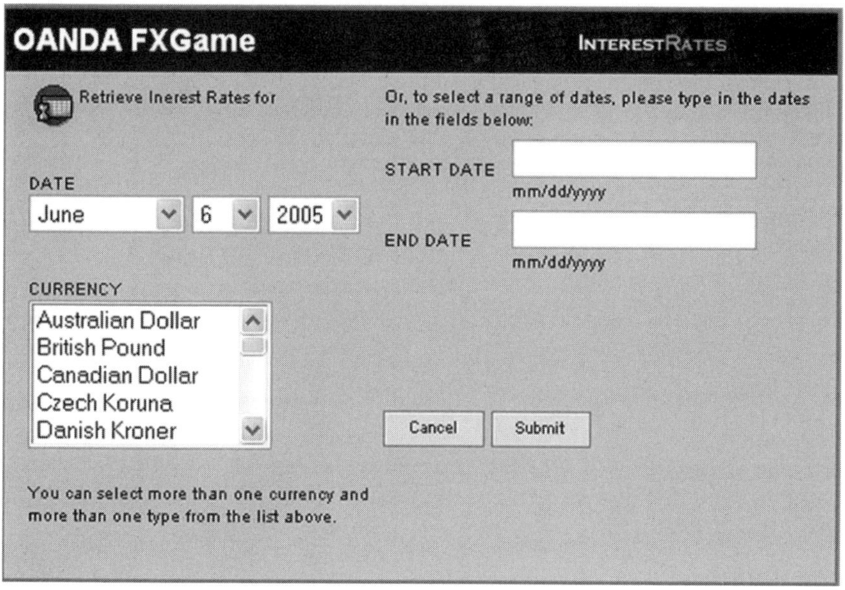

FIGURE 2.12 Oanda FXTrade: Interest Rate Selection
Source: Oanda.

Getting back to our discussion of the transactions, we can flip things around if we are aiming to take a long position in the USD (short EUR). The basic structure of the trade does not change. In this case we are simply borrowing EUR and converting them into USD. If the USD appreciates against the EUR (EUR/USD declines), meaning it would take fewer USD to repay the EUR loan we took out, then we would have a profit.

Things get a bit more complicated, however, when one is trading the crosses. A cross-trade, because it does not include the account's base currency (USD), adds a layer of complexity to the equation. Everything remains

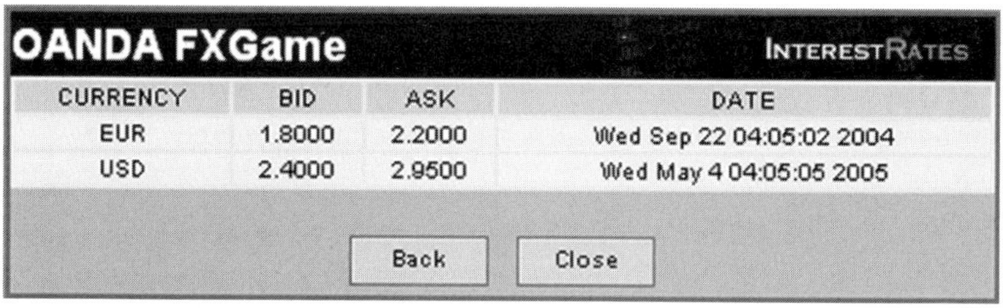

FIGURE 2.13 Oanda FXTrade: Interest Rate Comparison
Source: Oanda.

essentially the same when we enter the trade. If, for example, we were buying 100,000 EUR/JPY at 131.00 we would borrow 13,100,000 JPY (100,000 × 131), exchange that into EUR, and deposit it. We would pay interest on the JPY loan and earn it on the EUR deposit.

Cross Rates or Crosses

Any currency pair that does not include the USD in it is most commonly referred to as a cross-rate, or cross. Cross trades are just as relevant as the straight ones. The major crosses are:

EUR/JPY	EUR/GBP
EUR/CHF	GBP/JPY
GBP/CHF	AUD/JPY

The complexity of a cross trade comes when unwinding the trade. Assume EUR/JPY rises to 132.00, and see how the long position unwind would look:

Cross-Rate Trade

Unwind 100,000 EUR/JPY long.

(Entered trade at 131.00.)

100,000 EUR

||

Convert EUR back to JPY at 132.00.

(100,000 × 132 = 13,200,000 JPY.)

||

Repay 13,100,000 JPY.

(13,200,000 − 13,100,000 = 100,000 JPY remains.)

Note that there are 100,000 JPY remaining after the original JPY loan is repaid. That is our profit, but it needs to be converted back into USD for our accounting purposes, since we have a USD account. That happens by exchanging the JPY for USD at the current USD/JPY rate. If that rate is 107.00, then we have a gain of $934.58 on the trade (100,000/107.00). Of course, we must also take into account the carry when determining our net profit.

It should be noted that the cross trade transaction structure applies in all cases where one is trading in nonbase currencies vis-à-vis one's account. For example, a trader whose account is denominated in EUR would treat any non-EUR inclusive pair (like USD/JPY) as a cross.

Position Value and Profit/Loss

We have already gone through a brief discussion of profits and losses (often referred to as P/L or P&L), but it is worth taking a more thorough look at the topic and at position value in general. This is mostly a straightforward matter.

Using the stock market as the most easily understood example, the value of any position is Shares × Price. Profit for a given trade is determined by calculating the enter position value and comparing it to the position value when closed.

Long position profit equals

(Shares × Exit Price) − (Shares × Entry Price) − Transaction Costs

or

(Exit Price − Entry Price) × Shares − Transaction Costs

Buy 100 shares of IBM at 100 and sell at 110:

(110 − 100) × 100 − Transaction Costs = $1,000 − Transaction Costs

Short position profit equals

(Shares × Entry Price) − (Shares × Exit Price) − Transaction Costs

or

(Entry Price − Exit Price) × Shares − Transaction Costs

Short 100 shares of IBM at 100 and cover short at 90:

(100 − 90) × 100 − Transaction Costs = $1,000 − Transaction Costs

This is an easy formula and readily applied to just about any market. We simply replace Shares with the unit of measure for that market. That could be ounces of gold, barrels of oil, bushels of corn, the face value of a fixed income contract, or the multiplier of an index.

Even in forex, which can be considered a bit more complex than most others, the essence of trading boils down to starting value and ending value (as set by the market):

Non-USD Base (i.e., EUR/USD)

Long: (Units × R2) – (Units × R1) or Units × (R2 – R1)

Short: (Units × R1) – (Units × R2)) or Units × (R1 – R2)

where R1 is the starting rate and R2 is the ending one.
Buy 100,000 EUR/USD at 1.3000 and sell at 1.3100:

(100,000 × 1.31 = \$131,000) – (100,000 × 1.30 = \$130,000) = \$1,000

USD Base (i.e., USD/JPY)

Long: ((R2/R1) – 1)) × Units

Short: ((R1/R2) – 1)) × Units

Buy 100,000 USD/JPY at 110.00 and sell at 111.00:

((111.00 / 110.00) – 1)) × \$100,000 = \$909.09

Short 100,000 USD/JPY at 110.00 and cover at 109.00:

((110.00 / 109.00) – 1) × \$100,000 = \$917.43

As we know from the EUR/JPY example, cross trades require an additional step. The same calculation can be used as previously (the non-USD base is probably the easier, though either could be used), but the Profit/Loss figure would then have to be converted using one of the currencies involved to get it back to the account currency as demonstrated earlier.

You will note that we did not list a transaction cost in the forex calculation just mentioned. For the most part, spot forex trades do not have commissions or any other fees for execution. Recall, however, that there is carry based on the interest rate differentials. This carry can be either positive or negative. It is credited or debited on a daily basis (one can see those transactions in the FXTrade Activity Log), including weekends.

Discrete versus Continuous Carry Interest

Oanda calculates interest on a continuous basis for open forex trades. That means the trader pays or earns carry interest the whole time a position is open, regardless of trade length. Most other forex platforms handle carry only for overnight positions by doing end-of-day calculations on all open trades at some specific time (usually 4 or 5 P.M. Eastern).

The FXTrade platform comes with a handy profit/loss calculator the trader can use in advance of entering a trade to determine potential gains or losses. It is reached by selecting Tools, then PIP/Profit Calculator from the menu. That brings up a small window.

The PIP/Profit Calculator, as shown in Figure 2.14, (and similar tools on other platforms) allows one to easily make calculations. By simply changing the inputs one can simulate long or short trades in any currency with the entry (OPEN) and exit (CLOSE) points of one's choosing. The profit or loss figure (P&L) will appear at the bottom of the window.

Be aware, however, that as great a tool as the PIP/Profit Calculator is in the planning process, it has its limitations. The calculations will be spot

FIGURE 2.14 Oanda FXTrade: PIP/Profit Calculator
Source: Oanda.

on for noncross rates. They will be only estimates based on current rates for crosses, though.

MANAGING THE TRADE

There is more to trading than just executing trades. We are not yet ready to get into the decision-making process that drives entry and exit moves, but at this stage it is important to bring up the elements of trade management, specifically as it relates to ancillary order entry.

We addressed stop and limit orders earlier in this chapter, along with variations on their basic idea. While they can be used to enter trades at specific prices, it is more common for them to be used to define open positions. For example, a trader with a long position on can have a sell stop to exit the trade if the market were to go against the position and a sell limit to exit the trade at a profit.

As demonstrated earlier, entering a stop or limit order (no difference in FXTrade) is very similar to putting in any other type of trade. Let's walk through the process of setting a stop loss and a take profit.

First, we start with a fresh new trade—buying 1,000,000 EUR/USD. You can see from a look at the Trades tab in Figure 2.15 that the long trade was executed at 1.22774.

So we have an open long position in EUR/USD, which we want to protect against an adverse move (a decline). We can do that by placing a stop below the current market rate.

In this particular case we will take a 5-pip risk. That means putting our stop at 1.22724. Remember that since we are long, and will thus exit by selling, our order will get executed at the bid price. This is something to keep in mind when setting stops and limits.

So our order ticket is as shown in Figure 2.16.

We have an order to Sell at 1.22724. Note that the Duration box has been clicked and 1 month selected. This order will be good for 30 days, which is as long as FXTrade does. This is something that varies among the different trading platforms and systems.

Trades		Orders	Boxes	Positions		Exposure	Activity Log	
	TICKET	MARKET	UNITS	S/L	T/P	PRICE	CURRENT	PROFIT (USD)
Long	129281610	EUR/USD	1,000,000			1.22774	1.22759	−150.00

FIGURE 2.15 Oanda FXTrade: Trades Tab
Source: Oanda.

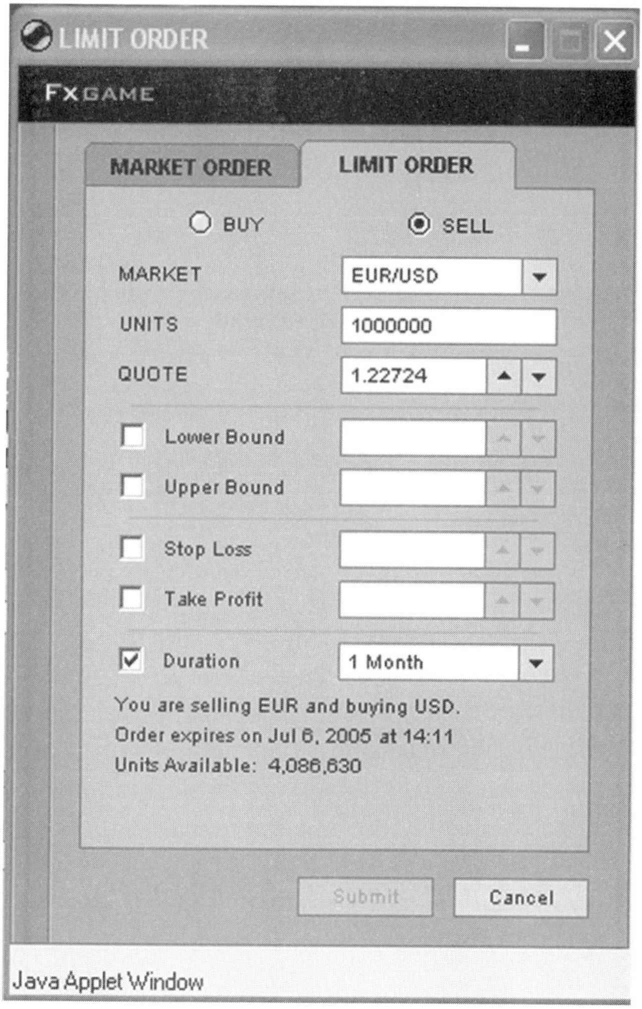

FIGURE 2.16 Oanda FXTrade: Order Ticket
Source: Oanda.

At the same time we will set a take profit at 5 pips above our entry price. That means a limit order to sell at 1.22824. Figure 2.17 shows that trade ticket.

These two orders bracket our position for 5 pips on either side. We are in a 1:1 risk/reward situation for this particular trade (something that comes up again later in the book). That means we will make or lose the same amount, in this case $500.

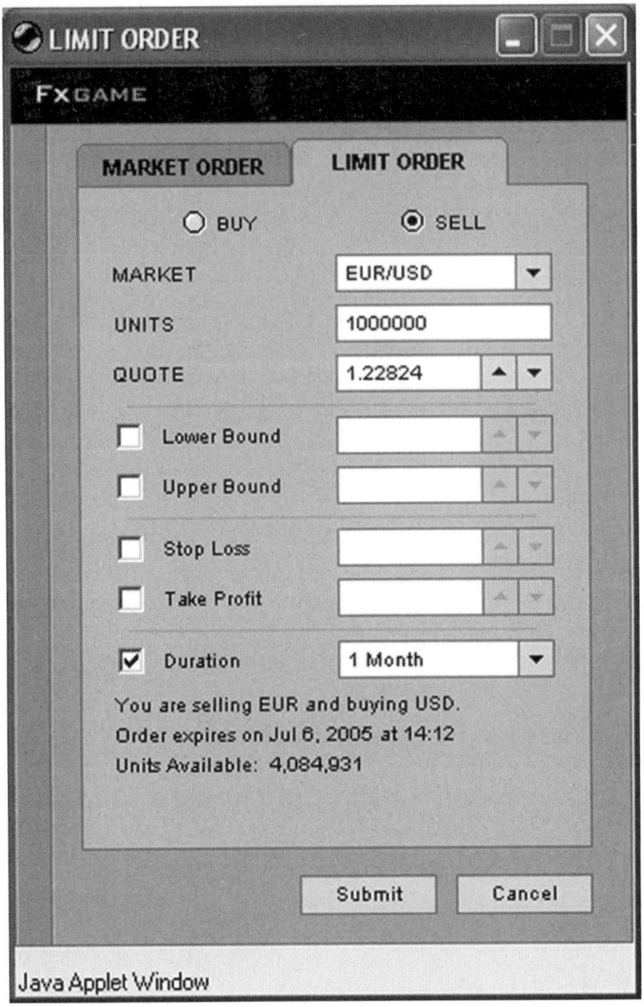

FIGURE 2.17   Oanda FXTrade: Order Ticket
Source: Oanda.

Please note that just because we chose 5 pips for the stop and take profit on this trade, does not mean that it is a recommendation of any kind. We address the process of defining stop and take profit in future chapters.

If we flip over to the Orders tab in our FXTrade platform we can see that the stop and limit orders we just entered are shown, as outlined in Figure 2.18.

Trades		Orders		Boxes	Positions		Exposure	Activity Log	
	TICKET	/	MARKET	UNITS	S/L	T/P	PRICE	CURRENT	EXPIRY
Short	129281621		EUR/USD	1,000,000			1.22724	1.22759	Jul 06, 14:11
Short	129281630		EUR/USD	1,000,000			1.22824	1.22759	Jul 06, 14:12

FIGURE 2.18 Oanda FXTrade: Orders Tab
Source: Oanda.

With our stop loss and take profit orders in place, we can rest easy. If we walk away from the screen and something happens, the trade will close out with either a $500 profit or a $500 loss (not counting the interest carry).

In this particular instance, the market went against our position. The 1.22724 stop was hit, so we lost $500, plus $0.29 in negative interest rate carry. That shows up in our Activity Log, along with a complete record of all the orders we entered and trades executed in the cycle (see Figure 2.19).

So we are now out of our long position. There's a catch, however. If we flip over to check the Orders tab (Figure 2.20), we can see that our take profit limit order remains.

This can be problematic. If the market were to rally up to 1.22824, that order would be executed and we would find ourselves short 1,000,000 EUR/USD. If that is our intention, then fine. Most of the time, however, that is not what we are after. We would like that order cancelled. If we are in front of the screen when the stop is hit, we can certainly cancel manu-

Trades	Orders	Boxes	Positions	Exposure	Activity Log		F
TICKET ▽	TYPE	MARKET	UNITS	PRICE	BALANCE	DATE/TIME	
129281759	Interest Payment	EUR/USD	1	-0.2910	189,076.51	Jun 06, 14:22	
129281759	Sell Order Filled	EUR/USD	1,000,000	1.22724	189,076.80	Jun 06, 14:22	
129281630	Sell Order	EUR/USD	1,000,000	1.22824	189,576.80	Jun 06, 14:12	
129281621	Sell Order	EUR/USD	1,000,000	1.22724	189,576.80	Jun 06, 14:11	
129281610	Buy Market	EUR/USD	1,000,000	1.22774	189,576.80	Jun 06, 14:11	

FIGURE 2.19 Oanda FXTrade: Activity Log Tab
Source: Oanda.

Trades		Orders		Boxes	Positions		Exposure	Activity Log	
	TICKET	/	MARKET	UNITS	S/L	T/P	PRICE	CURRENT	EXPIRY
Short	129281630		EUR/USD	1,000,000			1.22824	1.22725	Jul 06, 14:12

FIGURE 2.20 Oanda FXTrade: Orders Tab
Source: Oanda.

ally (in FXTrade, click on the order to bring up the screen shown in Figure 2.21, make sure CANCEL is selected, and click the Submit button). If not, however, we are left with a hanging order that could lead to an unintended position. Unintended positions can be quite damaging, especially with no stop loss.

Imagine, for example, that EUR/USD starts rallying. It moves up to 1.22824, our take profit point. The limit sell order, which is still active, gets

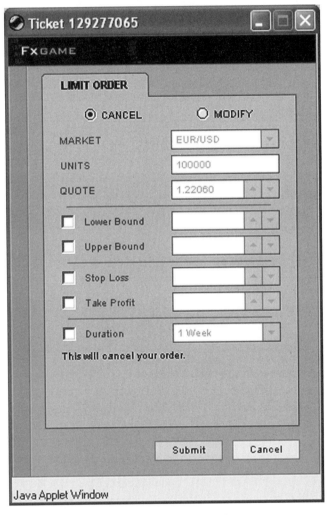

FIGURE 2.21 Oanda FXTrade: Order Ticket
Source: Oanda.

triggered. Suddenly we are short 1,000,000 EUR/USD. If the market immediately turns around, great! What if it keeps going higher, though? What if
some news item is causing a price rally? That could be dire indeed. We
could come back to the computer and find ourselves deep in the hole. A
100-pip rally—not out of the question—would cost $10,000.

So how do we avoid this sort of situation?

If you recall, earlier in the chapter we mentioned a one-cancels-other
type of order (OCO). That would be very handy in this situation. If either
the stop loss or the take profit order is executed, the other order is cancelled. That is a great safety feature.

Unfortunately, the OCO order setup is not available in all markets
or on all platforms. That includes FXTrade. There is another solution,
however. Oanda has provided a way to handle this type of situation,
which many (if not most) online trading platforms have as well. The solution is to enter stop loss and take profits that are tied with a specific
position.

Let's initiate another position, this time in EUR/JPY. We will buy
1,000,000 units at the market. Our order ticket is shown in Figure 2.22.

Note that in this instance we have entered Stop Loss and Take Profit
levels on the order screen, which we did not do before. This is a wonderful little feature that simultaneously creates two additional orders when
we make our trade. As soon as this market order is executed, we will
have an active stop loss order at 131.102 and an active take profit limit order at 131.202. They are created by the trading platform based on the figures we enter in this order ticket and put in the system as soon as the
order executes.

Based on our buy order, the Trades tab would be as depicted in Figure 2.23.

The trade has gone in as usual. Previously, however, there were no entries in the S/L and T/P columns (stop loss and take profit, respectively).
Those are now showing the levels we put in when placing the order. If we
flip to the Orders tab (Figure 2.24), we can see that they match two new
orders that have been entered.

There are a couple of differences between these orders and the ones
we placed in the previous trade example. Take a close look at Figure 2.24.

Starting on the left, notice that where before we had Short in the left-
most column, reflective of a sell order, we now have SL and TP, indicating
that these orders are matched to an existing position. The S/L and T/P
columns are now "n/a." Very importantly, the EXPIRY column now shows
GTC. These orders will stay active until the underlying position (our long
in EUR/JPY) is closed.

Using the Stop Loss and Take Profit when placing our orders also provides us with another nice little feature. As shown in Figure 2.25, the two

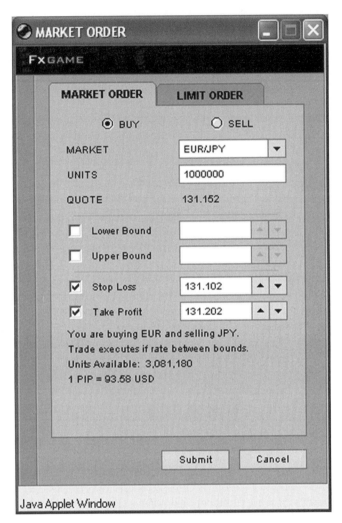

FIGURE 2.22   Oanda FXTrade: Order Ticket
Source: Oanda.

Trades	Orders	Boxes	Positions	Exposure	Activity Log			
	TICKET /	MARKET	UNITS	S/L	T/P	PRICE	CURRENT	PROFIT (USD)
Long	129281907	EUR/JPY	1,000,000	131.102	131.202	131.152	131.105	–439.93

FIGURE 2.23   Oanda FXTrade: Trades Tab
Source: Oanda.

Trades		Orders		Boxes		Positions		Exposure		Activity Log	
	TICKET	/	MARKET	UNITS	S/L	T/P	PRICE	CURRENT	EXPIRY
SL	129281907		EUR/JPY	1,000,000	n/a	n/a	131.102	131.125	GTC
TP	129281907		EUR/JPY	1,000,000	n/a	n/a	131.202	131.125	GTC

FIGURE 2.24 Oanda FXTrade: Orders Tab
Source: Oanda.

values are plotted on the chart. The lower line (normally red) is the stop loss. The upper one (normally green) is the take profit.

When using normal stop and limit orders to act as stop losses and/or take profits, the FXTrade system just puts in little boxes indicating the existence of a standing order at a certain price, entered at a certain time. Arrows are placed on the chart when trades are executed—like the upward pointing one on the chart in Figure 2.25. (*Note:* These lines and trade/order indicators can be turned on or off using the two circular buttons on the top left portion of the chart area. See Figure 2.26.)

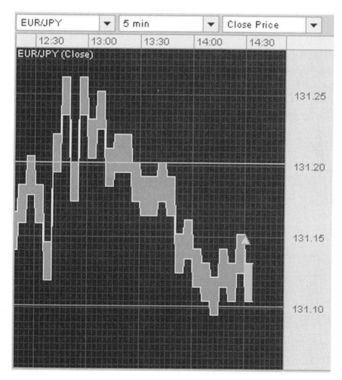

FIGURE 2.25 EUR/JPY Chart with Target and Stop
Source: Oanda.

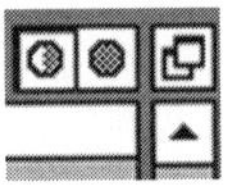

FIGURE 2.26 Show/Hide Trades Toggle
Source: Oanda.

Again, the market went against us on this trade and we were stopped out. (We're not doing very well on these trades!)

In Figure 2.27 you can see from the Activity Log that our stop loss was triggered. Recall from the earlier example (Figure 2.19) that our exit trade looked like a regular sell. It came through as "Sell Order Filled." We also saw both the stop loss and take profit orders we had entered. When using the Stop Loss and Take Profit entry feature of the order screen, we do not see the ancillary orders in the Activity Log. All we see is that we opened a new position (Buy Market), it was stopped out (Stop Loss) for a $468.01 loss, and that we earned a positive carry (Interest Earned) of $0.02. Nice and clean. Even better, we have no lingering order, as Figure 2.28 shows.

By now you should see how valuable being able to enter your stop and target levels at the time of trade entry can be. What's more, you do not even have to do it up front. You can add a Stop Loss and/or Take Profit to any open trade, or go in and modify existing ones. To do so, click on an open order in the Trades tab. Click the Modify radio button to activate the edit feature. When done, click Submit and you are finished. You will see the changes reflected in the trade, on the Orders tab, and on the Activity Log.

Trades	Orders	Boxes	Positions	Exposure	Activity Log		F
TICKET	TYPE	MARKET	UNITS	PRICE	BALANCE	DATE/TIME	
129281928	Interest Earned	EUR/JPY	1	0.0227	188,608.53	Jun 06, 14:30	
129281928	Stop Loss	EUR/JPY	1,000,000	131.102	188,608.50	Jun 06, 14:30	
129281907	Buy Market	EUR/JPY	1,000,000	131.152	189,076.51	Jun 06, 14:30	

FIGURE 2.27 Oanda FXTrade: Activity Log Tab
Source: Oanda.

Trades	Orders	Boxes	Positions	Exposure	Activity Log		
	TICKET /	MARKET	UNITS	S/L	T/P	PRICE	CURRENT	EXPIRY

FIGURE 2.28 Oanda FXTrade: Orders Tab
Source: Oanda.

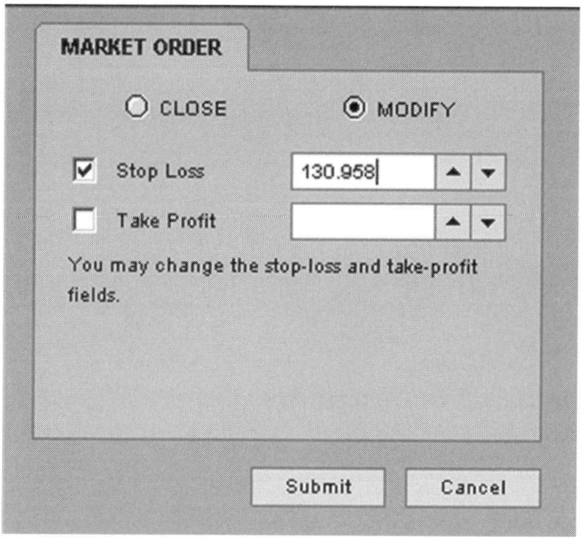

FIGURE 2.29   Oanda FXTrade: Modify Order
Source: Oanda.

Note: By clicking the order, leaving the Close radio button active and clicking the Submit button closes out the trade, so be careful when working with this box. (See Figure 2.29)

At this stage you should have a pretty clear understanding of how to deal with one trade at a time. It may be that is all you ever have to handle. We would be remiss in our discussion of trading management, however, if we did not broach the subject of multiple simultaneous positions and their impact on the overall trading account profile. With that, let us take a look at market exposure.

We start with a long position of 100,000 EUR/JPY initiated at 131.172 (Figure 2.30). Our exposure is clear. We are long 100,000 EUR and short 13,118,200 JPY (Figure 2.31). Now let's add another trade. We are going to buy 100,000 USD/JPY at 106.921 (Figure 2.32). Notice how dramatically this changes our overall situation (Figure 2.33). We have nearly doubled

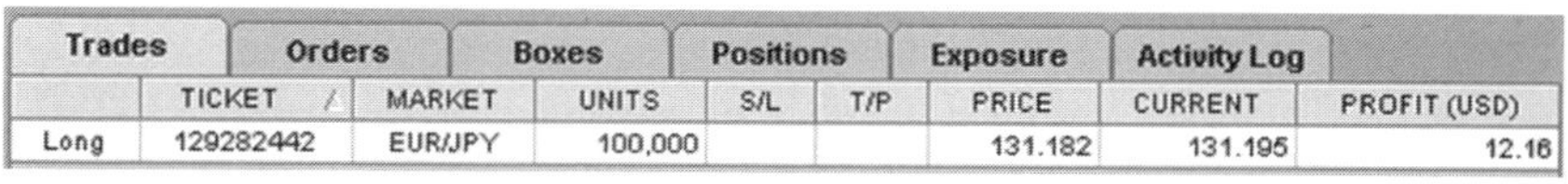

Trades	Orders		Boxes	Positions		Exposure	Activity Log	
	TICKET /	MARKET	UNITS	S/L	T/P	PRICE	CURRENT	PROFIT (USD)
Long	129282442	EUR/JPY	100,000			131.182	131.195	12.16

FIGURE 2.30   Oanda FXTrade: Trades Tab
Source: Oanda.

Trades	Orders	Boxes	Positions	Exposure	Activity Log
			MARKET	/	UNITS
Long			EUR		100,000
Short			JPY		13,118,200

FIGURE 2.31   Oanda FXTrade: Exposure Tab
Source: Oanda.

Trades	Orders		Boxes	Positions		Exposure	Activity Log	
	TICKET	/	MARKET	UNITS	S/L	T/P	PRICE	CURRENT	PROFIT (USD)
Long	129282442		EUR/JPY	100,000			131.182	131.195	12.16
Long	129282668		USD/JPY	100,000			106.921	106.884	-34.62

FIGURE 2.32   Oanda FXTrade: Trades Tab
Source: Oanda.

Trades	Orders	Boxes	Positions	Exposure	Activity Log
			MARKET	/	UNITS
Long			EUR		100,000
Short			JPY		23,810,300
Long			USD		100,000

FIGURE 2.33   Oanda FXTrade: Exposure Tab
Source: Oanda.

our short exposure to JPY, while adding a long risk for USD. This is something very easy to do if one is not paying attention. It is also a potential problem outside forex. Any pair of trades which are subject to a matched risk profile—corn and wheat, gold and silver, stocks and bonds, to name a few—can create portfolios out of balance in risk terms.

There are also situations where additional positions can radically change one's overall exposure. To demonstrate, we start with a long position in EUR/USD—100,000 initiated at 1.22734. Our starting exposure is then as shown in Figure 2.34.

Now, we are going to buy 100,000 USD/JPY, executed at 106.861. Notice in Figure 2.35 what happens when adding the next position to our

Trades	Orders	Boxes	Positions	Exposure	Activity Log
			MARKET	/	UNITS
Long			EUR		100,000
Short			USD		122,734

FIGURE 2.34   Oanda FXTrade: Exposure Tab
Source: Oanda.

Trades	Orders	Boxes	Positions	Exposure	Activity Log
			MARKET	/	UNITS
Long			EUR		100,000
Short			JPY		10,686,100
Short			USD		22,734

FIGURE 2.35 Oanda FXTrade: Exposure Tab
Source: Oanda.

portfolio. Notice that our short position in USD is much reduced. It is still there, but we have essentially created a synthetic long EUR/JPY trade with a small long EUR/USD position on the side. Instead of having a position in which we expect to benefit from EUR/USD rising and USD/JPY rising, our account performance is now dominated by the movement of the EUR/JPY cross.

In forex, this sort of shifting exposure is easy to see and track. It's right there on the screen in front of us, after all. In other markets where the drivers of account performance are not always quite so clear and quantifiable, it can be harder to always be aware of how shifts in trading positions can impact the overall risk profile. Value-at-risk (VAR) is one of the tools used in financial circles to understand the various exposures inherent in holding positions in multiple instruments and markets.

We address this whole topic in much greater detail in future chapters.

Homework

Continue executing trades. Do so with and without the stop and limit orders. Also do so in combination to see how the exposure changes.

CHAPTER 3

Price Action and Its Influences

In the previous chapter we jumped into the markets feet first and did an initial sample trade. In this chapter we start the process of understanding the markets and their behavior in preparation for later movement on to trading strategy.

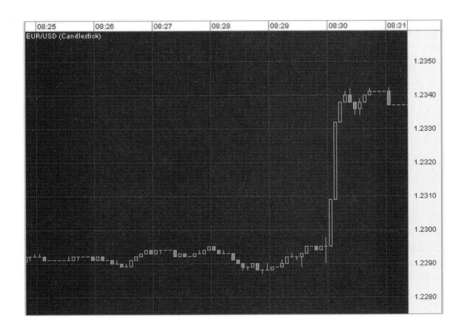

INFLUENCES ON PRICE

With the basics of trade execution and management out of the way, it's time to move on to the determinants of price movement. The things that contribute to price levels and action are numerous and diverse, and their influences can vary through time and across different markets. In this section we identify the different types of influences and the roles they play.

Fundamental Data

So-called "fundamental" information are generally the macro variables that go into determining the value of an asset or security. These variables can be thought of as elements that in many ways define the structure of price action. They do not always directly impact the price of a specific instrument in the short-term, but they can strongly impact the long-term price movement, the manner in which instruments are traded, and the reasons for doing so.

There are two ways these variables can influence prices. The first is in the broad, long-term sense where trends are considered. These sorts of inputs include:

- Interest rates.
- Economic growth (GDP).
- Government regulations.
- Laws and legal developments.
- Government budget surpluses/deficits.
- Trade balances.
- Commodity prices.
- Relative currency exchanges rates.
- Inflation.
- Corporate earnings.
- Weather.

These elements will generally all have long-term input into the pricing of any given market. They are often the basis for models designed to determine a market's underlying value. Some are more important for one market over another. They do not tend to move in sharp, dramatic fashion, so their influences also tend to be seen over longer periods of time.

That said, the release of economic data related to the influences listed and the immediate changes in things like weather can be seen to have serious impacts on the short-term activity in the markets. They come primarily in the form of data releases. Some of the most important are:

- Employment data.
- Trade data.
- GDP growth figures.
- Consumer and producer inflation rates.
- Retail and wholesale sales.
- Confidence and sentiment readings (U. Michigan survey, etc.).
- Income and spending.
- Production.
- Interest rate policy decisions.
- Earnings releases.
- Crop yields.
- Storms and other severe local weather.

The markets can react in very, very dramatic fashion to these releases when they are out of line with expectations. In general terms, the markets do not like to be surprised in any fashion. Uncertainty can be seen as the single biggest contributor to price volatility. It makes traders uneasy and prone to the kind of irrational behavior we discussed earlier in this text.

Following is a striking example provided by the non-farm payrolls release, which is released on the first Friday of each month at 8:30 A.M. Eastern time. Among the regular economic data reports, this is generally the most likely to create market volatility. It outlines how many jobs were created or lost during the previous month, the rate of unemployment, and the level of earnings for workers. These numbers are viewed as direct indications of economic health and pointers toward future interest rate activity. Figure 3.2 is of the December U.S. Treasury Bond Futures contract following the announcement of figures significantly different from expected.

As the 1-minute bars show, when the figures were released at 7:30 (the chart is on a Central time scale, one hour behind Eastern time) the market dropped more than two full points. One point on the T-bond futures contract represents a 1 percent change in the value of a $100,000 bond, so is worth $1,000. That means each contract fell more than $2,000 in about two minutes. Consider that the margin on a contract at the time was probably around $2,500. Traders long the bond ahead of the announcement could have lost more than 80 percent of their margin deposit on the trade in almost no time at all.

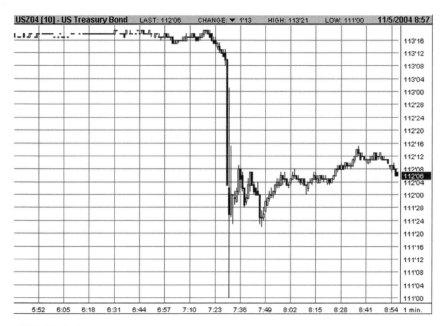

FIGURE 3.2 U.S. Treasury Bond Futures: 5-Minute Chart
Source: Futuresource.com.

It is also important to understand that in the futures pits such data events often result in fast market conditions. This means the action is so hectic that there may literally be trading going on at several different prices in various parts of the pit. This is a risk of having open positions at the time of a major news release. The market may snap back fairly quickly, as in Figure 3.2, but in the meantime the trader's positions may have been liquidated on a stop order at a substantial loss. The trader who sold at 111-00, as the figure indicates happened (the displayed prices are traded, not indicative), was no doubt cursing loudly when they saw the market rebound so quickly and dramatically.

Fortunately, all major economic releases are well documented. They are done on a preannounced calendar that is readily available. In the vast majority of cases, one can also find out ahead of time from any number of sources what the expectations are for the release. For an example, see Table 3.1.

Foreknowledge of pending data events may not prevent losses that can result from unexpected figures. It does, however, allow the trader to recognize and understand when risks are increased.

TABLE 3.1 Sample Economic Data Release Calendar

Time (NYT)	Loc	Description	Fcst*	Prev
3/18 12:00	US	Fed Chairman Greenspan Speaks	—	—
3/18 09:45	US	Mar Univ of Michigan Sentiment	94.8	94.1
3/17 12:45	CAN	Bank of Canada Dep Gov Longworth Speaks	—	—
3/17 12:00	US	Feb Philadelphia Fed Index	20.0	23.9
3/17 10:00	US	Feb Leading Indicators	0.1%	−0.3%
3/17 08:30	US	Weekly Jobless Claims	315k	327k
3/17 04:30	UK	Feb Retail Sales	0.1%	0.9%
3/17 00:00	JPN	Bank of Japan Monetary Policy Report	—	—

*(Fcst = forecast, Prev = previous)

Speakers

The next major and frequent source of influence on market activity is the collection of speakers that offer official or unofficial comments on the aforementioned economic items, and/or the public policies behind them. The biggest group of such statements, and the ones that generally have the most importance, are the ones that come from central bankers and finance ministry officials in the major economic centers. These are folks like the Federal Reserve chairman or treasury secretary in the United States, the European Central Bank president, the head of Japan's Ministry of Finance or the Bank of Japan, and similarly placed representatives of the other bigger industrial countries.

Such prominent officials generally speak at times well publicized in advance (like the Fed's Humphrey–Hawkins testimony). Market participants literally analyze the exact words these men and women use looking to decipher hidden meanings and figure out the future of interest rate and fiscal policy. The "irrational exuberance" statement from then Fed Chairman Alan Greenspan referring to the late 1990s stock market rally, and the response the markets had to it, is an example of just how big a deal these comments can be.

Heads of state can be included in this list as well. They tend to say less specific things, when they can be convinced to talk about the markets at all, but their speeches (like the State of the Union in the United States) can outline the overall direction of government policy, which certainly plays a part in the markets.

Numerous lower level government officials also make statements. This group includes the likes of regional Federal Reserve Bank governors and secretaries of major government agencies. The impact of any one specific speaker, however, will depend on several elements. Among other things, who they are, what they say, and the underlying context of the political, economic, and market situation all play a part.

In the markets themselves there are also a number of influential speakers. Not long ago stocks were heavily influenced by the comments of a select group of Wall Street analysts. This has abated somewhat, but there are still those whose word and activities carry weight. Warren Buffett is a perfect example. George Soros has been another at times. Any major money manager of high repute will fall into this category by virtue of the bandwagon effect. A number of traders, portfolio managers, and analysts have become media stars in recent years. As a result, their comments get heard by lots of people, making them influential.

Shocks

There is a group of market influencers that is harder to track and prepare for than the previously mentioned data and speakers. They may also have some cross categorization among the previous categories, but their timing is often unknown.

In this category are:

Natural disasters.

Merger/Takeover announcements.

Product recalls and related negative news.

Announcements of government action or investigation against companies.

Court case decisions (though the timing can sometimes be anticipated).

These sorts of events are surprises. They contrast with surprise data releases in that they do not operate on a schedule. As a result, anticipation is essentially impossible. As noted before, the market likes predictability, so shocks can have a huge impact on the price action, both long- and short-term. This is particularly true when the news is bad. Markets will often fall faster than they rise.

Order Flow

There are two types of order flow that impact the markets. The first is speculative. Put simply, that is all of the various money managers, market makers, traders, brokers, and others who are in the markets to make profits and/or provide liquidity. This type of volume tends to be volatile and fast moving. Speculators are the prime movers behind the spikes and drops as they react to the influencers noted in this section. A big trade can move markets, especially in thin volume conditions. That can either mean a short-term blip or become part of a bigger move depending on the circumstances.

The other type of order flow comes from nonspeculative sources. These flows come about as the result of activities related to business and trade. Companies move capital around the globe. They hedge costs and income flows against fluctuations in the markets, and they purchase and sell goods. While in terms of actual volume this nonspeculative activity may not match speculative trade, it is the reason why the markets exist in the first place. As with a big speculative transaction, a large nonspeculative trade can also influence short-term market action. Unlike the speculator, however, those who use the market to perform business functions can have a longer-term part to play in the way prices move. An excellent example would be a company doing a share buy-back. As the company continues to purchase shares, the buying will tend to have a positive impact on prices. This comes both from the actual buying as well as the impact this activity has on the company's outstanding share balance and earnings per share.

Intervention

Central banks around the world will, from time to time, take an active part in the financial markets. This may be direct and well publicized, such as when the Bank of Japan enters the market to exchange yen for U.S. dollars, thereby helping to keep the yen from appreciating too much against the dollar. It may also be more subtle, such as when the Federal Reserve buys and sells Treasury securities in the markets to expand or contract the money supply.

While this sort of activity may seem like any other large size transaction, in that a short-term impact would be expected as the transaction hits the market, there is an added element. When a central bank is trading, this has a deeper meaning. They are trying to influence the markets. Traders take that very seriously, so the impact tends to have a longer-term influence, regardless of whether the actual trades are deemed to have been effective.

Psychology

One additional, but not inconsequential, influence on prices and market movements is psychology. When we speak of market psychology, it is generally meant as an overall view of the sentiment among the mass of market participants. Thus the often-heard term "market sentiment." Do they think the market is fairly valued, overvalued, undervalued? Do they think the market is trending, and therefore likely to keep moving in its current direction? The reason this is important to know is because it can go a long way in determining not only the likely future direction of prices, but also how prices will react to some of those other influences noted in this section.

Market sentiment is an often-discussed topic among market analysts and traders. There are indicators designed to measure this in various ways. This is not something we discuss meaningfully now, though. The simplest way to keep track of market sentiment/psychology is to read and listen. What market participants say about the markets speak volumes. Also, monitoring how the market reacts to news and releases can be very helpful.

Homework

For one calendar week track the market reaction to economic releases. Review the calendar ahead of time and pick several releases. (For now, avoid speakers. They are harder to quantify. Once you have a better understanding, you can start listening to them with more ability to discern the importance of what is being said.) Determine what the market expectations are before each release, then watch what happens when the figure is announced. Document everything in a journal. This is something worth doing on a continuing basis to gain a full understanding of the array of major regular releases.

PRICE MOVEMENT

With an understanding of what causes prices to move, it is time to take a look at how they do so. For the sake of this discussion, the focus is on foreign exchange rates so as to maintain a standard point of reference throughout this text. Be assured, however, that markets of all sorts show similar characteristics in terms of price movement. The information presented herein is comparable for markets other than forex.

Period-to-Period Returns

The easiest point at which to start is in terms of return, alternatively referred to as percent change. If a market moves from 100 to 110 it has generated a 10 percent return. One then considers the time frame during which that change took place. It could be measured in minutes, hours, days, weeks, or any other time scale. If the aforementioned market move occurred over the course of a week, it would be a 1-week return.

Period Returns:
Influence of Time Frame

Using USD/JPY from January 1999 through December 2004 as an example, one can see that time frame influences the distribution of period returns. Note in Table 3.2 how standard deviation rises with period length.

TABLE 3.2 Time Frames Influence Period Returns and Their Dispersion

Period Length	Average Return	Standard Deviation
1 day	−.00475%	0.63530%
5 days	−.02455%	1.37209%
10 days	−.04137%	1.96393%
22 days	−.08031%	2.81958%

Period returns show common characteristics, regardless of time frame. There tends to be a high frequency of relatively small returns, with fewer larger ones. Relative is an important distinction. The actual size of those returns varies widely based on market and time frame, as could be demonstrated via a standard deviation measurement (see the sidebar). For the sake of simplicity and commonality, Figures 3.3 through 3.8 are a

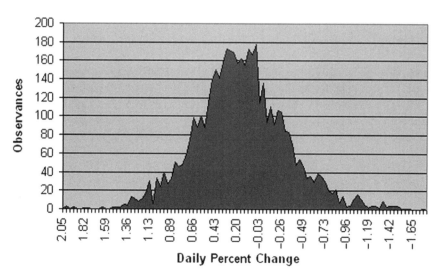

FIGURE 3.3 Distribution of Daily AUD/USD Changes 1999–2004
Source: Anduril Analytics.

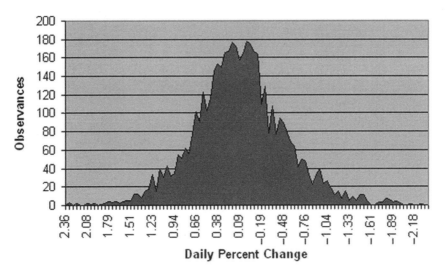

FIGURE 3.4 Distribution of Daily EUR/USD Changes 1999–2004
Source: Anduril Analytics.

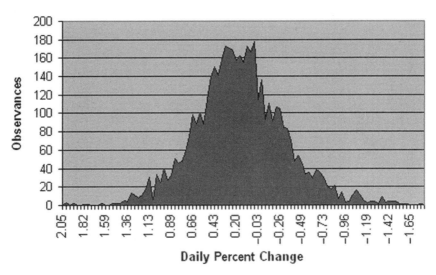

FIGURE 3.5 Distribution of Daily GBP/USD Changes 1999–2004
Source: Anduril Analytics.

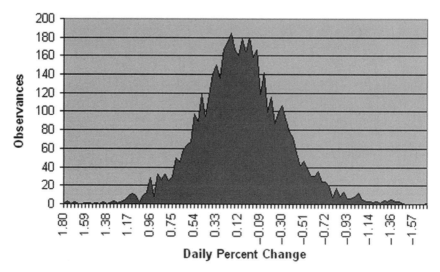

FIGURE 3.6 Distribution of Daily USD/CAD Changes 1999–2004
Source: Anduril Analytics.

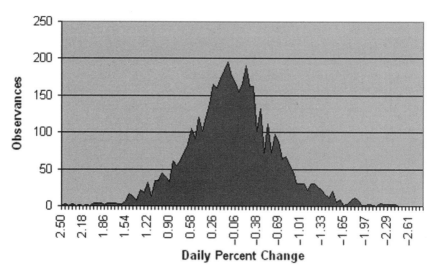

FIGURE 3.7 Distribution of Daily USD/CHF Changes 1999–2004
Source: Anduril Analytics.

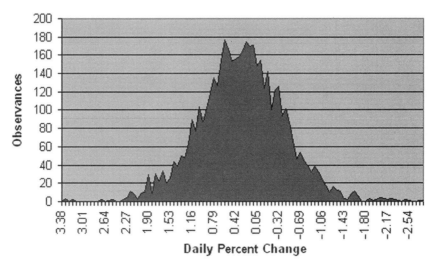

FIGURE 3.8 Distribution of Daily USD/JPY Changes 1999–2004
Source: Anduril Analytics.

series of daily return charts to provide a demonstration as to the distribution of price movement.

The observer will no doubt notice that the distributions shown on these graphs look very much like the bell shape of a standard distribution. They are a bit jagged as a result of the way the studies were done, but the basic idea is there.

That said, however, much discussion has taken place among researchers and academics as to exactly the type of distribution period returns matches. It is fairly well accepted that percent changes do not follow a normal pattern. The so-called "wings" are too fat. By this it is meant that there are more large period returns (up or down) than would be expected based on a normal distribution. It is for this reason that jump-diffusion and other similar models rose to popularity. They are based on the view that markets will generally behave fairly calmly (level volatility), but that they periodically have significant increases in volatility.

One can extend the discussion of period returns a step further by extending the time frames in question. Figures 3.9 through 3.14 represent 5-day percent changes, so in essence they are a combination of five 1-day returns. This is to say that each 5-day return is the compounded result of five 1-day returns.

In general terms the 5-day return charts look quite similar to the 1-day return graphs. There are small differences in the distributions, especially

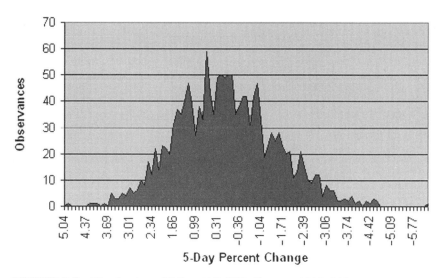

FIGURE 3.9 Distribution of 5-Day AUD/USD Changes 1999–2004
Source: Anduril Analytics.

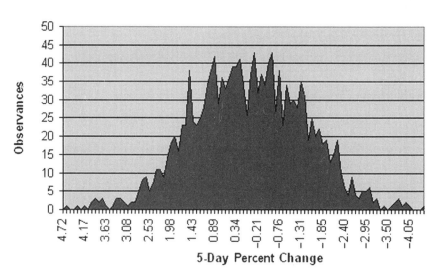

FIGURE 3.10 Distribution of 5-Day EUR/USD Changes 1999–2004
Source: Anduril Analytics.

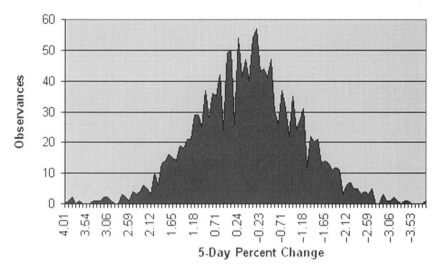

FIGURE 3.11 Distribution of 5-Day GBP/USD Changes 1999–2004
Source: Anduril Analytics.

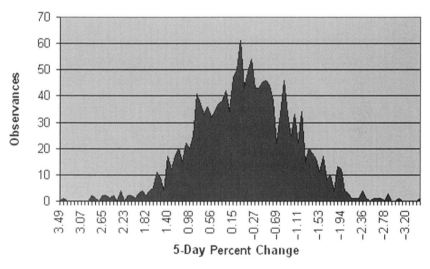

FIGURE 3.12 Distribution of 5-Day USD/CAD Changes 1999–2004
Source: Anduril Analytics.

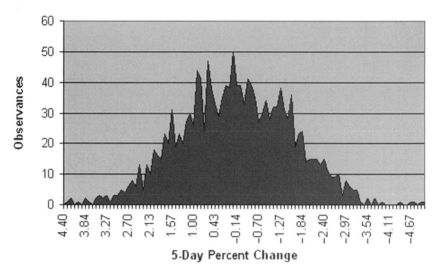

FIGURE 3.13 Distribution of 5-Day USD/CHF Changes 1999–2004
Source: Anduril Analytics.

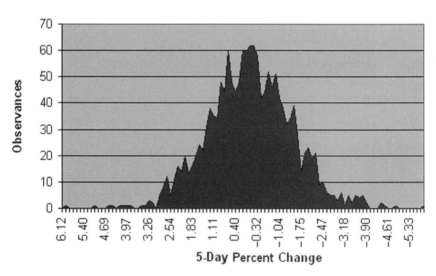

FIGURE 3.14 Distribution of 5-Day USD/JPY Changes 1999–2004
Source: Anduril Analytics.

in EUR/USD and USD/CHF which look "fatter" than the others, but are not ones of too much consequence. The interesting thing to observe is the scales on the bottom of the charts. One might expect that the returns achieved over 5-day periods would be roughly five times those of the 1-day periods. That, however, is far from the case. The reason for this is quite easily demonstrated.

Price Move Continuation

The reason 5-day returns are not anywhere close to being five times 1-day returns is that the market does not tend to move in straight lines. In fact, quite the opposite is the case. Take a look at Table 3.3.

The data in Table 3.3 indicate how often prices see follow-through from one day to the next. For example, the value for AUD/USD on Wednesday is 52 percent. This indicates that 52 percent of all Wednesday's prices moved in the same direction as they had done on the preceding Tuesday—Tuesday up and Wednesday up or Tuesday down and Wednesday down.

What the data in the table demonstrate is that returns do not tend to persist from period to period. There are a couple of exceptions— USD/CAD on Tuesday, for example—but in general terms the market tends to be roughly equally likely to rise or fall on any given day. That leads to the preceding 5-day return charts and how they do not show a distribution of returns as large as one would expect.

Period Ranges

The tendency of prices to move in anything but a straight line can be demonstrated as well by looking at the period ranges. Review the graphs in Figures 3.15 through 3.20.

TABLE 3.3   Price Continuation Day-over-Day

	Mon.	Tue.	Wed.	Thu.	Fri.
AUD/USD	52%*	44%	52%	44%	47%
EUR/USD	49%	45%	48%	42%	44%
GBP/USD	50%	48%	46%	47%	47%
USD/CAD	50%	**38%**	43%	50%	53%
USD/CHF	45%	46%	48%	45%	45%
USD/JPY	51%	47%	49%	46%	50%

Percent of time market continued in same direction day-to-day.

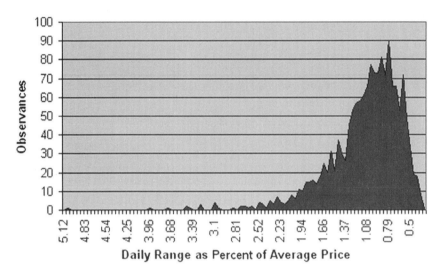

FIGURE 3.15 Distribution of Daily AUD/USD Ranges 1999–2004
Source: Anduril Analytics.

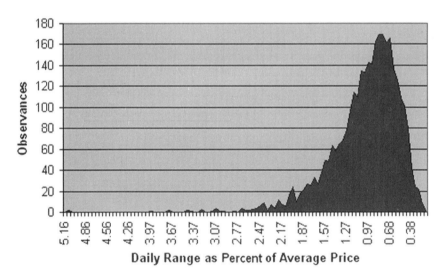

FIGURE 3.16 Distribution of Daily EUR/USD Ranges 1999–2004
Source: Anduril Analytics.

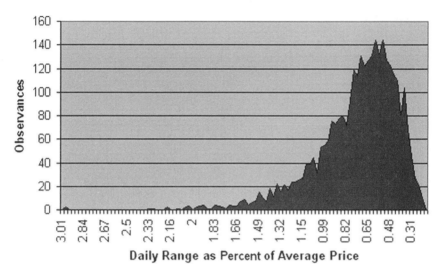

FIGURE 3.17 Distribution of Daily GBP/USD Ranges 1999–2004
Source: Anduril Analytics.

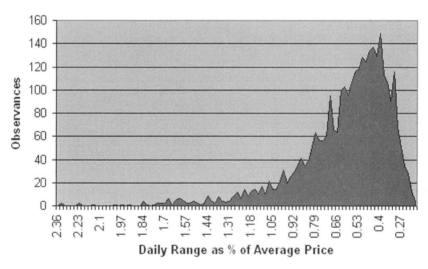

FIGURE 3.18 Distribution of Daily USD/CAD Ranges 1999–2004
Source: Anduril Analytics.

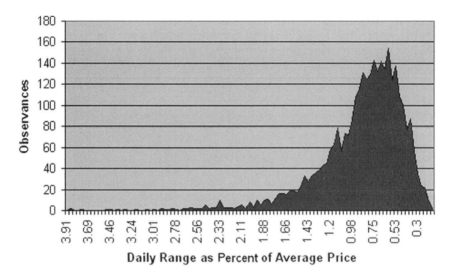

FIGURE 3.19 Distribution of Daily USD/CHF Ranges 1999–2004
Source: Anduril Analytics.

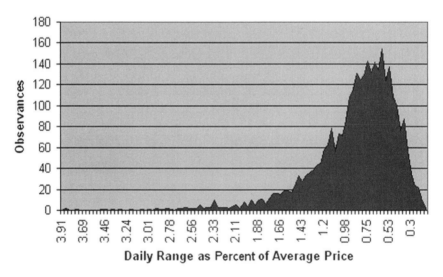

FIGURE 3.20 Distribution of Daily USD/JPY Ranges 1999–2004
Source: Anduril Analytics.

The charts show that daily ranges tend to be bigger than daily returns. In many ways they can be thought of as comparable to the 5-year return charts when discussing them in comparison to the 1-year return charts. After all, a 1-day range can be thought of in terms of a series of smaller period returns. Again, one can see in the ranges how prices do not move directly. It is quite rare to see a period in which the change is equal to the range.

Patterns—Intuitive and Otherwise

Despite the indications just mentioned that the markets move in rather uneven and unpredictable fashion, some patterns emerge. One of the most interesting and glaring is in what can be referred to as turning point days.

Refer to Monday and Friday, and the **bold faced** figures in Table 3.4. They indicate the key days each week. In all but one observation (Monday USD/CAD), the data demonstrate that the market tends to make extremes on the first or last day of the week. For example, on 61 percent of all Mondays USD/JPY made the weekly high and/or low, while on Wednesdays it did so only 25 percent of the time.

Various factors contribute to the Monday/Friday turning points. They are mostly intuitive in nature. Traders come in on Monday after the weekend prepared to initiate activity and on Friday they are looking to wrap things up for the weekend ahead.

What is less intuitive, however, is the distribution of trading ranges in terms of the annual calendar. See Table 3.5.

Table 3.5 lists the 20 smallest range days in EUR/JPY (the cross-exchange rate between the euro and the Japanese yen) during the period from January 2004 to December 2004. The Rng % column is calculated as (High − Low) / ((High + Low)/2). As could be expected, there are several dates in the collection that correspond closely to holidays, periods of less active trading and lower volumes.

TABLE 3.4 Turning Point Days

	Mon.	Tue.	Wed.	Thu.	Fri.
AUD/USD	55%*	34%	29%	37%	50%
EUR/USD	57%	26%	29%	30%	57%
GBP/USD	54%	33%	27%	28%	59%
USD/CAD	49%	35%	27%	30%	60%
USD/CHF	58%	28%	27%	31%	58%
USD/JPY	61%	30%	25%	31%	51%

*Percent of time the high and/or low for the week is made on a given day

TABLE 3.5 Small Range Days

Date	Open	High	Low	Close	Rng %
1/23/2004	134.37	134.37	134.26	134.27	0.08%
5/27/2002	114.94	115.06	114.68	114.89	0.33%
12/23/2003	133.27	133.44	132.99	133.01	0.34%
4/18/2003	130.09	130.46	130.02	130.31	0.34%
2/10/2003	130.18	130.49	130.02	130.13	0.36%
12/10/2002	124.66	124.91	124.46	124.77	0.36%
8/23/2002	116.09	116.45	116.02	116.33	0.37%
8/26/2002	116.25	116.4	115.97	116.37	0.37%
12/24/2004	139.98	140.36	139.83	140.27	0.38%
10/7/2004	136.71	136.96	136.43	136.62	0.39%
12/1/2004	136.8	137.08	136.54	136.8	0.39%
2/1/2005	135.12	135.56	135.02	135.3	0.40%
10/14/2002	122.54	122.73	122.24	122.72	0.40%
11/9/2004	136.26	136.7	136.15	136.34	0.40%
12/22/2003	133.54	133.75	133.21	133.28	0.40%
3/11/2003	129.15	129.51	128.98	129.3	0.41%
3/17/2005	139.74	140.04	139.46	139.81	0.42%
11/6/2002	121.78	122.09	121.58	121.95	0.42%
2/11/2005	136.29	136.34	135.77	135.97	0.42%
12/28/2004	140.28	140.62	140.03	140.27	0.42%

Now look at Table 3.6.

The 20 highest range days during the same time period as in Table 3.5 are shown in Table 3.6. Note that, here, too are a significant number of dates that fall close to major holidays. Given that these days tend to be lightly traded, one would not expect such large ranges. So why do these days happen?

The scatter chart of Figure 3.21 shows both what one would expect to happen under light volume situations and what can sometimes occur. The range is calculated in the same fashion as the preceding tables Rng%. The volume is a normalized figure in which each observation is calculated as a percentage of the average volume for the six-year period 1999–2004. Thus, the 100 percent point is at the average, which is why there are so many points plotted in that area.

The pattern of points on the chart has a general uptrend from left to right indicating that higher volumes tend to correspond to wider ranges. Note the collection of observations on the left side of the graph, however, which are from days where volume was less than half the period average. The distribution of those daily ranges is widely dispersed, not what most would expect. Why so?

TABLE 3.6 Large Range Days

Date	Open	High	Low	Close	Rng %
8/10/2000	97.16	98.94	96.54	98.6	2.46%
9/12/2000	91.06	92.97	90.67	92.31	2.50%
8/3/2000	99.46	99.87	97.37	98.16	2.53%
2/13/2001	109.31	109.65	106.88	107.39	2.56%
9/6/2000	94.16	94.21	91.81	92.09	2.58%
1/19/2001	111.28	112.12	109.23	109.3	2.61%
3/5/2004	135.49	138.96	135.25	138.71	2.71%
3/24/2004	131.66	132.15	128.61	128.8	2.72%
12/14/2001	112.49	115.49	112.36	114.94	2.75%
2/20/2001	106.84	107.3	104.38	105.46	2.76%
2/15/2001	106.8	107.22	104.25	104.35	2.81%
5/31/2001	102.87	103.05	100.07	100.75	2.93%
3/7/2002	114.52	114.77	111.25	112.14	3.11%
1/11/2001	109.07	112.36	108.9	112.19	3.13%
11/3/2000	92.91	95.16	91.98	92.6	3.40%
10/18/2000	92.09	92.61	89.45	90.38	3.47%
1/3/2001	108.78	109.48	105.34	105.45	3.85%
5/23/2001	106.26	106.31	101.99	102.85	4.15%
1/4/2001	105.26	109.89	105.15	109.85	4.41%
9/22/2000	91.55	95.75	91.47	94.98	4.57%

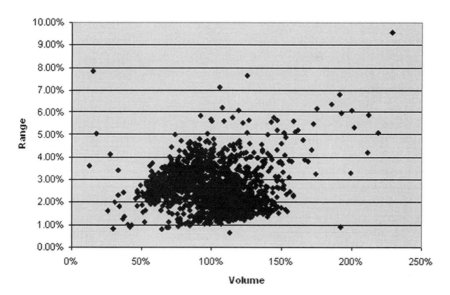

FIGURE 3.21 Dow Jones Industrial Average Range/Volume Comparison 1999–2004
Source: Anduril Analytics.

A conspiracy theorist might declare the explanation to be market manipulation by large traders. The idea there is that a big player can move the market when it is quiet and trading only light volume. Recall the earlier discussion regarding order flow and its impact. If a market is trading at low volumes, a large order coming in can have a significant impact on prices. A high volume trader could, therefore, push prices around. A more mechanical reason for such large price movements has to do with the nature of the markets in that they operate on a bid–offer basis. For example, there could be a price quote of 100-105. That means the highest price someone is willing to pay to buy is 100, and the lowest price there is selling interest at 105. Remember that there are volumes associated with each of those rates as well.

Using the bid side for the sake of furthering the discussion, assume that the buyer at 100 is willing to purchase 1,000 units. If someone comes in to sell 2,000 units, they would execute the first 1,000 at 100, the bid rate. That leaves 1,000 units to still be sold. The price the seller can get will depend on the depth of the market. It may be that there are other willing buyers at 100, enough to cover the remainder of the order. In an active market this is often the case.

What happens in a thin market, though? In such a situation, there may not be a willing buyer at 100. It may be that the next best bid is 99 for 500 units. Perhaps below that is another bid at 98 for 100 units, with another for 300 units at 97, and 200 more at 95. The trader looking to sell those 1,000 remaining units would have to fill part of the order at 99, more at 98, another bit at 97, and the last 100 at 95. In doing so, that one 2,000 unit trade knocked the bid down five points (there would be 100 units left on the 95 bid). More than likely, the offer rate would move lower in corresponding fashion.

Now this is a fairly extreme example for the sake of demonstration, but it illustrates the point. In markets with little volume it is possible for one or more large transactions to have an outsized impact on prices. This can happen around holidays and other vacation kinds of periods when fewer traders are active, and it can happen in markets that are thinly traded in the first place.

Most of the time these market situations do not add up to much excitement. Imagine, however, that some significant bit of news is released. The reaction could be seriously amplified in a thin market environment, leading to major volatility. What's more, this action tends to feed on itself. Sometimes it does not even take a single notable element, either. Refer to Figure 3.22.

The chart of the price action in EUR/JPY is from about mid-2000 to mid-2001. The circled bars are from the middle part of December 2000

FIGURE 3.22 Weekly EUR/JPY, 2000–2001
Source: Metastock.

to the first week of January 2001, normally a fairly quiet time of year, given the holiday season. In this instance, however, the market moved dramatically higher in large part because the thin volume conditions accelerated the price advance beyond what would normally have occurred.

The sort of information derived by work such as the turning-point study shows that the markets are not just random. There are patterns and tendencies to be found if one is willing to do the work to find them. As much as there is a bias toward viewing the markets in terms of numbers, it must be realized that behind every market is human interaction and decision making. Humans have patterns of behavior, and that gets reflected in price movement and trading activity.

Homework

Pick a market that interests you and a time frame for which you can readily acquire period high/low/close data. With that data, perform the following studies:

- Distribution of period returns.
- Distribution of period high-low ranges.
- Frequency of period move persistence (period 1 is up—period 2 is up, or period 1 is down—period 2 is down).

These are the same studies used in the examples from this section. They can be readily accomplished using basic spreadsheet and charting functionality.

Perform the following additional studies:

- Period time/range analysis: Determine if there is a clear pattern in the data for when the market tends to be most and/or least volatile in terms of period high-low ranges.
- Volatility persistence analysis: Determine if the volatility of one period (measured either by period returns or period high-low ranges) is followed by a similar level of volatility in the following period.

These are far from the only studies one can perform. Feel free to do additional ones. It will only serve to deepen your understanding of the market in question.

CHAPTER 4

Building the Trading Plan

In the first three chapters we set the groundwork by establishing a base of understanding and know-how. Now it is time to start the heavy lifting and get into the teeth of trading—the where, what, when, why, and how. That begins with the Trading Plan.

Transaction	Pair	Price	Units	PL	Balance
Buy Market	EUR/USD	1.23111	1,000,000	0.00	189,302.34
Sell Order	EUR/USD	1.23000	1,000,000	0.00	189,302.34
Sell Market Filled	EUR/USD	1.23000	1,000,000	0.00	188,191.03
Order Filled	EUR/USD	1.23000	1,000,000	0.00	188,191.03
Sell Market	USD/JPY	108.261	1,000,000	0.00	188,191.03
Sell Market	AUD/NZD	1.0709	1,000,000	0.00	188,191.03
Stop Loss	USD/JPY	108.400	1,000,000	−1,282.60	186,907.00
Stop Loss	AUD/NZD	1.0740	1,000,000	−2,185.50	184,722.31
Buy Market	EUR/USD	1.21975	1,000,000	0.00	184,734.51
Sell Order	EUR/USD	1.21850	1,000,000	0.00	184,734.51
Sell Order	EUR/USD	1.22200	1,000,000	0.00	184,734.51
Change Trade	EUR/USD	1.21975	1,000,000	0.00	184,734.51
Order Cancelled	EUR/USD	1.22200	1,000,000	0.00	184,734.51
Order Cancelled	EUR/USD	1.21850	1,000,000	0.00	184,734.51
Buy Market	GBP/USD	1.8117	500,000	0.00	184,734.51
Sell Market	NZD/USD	0.6974	500,000	0.00	184,734.51
Take Profit	EUR/USD	1.22200	1,000,000	2,250.00	186,980.39
Stop Loss	NZD/USD	0.6995	500,000	−1,050.00	185,928.75
Take Profit	GBP/USD	1.8195	500,000	3,900.00	189,841.04

WHAT'S A TRADING PLAN?

The starting point of effective trading is the Trading Plan. One can think of it as a Business Plan for the trader. Just like the Business Plan, the Trading Plan is a specific outline of current status, objectives for the future, and the expected path to reach those goals.

In plain language, the Trading Plan is a set of rules governing the trader's efforts in the markets. It brings together all of the whats, whens, wheres, whys, and hows of trading in an all-encompassing definition of what the trader is seeking to accomplish and how they will go about trying to make it happen. The Trading Plan is the starting point for every trader looking to succeed in the markets.

Please note that while we may be speaking here in terms of the trader as an individual, everything presented is equally applicable to a fund or company environment. The Trading Plan still must be constructed, albeit from a different perspective. Similar assessments to the ones following are required.

Why Does One Need a Trading Plan?

The very simple answer is that it allows the trader to measure their performance in a very clear, straightforward manner, on a running basis. Just as one uses a map to both establish the path to be taken and to judge the progress that has been made, the Trading Plan defines the trading system and gives the trader benchmarks for use in judging the execution of it.

Be aware that a Trading Plan and a trading system are two different things. The latter is, in brief, the way one determines entry and exit points—the timing of trades, if you like. The former is more overreaching in that it includes the trading system, plus other important things like money management. We will address the various parts of the Trading Plan, each in its proper place in the pages to come.

What Is the Purpose of the Trading Plan?

There are several reasons to have a Trading Plan, but probably the biggest is the way it simplifies things. A good, well-thought-out Trading Plan takes a great deal of excess thinking out of the trading process. Decisionmaking is very clearcut. The Plan defines what is supposed to be done, when, and how. Trading can be a very emotionally charged venture. That can lead to all kinds of less-than-optimal behavior as was demonstrated in earlier chapters. The Trading Plan takes that out of the equation. Just follow the plan.

The Trading Plan is also very, very handy in helping one to understand the reasons for performance problems. If one is suffering from losses beyond what would be expected (as defined by the Plan), there are only two possible reasons. Either the Plan is not being followed, or there is a problem with the trading system. That's it. Without the Trading Plan, resolving performance issues is a much more complicated process.

While a Trading Plan is intended to help the trader succeed in the markets, having a Trading Plan is not a guarantee of generating profits. A Plan is only as good as the components in it. The primary focus of the remainder of this text is to help make those components as strong as possible.

How Does One Develop a Trading Plan?

The process of building a solid Trading Plan can be fairly straightforward, or it can be complex and involved. That is entirely based on the trader and what he or she is looking to accomplish. Much of that is determined in the upcoming section on assessment. In essence, however, the remainder of this book takes one through the process of developing the Trading Plan, and covers the related elements involved in doing so.

Before we move on along, however, there is one piece of business—the Journal.

JOURNALS

As previously noted, there are two elements for sustained successful trading. One is having and executing a good Plan. The other is having a good trading system as part of that plan. Every trader should maintain journals for focusing on both those elements.

The first journal covers system development planning and research. In it you keep track of everything that goes into your work. This kind of journal can become an invaluable resource as it provides a record of all your testing to which you can refer at future times. It will keep you from duplicating your work and can also provide ideas for new lines of exploration.

The second journal is a log of all trading activity. This journal's objective is to monitor both the performance of your trading system and your ability to execute it with consistency (follow your Plan). Poor trading systems are less frequently the cause of poor trading performance than the inability of the trader to properly apply them. That's following the Trading Plan. The second journal is intended to make sure you do just that.

Journals are only as good as what gets put into them. If one fails to accurately track trades, it becomes hard to judge trading system performance. If one fails to record trading system tests, it becomes very easy to duplicate effort and frustrating when trying to recall the results of experiments for potential use going forward.

Homework

Start to maintain both a system research journal and a trading log. These both should be ongoing efforts, not just a one-off for the sake of completing an assignment. Be thorough and honest. Do not short-change yourself by failing to put in entries or through incompleteness.

PERSONAL ASSESSMENT

The backbone of a good Trading Plan is its reflection of the trader who is applying it. Plans, systems, and methods that do not mesh with those who attempt to trade them are often doomed to fail. For that reason, it is imperative that the first step in building a system is assessing the trader.

Trading is not something one does on a whim or in some willy-nilly fashion. It takes a thorough understanding of several things, not the least of which is your own personality and situation. To that end, the first step in the process is assessment. The topics related to methods and system building are addressed soon, but not before laying the groundwork that will help in guiding the trader to pick those most suitable to her or his individual situation.

In progressing through the steps that follow, make sure to include the questions and answers in your system research journal.

Step 1: First Things First—Why?

Can you state clearly what motivates you to be a trader? Is it the potential for large profits? Is it the excitement? Is it the challenge of puzzle solving? Maybe it's something else.

Do you know what your trading goals are? This doesn't necessarily have anything to do with money, by the way. It is just a question of what you hope to get out of being a financial market participant.

Motivation is a very serious consideration. At the top level, it can help you decide whether trading is even something you should be doing. The markets very quickly weed out those trading for the wrong reasons. For example, excitement and consistent profitability do not go hand in hand for many people. Although some do well operating in highly emotional states, most do not. It is quite often a good idea to find other sources for that rush.

At the same time, motivation can be directly applicable to the way one trades. For example, if you want to trade for a living, you are going to take a different approach than if you just want to handle your retirement account. This is a topic that will come up repeatedly in the sections ahead, and it is something that must be reassessed from time to time.

> For a discussion of the reasons why people get into trading, and the impact those reasons can have on their performance check out this article: www.trade2win.com/knowledge/articles/why-trade?

Step 2: Financial Assessment

Before one should even start to think about trading, it is imperative to determine whether it is reasonable to do so in the first place. Trading should be done only with risk capital. Risk capital comprises funds that, if lost, would not negatively impact the trader's financial well-being. In simple terms, one should not put at risk what one cannot afford to lose. This is a hugely important point. A trader who is playing with money he or she needs to live on does not operate from a solid footing in many regards, not the least of which is the stress it creates and the impact that it can have on decision making.

Once the question of how much money you can afford to lose is addressed, another similar question must be asked. How much are you *willing* to lose? At first glance, one might think this is the same question. There is an important difference, though. While some folks are risk takers who would answer the same to both questions, many people would not. An example would be the trader with $10,000 in available risk capital only willing to lose $5,000.

This second question moves us from the realm of the practical to the world of the emotional in that it addresses the individual's specific feelings toward money. Different people will place value on different sums in varying ways. In the just mentioned example, the risk capital was $10,000. One trader might be fine losing 100 percent of that amount, while another would consider a 50 percent loss devastating. It may be hard to look at it in that manner with such a relatively small sum, but what if the risk capital was raised to $10 million? That changes things, doesn't it? That first trader might not be so willing to lose 100 percent now. That's an awful lot of money!

The point being made here is that before one begins trading, it should be clear from both the objective sense and the emotional one what is at stake. This is Step 1 in the trader's ongoing process of risk evaluation and management, and it needs to be re-evaluated periodically.

One other financial consideration is account or portfolio size. One can start trading stocks with relatively little money, and it is possible to open an FXTrade account with an initial deposit of less than $100. This is not the case in all markets with all brokers or trading platforms, though. Many have minimums of $3,000 and higher, and there can be baseline account sizes for the use of margin.

Regardless of what the minimum requirement is, however, one needs to keep transaction costs in mind. A small account is impacted more significantly in terms of performance by transaction costs like commissions than is a larger one. Consider a trade with a $20 commission. That would be a 2 percent hit on a $1,000 account, but only a 0.4 percent impact on a $5,000 account. What's more, nonflat rate commissions (which still exist) tend to operate on a sliding scale where larger trades incur smaller commissions on a percentage basis. For example, in options trading there is often a fixed base fee, then a small per option fee.

Also, if one trades the futures market the account size becomes an issue in regard to margin requirements. If one is to trade E-mini S&P 500 contracts, the account must have at least enough to cover the initial margin requirement (approximately $2,500). It's also a good idea to have some cushion so one small loss does not mean having insufficient funds for future trades.

All of this is somewhat irrelevant when trading demo accounts, but it is very important when shifting into live action.

Step 3: Time Assessment

Trading requires time in a couple of ways. The first is the time dedicated to developing a trading system. This can be thought of as a one-off thing, but in reality it is more an ongoing process. Once a system is in place, time is required in terms of monitoring the markets for signals, executing transactions, and managing positions. How much time all these different elements require depends on the trading system. The trading system, in turn, needs to take into account the amount of time the trader has available.

With that in mind, the first question to be answered is how much time each day/week/month (whichever is most appropriate) can you dedicate to the various requirements of trading and managing a trading system?

Different trading styles require different time focus. As a rule, the shorter term the trading, the more specifically dedicated time required. A day trader, for example, runs positions that are opened and closed during the same session. This normally means a lot of time spent watching the market for entry and exit signals. An intermediate or longer-term trader who holds trades for weeks or more does not have to dedicate the same amount of time to watching the markets. He or she can usually get away with only spot checking from time to time. Of course there is a whole array of possibilities in between.

At this point it is also important to consider distractions. There is a major difference between having six hours per day of uninterrupted time to watch the markets and having six hours of time during which you will be making and receiving phone calls, having meetings, and otherwise not being able to focus on the markets and make trades when required. In the former case one could day trade. In the latter, however, day trading would probably be a disaster as the trader would most likely miss important trading situations on a frequent basis. This sort of thing needs to be taken into account.

The basic decision one has to make is in what time frame the trader can reasonably expect to operate on a consistent basis. The individual must be able to do all the data gathering, research, market analysis, trade execution and monitoring, portfolio management, and any other functions required of their trading system. That means a trading time frame has to be selected that allows the trader to handle all of these duties without the kinds of disruptions that can cause poor system input from the user, and therefore poor system performance.

Before moving on, the comment should be made that nothing says a trader cannot operate in multiple time frames. The point of this step is really to determine the shortest time frame realistically workable for the trader. He or she would then certainly be able to trade in ones longer-term than that base point. For example, just because one has the ability to day trade does not mean he or she cannot operate in a longer-term trade horizon.

One last thing to consider, especially where it relates to short-term activity such as day trading, is time of day. It is all fine and good if a trader has eight hours of uninterrupted free time available during which to trade. What if that time is between 6:00 P.M. and 2:00 A.M. Eastern, though? None of the primary U.S. markets is open then, so the day trading options are a little thin for a U.S.-based trader. (Forex might be an option).

It is also worth stating that sometimes trading is not a good idea. We all go through spells in our lives when we are distracted by any number of things (like the author writing this book!). This can be through illness, injury, family or relationship issues, or work-related stress. These tend to be temporary in nature, but nevertheless are a factor in our trading. If you cannot focus on trading the way you need to—and by that we mean following your plan—then no time frame is going to be the right one. It's perfectly fine to take time off and not trade.

Step 4: Expectations Assessment

Clearly, anyone who trades does so with the expectation of making profits. We take risks to gain rewards. The question each trader must answer, however, is what kind of return he or she expects to make. This is a very important consideration. as it speaks directly to what kind of trading will take place, what market or markets are best suited to the purpose, and the kinds of risks required.

Let us start with a very simple example. Suppose a trader would like to make 10 percent per year on a very consistent basis with little variance. There are any number of options available. If interest rates are sufficiently high, the trader could simply put the money into a fixed income instrument like a CD or a bond of some kind and take relatively little risk. Should interest rates not be sufficient, the trader could use one or more of any number of other markets (stocks, commodities, currencies, etc.) with varying risk profiles and structures to find one or more (perhaps in combination) that suits the need. The trader may not even have to make many actual transactions each year to accomplish the objective.

A trader looking for 100 percent returns each year would have a very different situation. This individual will not be looking at the cash fixed income market, but could do so via the leverage offered in the futures market. Similarly, other leverage based markets are more likely candidates than cash ones, perhaps including equities. The trader will almost certainly require greater market exposure to achieve the goal, and most likely will have to execute a larger number of transactions than in the previous scenario.

As you can see, your goal dictates the methods by which you achieve it. The end certainly dictates the means to a great degree. Please see Figure 4.1.

There is one other consideration in this particular assessment, though, and it is one that harks back to the earlier discussion of willingness to lose. Trading systems have what are commonly referred to as drawdowns. A drawdown is the distance (measured in % or account/portfolio value terms) from an equity peak to the lowest point immediately following it. For example, say a trader's portfolio rose from $10,000 to $15,000, fell to $12,000, then rose to $20,000. The drop from the $15,000

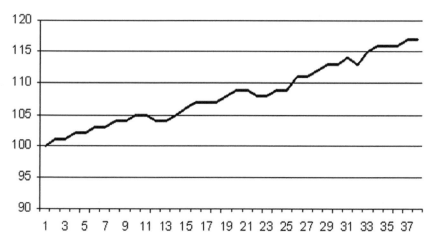

FIGURE 4.1 Low Drawdown Equity Curve

peak to the $12,000 trough would be considered a drawdown, in this case of $3,000 or 20 percent. Please see Figure 4.2.

Each trader must determine how large a drawdown (in this case generally thought of in percentage terms) he or she is willing to accept. It is very much a risk/reward decision. On one extreme are trading systems with very, very small drawdowns, but also with low returns (low

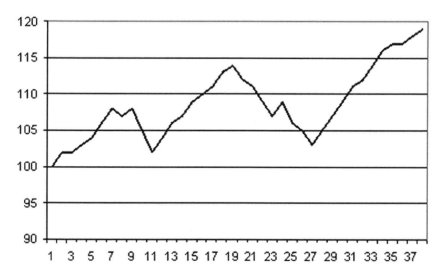

FIGURE 4.2 High Drawdown Equity Curve

risk—low reward). On the other extreme are the trading systems with large returns, but similarly large drawdowns (high risk—high reward). Of course, every trader's dream is a system with high returns and small drawdowns. The reality of trading, however, is often less pleasantly somewhere in between.

The question might be asked what it matters if high returns is the objective. It is quite simple. The more the account value falls, the bigger the return required to make that loss back up. That means time. Large drawdowns tend to mean long periods between equity peaks. The combination of sharp drops in equity value and lengthy time spans making the money back can potentially be emotionally destabilizing, leading to the trader abandoning the system at exactly the wrong time. In short, the trader must be able to accept, without concern, the drawdowns expected to occur in the system being used.

Before progressing further, it must be noted that there is potentially an important link between the time frame topic of Step 3 and the expectations issue here. It was noted earlier that in some cases more frequent trading can be required to achieve the risk/return profile sought. If the results of Step 3 and Step 4 conflict, a resolution must be found. And it must be the questions from this Step that must be reconsidered, as the time frames determined in the previous one are probably not very flexible (especially going from longer-term trading to shorter-term participation).

Step 5: Market Knowledge Assessment

By going through the assessments in the last couple of steps (time and expectations) one should start getting an idea of what market or markets are best suited for the kind of trading being formulated. Table 4.2 will help narrow the focus a bit further.

The question then becomes one of knowledge of and comfort with the markets on the list of prospects you develop. It is always easiest to trade in a market where there is a firm understanding of the operations and the instruments in question. In such a circumstance the trader can focus on other things. The trader looking to work in a market new to them, however, has a learning curve to overcome first and foremost.

Picking up the basics of any given market and/or instrument is fairly easy, as there are plenty of resources in that regard. Getting comfortable, however, is often more a question of experience and observation. That takes more time.

Before one trades a market, certain things need to be understood.

- Addressing the point from Step 3, the trading day should be known. Foreign exchange is still the one true 24-hour market, but several oth-

TABLE 4.2 Market Matrix

Market	High Volume Time Frame	Cash/Spot	Futures	Options
Equities	9:30–4:00 ET for U.S. exchanges (similar local times for other global markets)	**Primary**	Yes (single stock futures)	Yes (cash)
Indices	8:20–4:00 ET for U.S. exchanges (similar local times for other global markets)	Yes (Exchange-Traded Funds, SPDRs, QQQ, etc.)	**Primary**	Yes (cash and futures)
Fixed Income	8:20–3:00 ET for U.S. exchanges (similar local times for other global markets)	Yes (but not usually traded actively by individuals)	**Primary**	Yes (futures)
Forex	24-Hour (best overall volume during N.Y./London overlap, but has other high volume times for regional currencies)	**Primary**	Yes	Yes (futures via exchanges, but spot variations are proliferating)
Commodities	Varies by market	Not for traders	**Primary**	Yes (futures)

ers have closed the gap. Even in forex, though, there are times of day, especially in certain currency pairs, when trading is thin. The longer-term traders might not concern themselves with this sort of thing, but it is vitally important for shorter-term participants to be aware of these sorts of liquidity and volatility considerations when choosing a market for trading.

- In consideration of the questions raised in Step 2, the capital requirements for effectively trading a market are important to understand. Many markets these days can be traded with small accounts, but that does not necessarily mean one can have a reasonable expectation for performance. Transaction costs can be an important consideration, and margin requirements have an impact. A poorly capitalized account can severely hamper performance, so it is important for the trader to operate only where the risk capital available is sufficient to trade well.

- Taking into consideration points raised in Step 4, the trader must understand the instrument(s) being traded in terms of price increments. Stocks are easy in that a 1-point movement in share price is $1 per share. The futures markets are considerably more diverse in terms of contract specifications and point values. Forex pip values vary according to the market rate and the size of the position. In order to understand both risk and expectation, it is important to know these values. It is also very important to have a good idea of the kind of price volatility that can take place in the instrument(s) being considered during the anticipated time frame.

Refer to the support site for this book (www.andurilonline.com/book) for more in-depth information on the various markets and instruments.

Step 6: Skill Assessment

Trading can be as complicated or as simple as one wants. Some traders use methods that require very little technical proficiency. Others run systems based on advanced math and computer programming. Where a trader falls in this spectrum determines what methods are likely to produce positive results.

Modern trading does increasingly require at least a modicum of technical savvy. In general terms, however, if you can operate a computer sufficiently well to get on the Internet, you can trade. Everything else is just a bonus, albeit sometimes a quite handy one. There are numerous software packages available from the ubiquitous Microsoft Excel to specialized data gathering and charting packages to artificial intelligence applications (neural nets, etc.). One can find successful traders who use any level of technology, including those who still do things entirely by hand.

The point is not that one is better than another, or that you need complicated tools with all sorts of bells and whistles, but rather that there is something out there for anyone. Each trader just needs to find what is comfortable and useful, and what is not going to eat up the trading funds in costs.

Of course the great thing about skill sets is that they can be expanded. All it takes is a little learning. As an individual gains experience and exposure to trading and the markets, he or she is bound to pick up new knowledge and understanding. It is an evolutionary process.

Homework

As the first set of entries in your system research journal, address the questions and issues brought up in this section. Answer the questions posed and use those answers to make an overall determination as to how you think you should best operate in the markets.

THE PLAN

Now that we have gone through the assessment process it is time to take that information and awareness to the next step—forming the actual Trading Plan. Our plan must account for a number of things:

- Trading objectives.
- Market(s) and instrument(s) traded.
- Trading time frame(s) utilized.
- Software, hardware, and other tools required.
- Amount of risk capital put into play.
- Broker(s) and/or trading platform(s) used.
- Risk management strategy.
- Trading system(s) employed.
- Trading routine.

We cover each of these elements of the Trading Plan briefly in the pages that follow. The risk management and trading system sections, however, are more expansive discussions, so they are addressed in more detail in the chapters that follow.

Trading Objectives

What have you determined to be your goal(s) for trading? Most of the time this can be expressed as profits (either in currency or percent return) per unit of time. For example, you might choose a goal like making $500 per month, or achieving average quarterly returns of 5 percent. Maybe you want to frame your objective in terms of risk adjusted return, and so set a goal based on the Sharpe ratio or similar measures (covered later).

Whatever you select, based on the assessments you did in the previous section of this chapter, make sure you have something both definable and measurable. Do not short-change yourself by setting a goal like "make money." Remember, part of the value of a Trading Plan is in its ability to help in performance assessment. If no measuring sticks by which to compare actual results with planned ones are included, the whole purpose is defeated.

Market(s) and Instrument(s)

Will you trade options on equity indices? Are you going to use the futures market to trade in gold? Will you be trading spot forex? Maybe it is all of the above. Regardless, make sure you outline clearly your intentions in your Trading Plan. When getting started, it is generally best to stick with one market and/or instrument. Additional ones can be added as knowledge and comfort increase. As noted throughout, we primarily use forex for the examples going forward.

Trading Time Frame(s)

What is the time frame in which you will be trading? Are you going to be a day trader? A swing trader? A long-term trader? Again, it probably is best for the new trader to work exclusively in one time frame to gain a good understanding of operating in that manner.

Software, Hardware, and Other Tools

Outline the things you will use in your trading. This includes the computers system or systems, the software, the data feeds, and the Internet access that will drive your trading and analysis. Make sure that you have some kind of backup plan in place should your primary system fail during a critical time. There is nothing worse than being unable to make trades or adjust orders because your Internet service is down.

New (and experienced) traders can get caught up with all the fancy software and other stuff that is available. Try to avoid going overboard. Trading does not really require all that much beyond a way to enter and monitor trades and keep track of prices. As you develop your analytic techniques and methods, you may find that a certain kind of software package, source of data, or some other tool or resource is a good addition to your trading repertoire. Be selective, though.

Risk Capital

This was addressed fairly comprehensively in the assessment earlier. During the early learning and development process, one should stick to demo accounts. Once you have a firm handle on trading and are comfortable with your trading system, then you can shift over to real money trading.

Broker/Trading Platform

You defined earlier what market(s) and instrument(s) you will trade. That dictates, to a certain degree, how you go about trading in terms of where you get your trades executed. There are a number of different options available regardless of what you plan on trading.

A good resource for finding a broker or trading platform to suit your needs is Trade2Win (www.trade2win.com). The site has member reviews of brokers (and other trading resources), plus discussions of them in the message boards where questions are answered.

As we have throughout the text so far, we will continue to use Oanda's FXTrade system for trading examples.

Risk Management Strategy

This is covered in the chapters to come.

Trading System(s) Employed

This is covered in the chapters to come.

Trading Routine

Trading is a process. There are steps that must be completed along the way. Your routine must incorporate them. Certain things will be defined by your trading system or strategy, such as how and when market analysis is done and when orders get placed. For example, a longer-term trader might do the requisite analysis over the weekend and place the orders first thing on Monday.

Other things are more general, such as when and how you record your trades for accounting purposes. This is important for tax records. It is also important in the case of disputed transactions, which do sometimes occur.

Be sure to include in your trading routine the process by which you evaluate your trading. This means not only gauging how your trading system is performing based on expectations, but also how you are sticking to the Trading Plan. This is a learning tool in your development as a trader, which can lead to improvements in your trading system, style, or methods. It is also a way to keep on task with your Plan. Remember how we said earlier that having a Trading Plan allows the trader to determine the cause of poor trading performance.

Modifications

The Trading Plan is a work in progress. That is something to keep in mind. As things change, the Trading Plan must change, too. Go through the assessment process periodically, especially when you have changes in your financial or life situation. Also, as your research leads to changes in your trading system or methods, be sure to reflect those adjustments in your Trading Plan.

Remember, the main purpose of the Trading Plan is to keep you on task and operating in an effective and efficient manner, given your operating parameters. It is, however, only as good as you make it, and it is completely useless if it is not applied in practice.

Sticking to the Plan

A Trading Plan has value only if it is utilized as intended. It does you no good to have one if you do not stick to it. We all know this, yet traders find reasons to deviate from their Plan, almost always with negative consequences. Why? There are several reasons.

- *The Plan does not match the trader*: A Trading Plan is a personal thing intended for a specific trader, based on their personality and circumstances. If it is not created honestly based on reality rather than hope, then it will not match the trader, and likely it will be neglected.
- *Lack of patience*: Trading Plans are intended to be long-term, at least relatively so. Many traders give up on their Plan, or often more specifically the trading system in the Plan, after a period of subpar performance rather than sticking it out through the inevitable rough times.
- *Lack of discipline*: Trading according to a plan requires continual performance of a set of actions in a proscribed manner. Doing so takes discipline. Traders lacking discipline do not stick to Trading Plans. (The word "discipline" is probably the most frequently used in regard to trading success.)
- *Self-destructive behavior:* Sometimes traders have deeply ingrained issues of a psychological nature that tend to sabotage them. It is something that can be overcome with work, but first it must be recognized and addressed.

These are not the only reasons traders fail to stick to Trading Plans, but they do represent a large portion of the explanations for its happening. The point is that a Trading Plan is little more than a document if not put into practice.

Homework

Document your Trading Plan, from start to finish based on what was discussed in this chapter, in your system research journal. Leave space for the risk management and trading system sections. They will be filled in later.

CHAPTER 5

Risk and Money Management

Before getting into decision making in trading and defining the systems, methods, and techniques whereby buy and sell decisions are made, the topic of risk must be defined and addressed. That is what this chapter is all about.

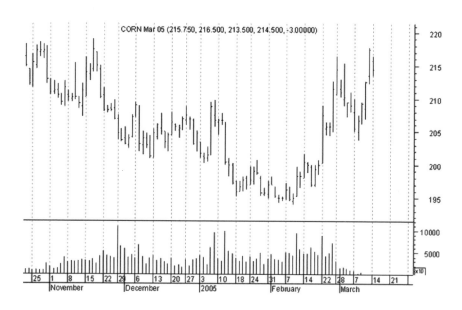

WHAT IS RISK?

Before we started on the topic of the Trading Plan, we had discussed how to execute trades, what makes markets move, and how they do so. In this chapter we continue along the logical path and take a look at how price movement can impact the market participant, or more specifically how it can impact one's portfolio or trading account. It is price movement that provides opportunity to the speculator. At the same time, however, the same price movement (or at least the potential for it) creates risk, a risk that is not restricted just to speculators. Anyone who participates in the markets, be it in a hedging, issuance, investment, or any other purpose, must be aware of and address the risk inherent in doing so.

Risk can be defined as the potential for something undesirable to take place in regard to some activity (or lack thereof). It is often thought of in terms of chance or probability. For example, when one is driving a car, there is a risk of being in an accident. Mostly the odds of its happening are low, but if the weather is bad, or the lighting poor, or the driver impaired, the chance of something untoward happening is higher. The driver can reduce the odds of crashing by not driving under adverse conditions and by being aware, alert, and conscientiously focused when operating the vehicle.

This example can be directly carried over into trading, where risk is thought of in terms of either capital or rate of return. Taking positions in the financial markets, just as in driving, always implies a level of risk. Granted, trading is unlikely to lead to bodily harm (unless your spouse finds out you lost the family vacation money!), but the basic idea holds. There is a chance for an adverse outcome to any venture into the market.

Just as in driving, though, there are factors that increase the risks. Weather is just one of those factors (at least for some market participants). There are data releases, external shocks, prominent speakers, trade flows, and all the other things discussed in Chapter 3. And just as in driving, sometimes the trader can be impaired for one reason or another, increasing the chance of poor results (recall that discussion in the Assessment portion of Chapter 4). But as in driving, the trader can reduce the odds for negative performance by being alert to the situation, applying leverage in a reasonable fashion, and diligently following the Plan.

In academic terms, risk is generally thought of as the chance of not achieving the expected outcome. This is defined in a bidirectional fashion. There is a risk of a higher return than expected, just as there is the risk of a lower than expected return. Statistical measures are employed in this regard to attempt to approximate that risk, some of which we bring into play later on as we look at trading system performance.

Relatively few traders, however, consider making higher than expected returns a risk. This is not to say it is the best approach to take, but risk is mostly defined in terms of loss of capital (negative return). This can be addressed in two parts. One is the probability of losing. The other is the size of the loss.

The probability of loss is most often assigned to the timing of position entry and exit. That is a function of the trading system, which is discussed in the chapters ahead. As was outlined in Chapter 3, though, predicting the market return of any given period, even in a binary up/down fashion, is a difficult proposition at best. Traders do their best to put the odds in their favor, or at least to know what the odds are likely to be. That said, no one really knows what will happen on any given trade, so the control of whether a specific trade is going to be a winner or loser is out of their hands. Even a trading system with a 99 percent success rate is subject to a negative result, and it is virtually impossible to accurately predict when that one loser is going to occur.

What a trader can do, however, is manage the size of the loss, should one occur. The trader can also manage the impact of a series of losses on the portfolio. Table 5.1 and Figure 5.2 show why this is important.

Table 5.1 outlines the gain required to be made in order to overcome a given loss. For example, if one's portfolio were to suffer a 25 percent drop in value, it would take a 33 percent increase to get back to where it started $(100 - 25 = 75, 25/75 = 33\%)$.

Figure 5.2 depicts the same thing in visual form. Notice how the required return to break even after a loss increases at an exponential rate. This is why controlling losses is extremely important.

TABLE 5.1 Loss to Breakeven
Return Requirement

Portfolio Loss	Gain to Get Even
1%	1%
5%	5%
10%	11%
20%	25%
25%	33%
30%	43%
35%	54%
40%	67%
45%	82%
50%	100%
75%	300%

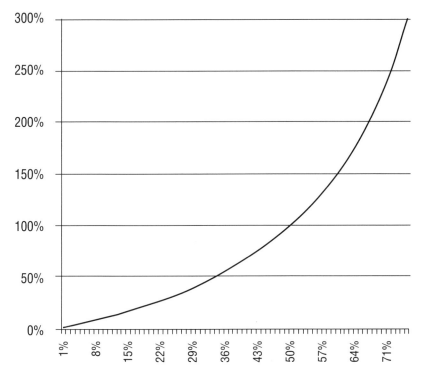

FIGURE 5.2 Required Percent Gain to Break Even for a Given Percent Loss

The sections to come in this chapter delve into the process of managing potential declines in portfolio and/or position value. Before we do so, however, one important thing needs to be addressed that lays the foundation for everything else.

Risk Tolerance

Before one can set about properly outlining a meaningful risk or money management strategy, one first has to understand and define her or his risk tolerance. Some people are naturally risk-averse. They will tend to only feel comfortable exposing small amounts of their portfolio to the potential for loss. Others are more risk-tolerant and can stomach wilder portfolio swings.

There is much that goes into this tolerance determination—age, personality, income, life situation—but the central point is that risk management must take it into consideration. (It should be noted that institutions also have varying risk tolerances, albeit based on a few different variables.) Risk tolerance goes a long way toward determining the manner in which a trader can operate. Once risk tolerance is understood, the other elements of the discussion that follow in this chapter fall into place.

Homework

You left an opening for your risk management strategy in your system research journal where you outlined your Trading Plan. We are going to start fleshing that out now by defining your risk tolerance. Answer the following questions in your journal:

- What percentage of your total portfolio or trading account are you willing to lose before you stop trading?
- What percentage are you willing to lose in any given period? (Define period in terms of your trading time frame: day for day traders, week for swing traders, month or some longer period for intermediate and longer-term traders.)
- What percentage are you willing to lose on any given trade?
- How much of a peak-to-trough drawdown will you accept? (See the Expectations assessment from Chapter 4).

MONEY MANAGEMENT—TRADE

Neatly stated, money management is the process by which one defines and regulates the risks of trading. Money management can also be viewed as the process by which one simultaneously attempts to minimize the risk of loss and maximize the opportunity for gain.

From a practical perspective, money management must be approached on three levels. The first is in the Trading Plan, where the trader defines the overall approach to risk. The second is in the trading strategy or strategies utilized as part of the Trading Plan, where money management is involved in such things as position sizing. The final level is on the actual trade-by-trade basis, where the steps can be taken to control the possible loss suffered due to adverse market action. The second level is discussed in detail as part of the chapters on trading system development. The remainder of this chapter concentrates on the first and third levels, starting with the latter.

Stops

Stop orders (stops) were mentioned in Chapter 3 as part of the discussion of market orders, and examples were shown to demonstrate their use.

They are a tool commonly employed by traders with open positions. One with an active long position can place a sell stop below the market price to prevent a loss in excess of a certain amount. For example, a trader who buys 100 shares of IBM at 100 might put a stop at 95. That stop would be triggered if the market moves down to 95, at which point the shares would be sold. The trader would lose $500 on the trade, but would be protected from a larger loss should IBM continue to move lower. In the same manner, a short position would be protected by a stop placed above the current market price.

In some cases, traders will adjust the stops as the market moves in the intended direction to lock in profits. Let us say, for example, that a trader sells gold at $400 and places a stop at $410, meaning her position would be exited if the market rose to $410 or higher. If gold drops to $350, the trader could move her stop down to something like $370. That would lock in $30 in profits, while keeping the trade open for further gains. These kinds of orders are called trailing stops. As the market moves, the stop is trailed along.

It must be noted, however, that stops are not guarantees. Remember that a stop order becomes a market order when the order price is reached or exceeded. If the market is moving rapidly at the time the stop level is hit, the actual execution price of the trade could vary from the order price.

Market Wisdom

One of the most prevalent bits of advice to new traders is to always use stops to protect one against extreme losses. This is a good policy in the majority of cases. Unless one's trading system eliminates the need (some do), it is highly advisable to have a stop.

It should be made clear, however, that there is a difference between a stop intended as a money management control and one that is used in a trading system to exit a position. The former is to protect one from extreme losses due to adverse action. That is the focus of this chapter. The latter is to exit a trade when the market indicates that it is time to do so based on the decision-making process of the system in question. That is addressed in later chapters.

For example, if one has a sell stop at 9.75, one could see that filled at 9.76, 9.70, 9.50, or any number of other places. Generally, it will be close in active, liquid markets, but you cannot assume a specific price for a fill, even in electronically traded markets.

This sort of risk is especially apparent where there are discrete openings and closings, as in the stock and futures markets. If prices

move between one day's close and the next day's open, as could happen
if there were a significant news item, the stop can get filled significantly
away from the order price. It is unavoidable when it happens, and is
something to take into account when one is developing a strategy for
stop placement (or for even trading a market).

Lock Limit

Lock limit is a situation that develops in the futures market when the natural clearing market price (the price at which trade will be facilitated) is
beyond the daily limit and trading essentially halts with price locked at
the limit. It is locked there because no transactions can be executed beyond the limit and traders are unwilling to trade inside the limit.

Using corn as our example, imagine that the closing price on Monday
was $5.15 per bushel. On Tuesday it is reported that a severe blight has
struck the corn crop, creating a supply short-fall. Prices jump to the $5.35
limit ($5.15 + $0.20). The expectation is that the $6.00 level will be hit.

In such a situation, the market will go lock limit because trade cannot
take place above $5.35 and no trader will sell below that point knowing
the market is very likely to go higher. So trade essentially stops.

Lock limit can be broken during the day if things calm down, or it can
go on for days. In our example, if corn were to indeed go directly to
$6.00, it would mean four consecutive limit moves.

Adverse overnight moves are not the only thing that can cause order
fills well away from the expected level. In many markets, especially futures, there are price movement limits known as daily trading limits.
These are daily barriers based on the previous day's close beyond which
prices may not trade during a given daily session. For example, corn futures, which trade on the Chicago Board of Trade (CBOT), have a 20 cent
per bushel limit, which is equivalent to $1,000 per futures contract. That
means the price cannot rise or fall more than 20 cents on any given day.
These limits can lead to a truly unnerving situation known as a *lock limit*.
(See the box.)

There are other forms of trading limitations across the markets, sometimes referred to as circuit breakers. They range from restrictions on the
types of trades allowed (as in the well-known "up-tick" rule in the stock
market whereby one can sell short only at a price higher than the last one
transacted) to actual trading halts if certain daily barriers are hit (as insti-
tuted in the U.S. stock market following the Crash of 1987).

The reasoning behind daily price limits and circuit breaker type actions is to calm the markets in the face of extreme volatility. The idea is
that if traders are given some time to gather themselves and settle, this

should lead to less frantic activity. While fine in principle, these restrictions on trading can actually increase a trader's stress level. No one wants to be left wondering if, when, and at what price they will be able to exit a position that is under pressure. It is a horrifying situation.

Hedging

Hedging is the process by which one uses a second position to offset some of the risk associated with a particular trade. It is not a common part of trading when one thinks primarily of speculating, but some do make use of it. In this regard, the type of hedge a trader would use is to offset one or more risks that are not specific to the instrument being traded, but that may have influence on its price activity.

What Is a Hedge?

A hedge is a secondary position taken on in conjunction with a primary one to reduce or offset a particular kind of risk associated with the primary position. Those risks include:

- Currency risk.
- Interest rate risk.
- Commodity price movement risk.
- General market decline risk.

Hedging is done by holders of assets to protect against adverse price moves. For example, an oil producer might sell crude oil futures (take a short position) to protect against a drop in the price of oil.

Hedging is also done by those looking to buy assets or holding short positions so as to protect against a price increase. For example a trader shorting a gold stock might buy gold futures to protect against a rise in the commodity.

Hedges are often, but not exclusively, done via futures and/or options.

For example, a trader who expects IBM to report good earnings might take a long position in the stock to profit from a move up in price, and simultaneously short S&P 500 futures or buy S&P 500 put options. By taking a short position in the index (in some ratio to the IBM position), the trader would profit from a fall in the overall stock market, which offsets that risk (the so-called systemic risk) as it relates to the long IBM position. The trade is then left with only risks related to IBM itself (nonsystemic risk). On the flip side, if the market rallies then the short position in the S&P 500 loses money (at a minimum the option premium). In this way, a hedge is like an insurance policy: It protects against a certain kind of exposure, but also has a cost.

The primary reason the vast majority of traders do not hedge is their time frame. Most traders are fairly short-term in nature. Hedging in that time horizon may not make sense given the relatively small size of the moves in question, and the costs of the additional transactions for entering and exiting the hedge. For example, interest rates tend to change gradually and their rise or fall takes some additional time to impact the general economy and other markets. A trader who is in and out of positions in days, or perhaps even weeks, is unlikely to be impacted by those changes. In that case, is there a value in hedging?

That said, for some traders hedging is a useful tool to define and limit position risk. For more information on hedging and related topics, check this book's resource page at www.andurilonline.com/book.

Spreads

A hedge is defined by what is trying to be accomplished, specifically, to offset one or more specific risks associated with the position being held. It is, as noted, comparable to taking out an insurance policy. In some instances this is confused with creating a spread position.

A spread position is one in which offsetting trades are made in two or more related but different instruments in an attempt to profit by the changes in the price or some other differential among the instruments in question. This is not the same as a hedge, though some tend to equate the two. The spread does not have the same insurance policy characteristics.

An example of a spread would be buying a 2-year note and selling a 10-year note. In such a case, the trader is making a bet that the interest rate spread between the shorter-term and longer-term maturities is going to widen (yield curve will steepen). Another kind of spread trade would

---

Fixed Income Securities

The yield of a fixed income security, like a 10-year note, moves in inverse relationship to its price. As prices go up, yields fall. As prices fall, the yields rise. The extent to which changes in yield create changes in the price of a fixed income instrument is a function of *duration*.

The yield curve is a depiction of yields at each given maturity from shortest to longest. It is referred to as a curve because it is rarely straight. A normal yield curve is upwardly sloping—long-term interest rates are higher than shorter-term rates. An inverted curve is the opposite—short-term rates are higher than long-term rates. (It is often said that an inverted yield curve is a predictor of an economic downturn.)

be to buy gold and sell platinum in expectation that the price of the former will rise more than the price of the latter (or fall less).

To make a direct hedge/spread comparison, let us start with a long position in General Motors stock. We bought the shares because we think GM is going to see excellent earnings growth in the quarters ahead. We are concerned, however, that the market as a whole might not perform very well in the near future, which could put pressure on the price of the stock. As a result, we buy S&P 500 put options, so that if the market does fall, we are protected. That is a hedge.

In this case, where we want to guard against a broad stock market decline, we would NOT want to take a short position in another auto stock such as Ford. While it *might* provide us *some* protection, one stock is hardly likely to provide a good representation of the market as a whole, or even necessarily a market sector. It is an inefficient hedge, as Ford-specific factors (nonsystemic) could be the dominant reasons for variation in the price of Ford stock. Think about something like a product recall, which would certainly pressure Ford's earnings but is unlikely to influence the general state of the automotive sector over much.

If, on the other hand, we think that GM is likely to take market share away from Ford, then we can take a short position in the latter in conjunction with our long position in GM. In that scenario we would expect GM stock to outperform Ford stock, regardless of how the overall market performs. That is a spread trade, which is also sometimes referred to as a matched pair trade.

A Spread Trade in Action

Assume that we buy 100 shares of GM and sell 100 shares of Ford, both at a price of $60.

If GM rises to $70 and Ford falls to $50, we make $2,000 ($10 × 100 × 2).

If the situation reverses and Ford rises to $70 and GM falls to $50, we lose $2,000.

In theory, we could make an infinite profit as there is no cap on how high GM stock could go in the face of Ford declining, remaining the same, or not rising as quickly. At the same time, we could have an infinite loss since there is also no limit to how high Ford could rise in the reverse scenario.

The difference between the two positions is subtle, but important. In both case we are taking opposing positions in securities we expect to move in essentially similar directions, though in the spread case we may expect GM to rise and Ford to fall. In the hedge situation, however, we are trying to limit our downside, at least as caused by one potential risk factor, which also likely cuts down our profit potential. The spread trade, however, is basically open-ended. The spread can go in either direction a virtually limitless amount.

Offsets

Another action that is sometimes referred to as a hedge, but is not, is to take simultaneous long and short positions of the same size in the same instrument (generally at different prices, but not always). This is referred to as an offset because as long as both those positions are held, the trader will neither gain nor suffer from any price movement. The market risk is nullified.

Offsets are NOT hedges. A hedged position still has a risk exposure somewhere by which the potential for profit remains. Offsets do not while both trades remain open. Once one leg is closed, the remaining position reverts back to a standard long or short trade like any other. Figure 5.3 demonstrates.

Assume both long and short trades are entered at 100. The profit/loss profile for both trades are represented by the diagonal lines. Together, however, as the horizontal line on Figure 5.3 shows, the combined position will always have a net gain of zero. If there were a difference in price

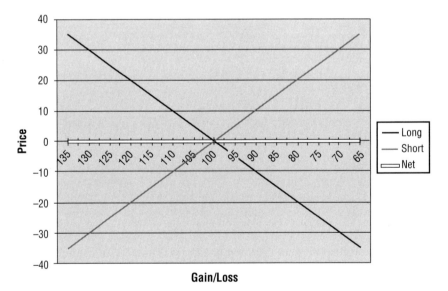

FIGURE 5.3 Offset Position Profits (Long and Short Entered at 100)

between the long purchase price and the short sale price, then the Net line would not be zero, but rather the value of Short Price – Long Price. (+1 if, for example, the long occurred at 100 and the short at 101).

So the question one is left with is why would anyone have an offset like this? The reason is that the trader expects to profit on both trades, or at least make more on one than is lost on the other. It is like a spread trade. That is all fine, but it does not change the basic fact that while both positions are open, the net effect of price movement on the portfolio or account is zero. Were the long to be exited at 105, it would register as a 5-point gain, but the remaining short position would be 5 points down. If the market were to turn around, and move lower, then the position could be exited in such a manner as to create a net overall gain for the portfolio. If, however, the market were to move higher and eventually exited above 105, the overall impact on the account would be as if a short position were taken at 105 (100 + the 5-point long profit) when the trader is considering the net profitability of the combined trades. (This sort of strategy might be employed in a narrowly traded market. Keep in mind transaction and/or carry costs, though.)

A Forex Twist

Recall that in Chapter 2 we took a look at our net currency exposure when we were having multiple open forex trades. It showed us how we can inadvertently alter our whole risk profile without necessarily realizing it. This is something that can come about when one is thinking in terms of hedging.

Consider, for example, a trader who is short EUR/USD because she believes the dollar will be stronger than the euro (recalling that a decline in EUR/USD means the USD is appreciating and the EUR is depreciating). At the same time, however, she is concerned that there might be a general decline in the USD, thanks to some upcoming data release. So she decides to neutralize her overall USD exposure by selling an equivalent USD amount in USD/JPY.

What did our trader just do? If you answered Create a USD offset, you are right! She no longer has any exposure to USD movement at all.

What she does have now, however, is a completely new risk profile. She may be net neutral USD, but she started off with a short position in the EUR and added a long position in JPY. That creates a short EUR/JPY position in the account. Instead of our trader's profit or loss being defined by the strength or weakness of the USD against the EUR, as was the original intent, it will be dictated by the strength or weakness of the EUR against the JPY, at least as long as both trades are open (and no others added).

To protect against a general USD decline, our trader should have, instead, sold the dollar index or bought put options against it.

MONEY MANAGEMENT—PORTFOLIO

Money management can be much more involved than just defining the risk of a specific trade or position. Unless the trader ever has only one position on at a time (a good idea for a new trader), there will be times when they will have or seek to have open trades in multiple markets and/or instruments. That is where complexity comes in and where the trader must have a very clear understanding of what risks are being taken.

The portfolio side of money management is where one must step away from taking a trade-by-trade view of things and shift to a wider focus. Failure to do so leads to a myopic outlook in which one fails to understand the manner in which combined positions can increase or decrease one's overall risk. In this section we take a look at ways traders can cause themselves these kinds of risk profile problems, and how they can be avoided.

Correlated Markets

Refer to Figures 5.4 through 5.7. Figure 5.4 is a plot of gold from the start of 2003 into early 2005. Figure 5.5 is EUR/USD (U.S. dollars per euro) for the same time frame. Since gold is priced in dollars, there is a tendency for the metal to appreciate as the currency declines in value (recall that a rise in EUR/USD means the dollar is losing value against the euro). It is easy to see the general correlation when viewing the charts shown in Figures 5.4 through 5.7.

Another example of this is equities and fixed income. Stocks and bonds (or notes) tend to trade in the same direction since declining interest rates are generally positive for corporate earnings (and mean lower discount rates when one is calculating discounted cash flows in that kind of valuation analysis). One can see that in the charts of the S&P 500 index and 10-year Treasury note price, respectively. While the amplitude of the changes may differ, sometimes dramatically, both instruments trended in the same direction from 1982 to 2005.

In the increasingly global financial environment, markets are linked to one another and influenced by similar things, which means they can move in similar ways. That results in positive correlation. This is of extreme importance to the trader in assessing overall portfolio risk. It is very easy to have highly correlated positions without thinking about it until suddenly there is a large loss when both positions go negative at the same time.

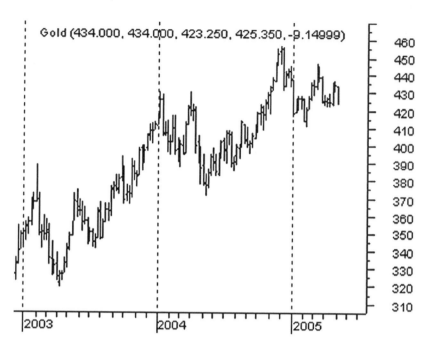

FIGURE 5.4   Gold 2003–2005
Source: Metastock.

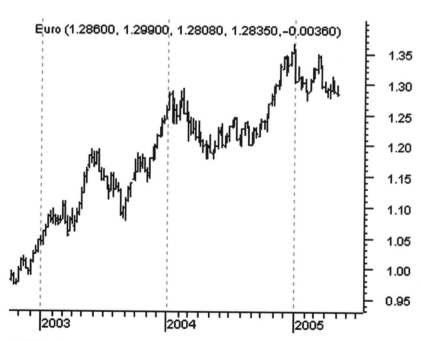

FIGURE 5.5   EUR/USD 2003–2005
Source: Metastock.

If one were to actually calculate the correlation coefficient for gold and EUR/USD or stocks and bonds during the time frames depicted in Figure 5.4 through 5.7, the result would not be 1.0. It is never going to be in any pair of markets or instruments. But it need not be to create excess risk. If one holds a position in two markets or instruments that are even modestly correlated, the overall risk to the portfolio can be significantly increased, theoretically up to double. This is often overlooked because if things go well (both positions profiting simultaneously), the return on the portfolio is higher than it would be otherwise. Recall from our definition of risk that traders do not usually think that higher than expected returns are a risk. That is just a bonus.

The risk of correlated positions is often brought home only when something happens that sees both positions go negative at the same time. It could be a news report or a data release, or just the normal course of trading activity with no overt cause. Whatever the reason, the trader is left staring at a larger than anticipated loss and cursing their foolishness at taking so much risk. One should try to eliminate (or at least severely reduce) the unfortunate experience of looking back with hindsight and realizing that something different should have been done.

The markets, however, do not always track one another. Even well correlated ones will diverge from time to time. Refer back to points A and B on the S&P 500 and 10-Year Note (Figures 5.6 and 5.7) as an example. While the 10-year dropped sharply between the two points, the S&P barely ticked lower at all. (It is interesting to note that the fall from point A to point B in the 10-year took place in 1999—an omen of the collapse in stocks that would come in 2000?)

These sorts of disconnects between the markets happen frequently. Refer to the Gold and EUR/USD examples (Figures 5.8 and 5.9).

These charts are taken from the first half of 2004, as a subsection of the earlier charts, which showed fairly well correlated movement. Notice that these charts are not nearly as well correlated in the first half of the plot period. During January and February gold was in a down trend while EUR/USD actually made a new high. Then the two flipped courses. Gold rallied through March while EUR/USD dropped steadily. It is exactly this kind of action that demonstrates why the trader must always be aware of the current linkages and correlations when putting on positions in multiple markets and/or instruments.

Lest the reader is left with the idea that having multiple trades active is a bad thing and to be avoided, it must be said that doing so can also lower the risk in a portfolio. That is the whole point of modern portfolio theory. One can actually combine multiple positions to create

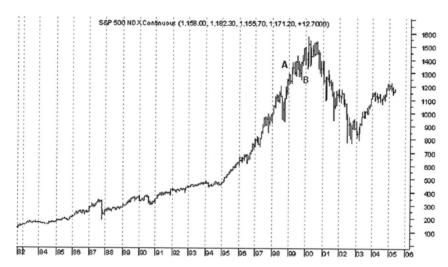

FIGURE 5.6 S&P 500 1982–2005
Source: Metastock.

FIGURE 5.7 U.S. 10-Year Note 1982–2005
Source: Metastock.

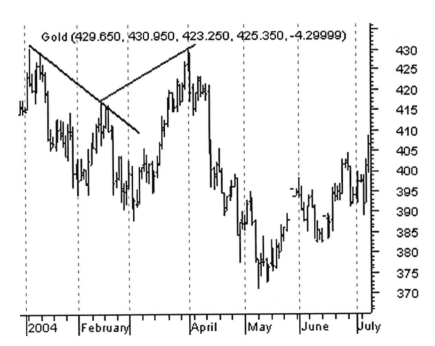

FIGURE 5.8   Gold 2004–2005
Source: Metastock.

FIGURE 5.9   EUR/USD 2004–2005
Source: Metastock.

less risky portfolios. From a trader's perspective, this normally equates to having positions on with negative correlations, or at least near zero ones.

Modern Portfolio Theory (MPT)

This theory suggests that thinking in portfolio terms is better from a risk–return profile than doing so in terms of individual securities. One can use expected returns and volatility of various combinations of securities to determine which provide optimal risk–reward scenarios. These portfolios can be plotted out, creating the efficient frontier. The investor should select a portfolio on that frontier.

This can be extended by the use of leverage, leading to the formation of the capital market line and so-called "super-efficient" portfolios.

Most traders—when thought of as speculators rather than investors— do not think in terms of portfolios in this fashion, however.

The really important thing to take away from this correlation discussion, though, is that the trader must be thinking in terms of the future. It is all fine and good if one market has a particular correlation coefficient when compared to another over the past whatever period of time, but it means nothing if the markets do not have the same linkage going forward. Trading is about expectations and so, too, is risk and money management. When looking at the correlations between two positions (active or proposed), the trader has to make an assessment (forecast, if you like) as to whether that linkage will change, and if so, how. To do otherwise is like driving a car while looking only in the rearview mirror.

That ties us in with the next topic.

Value at Risk (VaR)

Value at risk is a method for evaluating a portfolio's overall risk for a given time frame. It was designed for large institutions like banks so they could better manage the cumulative effect of their various positions across multiple markets. What VaR indicates is the extent to which a portfolio's value could fluctuate in a specific time period with a given level of confidence. For example, a specific portfolio of $100,000 might have a 1-day VaR of $5,000 at 95 percent. Translated, that means there is about a 95 percent chance that the portfolio in question will change in value somewhere between +$5,000 and –$5,000. This is an immensely valuable thought process for the trader as he or she monitors the status of the total position exposure.

The application of VaR at the institutional level can be highly complex, given the potential for large numbers of markets and instruments involved. Imagine an investment bank that trades stocks, fixed income, and foreign exchange, both in terms of generic positions and derivatives. There are a lot of intricacies in risk determination involved and the models used are complex.

For the individual trader, VaR is not quite as involved, given the smaller number of positions in question. Even still, determination of VaR as commonly expressed is more likely to be the pursuit of the quantitatively bent individual. It involves determining probabilities for price moves (remember the graphs in Chapter 3?) and combining them with correlations between the markets and/or instruments in question. Models can be utilized in the process.

We do not have the space here to go into a complete discussion of VaR. Refer to www.andurilonline.com/book for a list of references by which you can learn more if you are interested. What you should, however, keep in mind is the idea of VaR—Value at Risk. Every trader needs to understand what can and is likely to happen to her/his portfolio in whatever time frame in appropriate. To do otherwise is akin to piloting a ship through a sea full of icebergs on a foggy night. Does the *Titanic* come to mind? It was thought to be unsinkable, just as so many traders believe their portfolios to be. Then they hit those icebergs and are left in complete shock as their portfolios sink.

Risk of Ruin (RoR)

The VaR concept ties in with the concept of risk of ruin. Simply stated, the risk of ruin is the chance of blowing out one's account (for the record a blow out, when referring to one's account, is not a good thing). As discussed earlier in this chapter, each of us has a different idea of what exactly that means, so the RoR will vary from trader to trader.

For example, given that they use the same trading system in the exact same manner, the trader who considers "ruin" to be losing 50 percent of the account or portfolio value, would have a higher RoR than one who views ruin as meaning a 75 percent loss. After all, it is less likely to lose 75 percent than 50 percent (hopefully!).

The concept of RoR is closely tied in with the specific performance profile of the trading system or systems being employed. As such, it is addressed more specifically in the chapter on trading system performance assessment. We mention it here because traders have to know what the result of excess risk can be.

Homework

As noted, understanding market linkages is important. Pick a market that is of interest to you. Then, select two other markets, one that you would expect to be strongly correlated to the primary market, and one that would not be expected to show much linkage at all. Then, select three time frames and perform a basic regression analysis to determine whether your beliefs were correct or not.

Also develop a list of influences applicable to each market of the kind outlined in the Influences on Price section of Chapter 3 to compare the three. Then, compare the performance of each market in relation to the data, news, and other influences you identified.

Record all your findings in your system research journal.

THE PLAN

The idea of risk or money management for the trader is inherently a negative one. For those who are used to thinking in terms of positives, this can be a very unusual situation. Nevertheless, it is very important to approach trading in the proper manner. It is very easy to get caught up in fantasizing about big profits, but the successful trader spends their time focusing on the odds of losing and how much. Why? Because there will always be opportunities to make trading profits, but only if one remains in the game. The trader who takes on too much risk increases the odds that he or she will be knocked out of the game. Thus, money management.

Earlier in this chapter you were given the assignment of determining your own risk profile and defining it. Now is the time to put that into an action plan to guide your trading. This final section of the chapter presents a series of questions that should be addressed with the answers placed directly into your Trading Plan in the section you skipped last chapter.

1. *How much of a loss in account value are you willing to accept before halting your trading?* Decide where your "uncle" point is—the loss at which you just shut everything down and stop trading. This is something which hopefully never occurs, but if it does you should have a contingency. That's part of the planning process. The ideal here is to pick a point beyond which you have to draw the conclusion that there is either a problem with your trading execution or with your trading system. Either way, it is good to stop and assess things, which is what this kind of circuit breaker does.

The decision as to exactly where to put this point combines in some fashion elements of your personal comfort and expectations for the performance of your trading system. The latter will be addressed in the chapters to come. You may, however, decide on a personal cut-off regardless of your system.

2. *What kind of peak-to-trough drawdown are you willing to accept?* This speaks to the earlier discussions of personal risk tolerance. It also brings in the loss to breakeven analysis mentioned at the start of this chapter. In short, it is the degree to which you are willing to accept bouncing around in your portfolio's or account's value. Are you the slow and steady type, or do you not mind riding the roller coaster? Your decision here will influence the types of trading systems you are likely to trade as well as the per trade and overall risk you are willing to take.

3. *How much risk, as a percentage of your account or portfolio, will you take on a per trade basis?* Some of the best traders of all time limit their per trade risk to no more than one to two percent of their account. This might seem like a very small value, but it must be considered in terms of frequency of trade. One who is a day or swing trader, or who operates in a similarly short time frame will have more trades over a given time frame than will a longer-term trader. That being the case, they have a higher probability of experiencing a significant run of negative performance than would the less frequent trader.

Consider that the likelihood of x consecutive losing trades, with a probability of losing of p (probability of a winning trade is $1 - p$) is equal to p^x. Thus, if we have a 50 percent loss percentage and are considering a run of five consecutive trades, the straight-up probability of that occurring is $.5 \times .5 \times .5 \times 5 \times .5 = 0.03125$ (assuming the per trade probabilities are independent).

This figure is a bit misleading, though. While it is true that it is unlikely to get five consecutive losses, that is only applicable when all you look at are five trades.

As one goes beyond five observations, the odds of having a run of five consecutive losses increases, to the point of reaching 100 percent when the number of trades gets large enough. For example, a day trader making 1 trade per day (about 260 each year) would be almost certain of having *at least* one run of five losing trades in a row. You can run scenarios to look at the probability of an x-loss run, given a trade total and success rate with the calculator available at: www.anduriloneline.com/book/calculator.aspx.

Having this sort of information at hand is extremely useful when one is making risk management decisions. It probably is not a good idea to risk 10 percent of your account per trade when you have a 75 percent likelihood of seeing at least one run of five or more consecutive losing trades. That's a fast way to destroy one's account.

We have not yet begun working through trading system performance measures, so you are a bit limited in terms of having numbers to use in this way. Nevertheless, you can still make some approximations based on the time frame you are planning on using. We will revisit this portion of the plan later.

4. *How much of your account or portfolio will you have at risk in total at any given time?* If you plan on trading only one position at a time, then the answer is the same as in question 3. If, however, you plan on having multiple trades open, you need to define what kind of net exposure you will take (essentially VaR). You can still use the estimations we discussed in 3. as a guide to where your risk level should be, but you will probably have to make an adjustment. Rather than thinking in terms of trades, as we were previously, you must think in terms of time frames. The time frame in question would be based on the combined holding period of the positions in question. For example, a swing trader who has a one- to three-day holding period on any given trade might think in terms of two- to three-day periods. In that manner, they could perform the same kind of loss-run assessment as done in question 3, but with a different perspective.

This is where the correlation discussion we had in the preceding section and its follow-through in VaR come back into play. Trading positions that are highly correlated are going to create a higher VaR at any given time. Uncorrelated positions (remember we're talking on a forward looking basis) will generally decrease the VaR level. It is this VaR that is your most optimal measure for determining where you should make your portfolio risk cutoff.

Risk Management Plan Application

We have said before that the plan not applied is a worthless plan. While working through the risk management portion of your Trading Plan, take seriously the decisions you are making and the way they will be applied. Keep things as simple as possible. The stress of trading, which can be experienced regardless of whether you are winning or losing, can wreak havoc on your risk management strategy. In fact, that is the portion of the Plan most likely to go out the window.

Consider two very simple examples.

Joe has just made a very nice gain. Sue, on the other hand, just experienced a significant loss. Both may feel compelled to trade bigger on their next position. Joe is feeling good. The adrenaline is pumping. "Why not trade bigger? The system is doing well. Let me see if I can improve my returns."

Sue, on the other hand, might think about making that loss back. "It's a good system, after all. Why not trade a little bigger this time and make up for the loss?"

Notice that neither is thinking about deviating from the trading system at this point, just the risk management strategy. They have both stopped thinking about the potential for loss on the next trade.

The important thing to take away from this chapter is that one must either think of risk on the front end of the trade or face the prospect of realizing the riskiness of market participation at some future point. It can be equated to car upkeep and maintenance. You can either do the little things to keep your car in good shape (oil changes, regular service, etc.) or you can wait for a major problem to crop up, which will cost far more in time or money than if you had just done what you should have done along the way.

At this stage we have sufficiently begun to address the requirements for risk management in our trading. Some items have been left for further discussion at later points. They will be revisited through the process of trading system design, development, and testing as we move ahead with our Trading Plan. It is time to move forward to trading system development.

CHAPTER 6

Market Analysis

A t the heart of every trading system, from the simplest to the most complex, is market analysis. It is the basis for the decision-making process. This chapter outlines the primary methods employed.

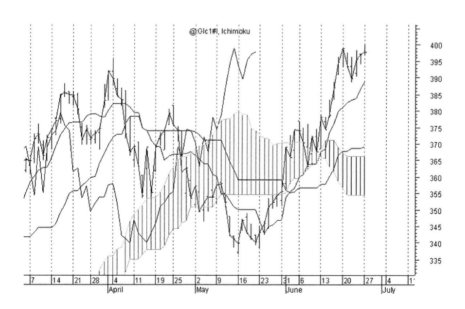

ANALYZING THE MARKETS

When one is considering trading as a speculative profit seeking venture (as opposed to a business activity, in some cases), there must be some mechanism by which one determines what actions to take, or indeed to take none. This process is market analysis. Every trading system incorporates it in some way.

In this chapter we explore the three primary methods used by traders and market participants—fundamental analysis, technical analysis, and quantitative analysis. The first two are often considered polar opposites, and their exponents can be often heard to sing their praises while damning the other in turn. Many fail to include the third, quantitative analysis, in the discussion. The well-known market commentator Ralph Acampora, however, in a presentation to students and faculty at the University of Rhode Island, described market analysis in terms of a triangle. The three may be employed differently, but they are nevertheless linked together, as shown in Figure 6.2.

Do not read anything into the position of any of the three in either absolute or relative terms. No implication is made in the design of the triangle.

This chapter spends considerable time specifically covering the analysis types individually, and in some cases jointly. Before getting to that point, though, it is important to take some time to discuss exactly what are the implications of market analysis.

Representation Bias

The map is not the terrain. Perhaps you have heard that expression. It basically means that no matter how detailed the map, it still is nothing more than a representation of something. It is not the actual thing

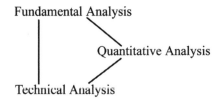

FIGURE 6.2 Analysis Triangle

itself. To think otherwise is to fall victim to what is considered *representation bias*.

Traders have to keep in mind that no matter what data, charts, or other kind of information they use in their analysis, it is not the market. It is only a representation of what could be only a single element of the market. Price, for example, is merely an indication where one or more parties are willing to transact or have transacted, no more than that. Moreover, since the market is in constant flux, any such representation is by definition a snapshot in time. It is history. A price chart is no more than a map of where transactions were or could have been made (traded versus indicative quotes) over some time period.

The simple fact of the matter is that no one can know everything. The financial markets are highly complex and amorphous. One could say with some validity that everyone on the planet is involved in them, directly or indirectly contributing to the supply/demand situation that underlies the markets. This is a very important thing to remember as one goes through this chapter.

One other quick thing should be mentioned before going forward. Market analysis is commonly thought of in one of two fashions: top-down and bottom-up. The former is when one looks at the broad view, then uses it to take positions in specific instruments. An example would be to determine an overall positive or negative outlook for the U.S. dollar, then pick a specific currency pair to trade (like EUR/USD). The bottom-up approach is one whereby the trader focuses on specific instruments (like stocks) and does not spend too much time looking at the wider view (the indices or overall economy, for example). Both approaches can be effective. It is a question of preference.

FUNDAMENTAL ANALYSIS

Fundamental analysis is most often associated with the stock market. In that regard it is the effort by which one attempts to determine the value of a company, and thereby its per share price. That is merely one application, however. Fundamental analysis is applied in essentially every market in one fashion or another. This is often seen as economic analysis, though other elements come in as well, depending on the market in question.

We start the discussion of fundamental analysis at what could be considered the top level, and then progress down to more minute elements that impact specific instruments. In a sense, we will be taking a top-down look at how fundamental analysis is applied.

The Business Cycle

Also referred to as the economic cycle, the business cycle is the pattern of economic growth and contraction that takes place over time. The use of the word "cycle" can be a bit misleading, as the pattern is not one of regular and consistent recurrence. Rather, these cycles tend to vary in overall length, as well as in the duration and amplitude of each phase. The basic idea that an economy goes through periods of expansion followed by periods of stagnation or decline is what is important to keep in mind, though.

Gross Domestic Product (GDP)

GDP is the total value of all goods and services produced by a country (or territory) over the course of a specific time period. Nominal GDP is the actual figure, while real GDP attempts to adjust the base figure for the impact of inflation on prices.

In basic terms, there are two primary phases of the business cycle. One is growth, which is the expansion of the gross domestic product (GDP). It is in this phase that unemployment declines, there is a rise in consumer and business, company profits grow, and all those generally good things associated with prosperity happen.

Recession and Depression

A recession is defined as two or three (depending on to whom you speak) consecutive quarters of negative GDP growth. Recessions are considered normal events in the course of the business cycle.

There is no agreed upon definition of depression, but it can be thought of as a sustained recession that also features depreciation in assets, goods, and services (negative inflation).

On the flip side is contraction, negative GDP growth. That is when unemployment rates rise, bankruptcies increase, profits decline, individuals and companies have less to spend, and generally things are not pleasant. Depending on the severity and/or duration of the contraction, this period can be termed a recession, or perhaps even a depression.

There are, of course, degrees for each cycle. Some growth phases are faster than others, and in fact growth rates tend to start slowly, increase to some peak, then fall off. The same is true in the contraction phase. Some are more severe, and others less. Of course, there are the transition periods. Economies do not go instantly from growth to contraction or vice versa, after all.

Many factors influence business cycles, in terms of both the length of the phases and transition periods and the magnitude of growth and contraction rates. They include (1) interest rates, (2) monetary and fiscal policy, (3) inflation, (4) currency exchange rates, (5) commodity prices, (6) government regulation, (7) currency exchange rates, and (8) foreign trade, among others. At the same time, each of these elements is impacted by the business cycle and has a high degree of interaction and influence with and among one another. This section of the chapter discusses those items individually, and in relation to one another, and eventually brings it all down to the level of the individual company.

General Economic Analysis

You will recall from Chapter 3 that the list of influences on price movement features a heavy dose of economic data. It is a fact of life that overall economic activity influences everything in the financial markets. If, for example, the economy is in the contraction phase of the business cycle, interest rates will probably move lower, exchange rates will likely be negatively impacted, demand for goods and services can be expected to decline, inflation will generally be lower, and companies will see earnings come under pressure, which means lower stock prices. In most cases, the opposite is true during economic expansion, and transition phases can see mixtures of the two. For this reason, it is important for the trader to understand where the economy is in the business cycle, and what the future may bring in that regard. Because of this, a great deal of effort and energy is put forth monitoring and forecasting economic conditions.

Quarterly GDP data are readily available for the purposes of business cycle analysis. The problem, however, is that GDP data are not very timely. The final figures for any given quarter are often not released until nearly a whole next quarter has passed. Therefore, those seeking to know the current health of the economy have to find ways to measure GDP growth with less time lag. This is done through monitoring, on an ongoing basis, the components of GDP.

The components of GDP are (1) private consumption, (2) business investment, (3) government spending, and (4) net exports. An array of government and private sector reports and information can be used to measure these components. The trade figures, for example, are watched very closely. One need look no further than any publicly available monthly economic data release calendar to see how many of these data items are reported. You can be sure that they are all finding their way into any number of models used to forecast GDP.

In terms of taking a forward look to see where GDP growth is likely to be in the future, there is also a collection of items that are collectively referred to as leading indicators. They are measures considered guides to the future growth of the economy. With them, one can have a useful (if not always accurate) crystal ball for developing GDP growth expectations. The Conference Board (www.conference-board.org) has collected several of them together into a leading index for the United States (and other countries). This index includes:

- Average weekly claims for unemployment insurance (taken inverted).
- Building permits (for new construction).
- Average weekly manufacturing hours.
- Manufactures' new orders for nondefense capital goods.
- Manufactures' new orders for consumer goods and materials.
- Index of Consumer Expectations.
- Real money supply.
- Interest rate spread (yield curve).
- Stock prices (measured by one or more indices).
- Vendor performance.

As you read through this list, you can no doubt see how many of the items clearly indicate the potential for future economic production. For example, Building permits indicates the pending need for materials and labor in the construction arena. That makes them very significant figures for one attempting to predict future GDP growth.

Traders and market analysts will take one of two approaches in regard to GDP growth figures (assuming they use fundamental analysis in their work). One will be to specifically include it in their specific analysis of whatever market they are looking at. By that we mean models. For example, GDP growth rates can be an input in corporate revenue growth models. Other traders will use the economic outlook more as a guideline or bias setter.

Interest Rates

While closely related to and integrated with economic growth, interest rates move independently from the economic cycle. They fluctuate freely via trade in the fixed income markets. As such we have here both a component of fundamental analysis (interest rates being a contributory element in the analysis of several markets), and a market in its own right. What that creates is a highly dynamic element for the fundamental analyst as interest rates move continuously and are influenced by other market elements.

Most specifically, interest rates (a component factor of fixed income security prices) are highly sensitive to inflation. Consider a bond that pays out annual interest of 10 percent on a fixed principal amount (par value). The real value of those interest payments will depend on the level of inflation. The higher the inflation rate, the lower the real interest rate, and vice versa.

Nominal versus Real Rates

The nominal rate of return is the actual payment, for example a $1,000 bond paying $100 in annual interest has a nominal rate of 10 percent. The real interest rate is the inflation adjusted rate of interest. In the preceding example, if inflation was 3 percent, the real rate of return on the bond would be 7 percent.

In order to keep their real rate of return at a steady level, fixed income investors will demand higher nominal rates from their fixed income securities. For example, at a 3 percent rate of inflation, a 7 percent yield for a bond might be fine, but if inflation was 5 percent, the required yield may be 9 percent, keeping the investor's real rate of return at 4 percent. As bond prices and yields are inversely related, bond prices fall as inflation rises so as to provide the higher yields demanded by investors.

Since inflation is so important to the interest rate market, it should be no surprise that traders using fundamental analysis spend considerable time looking at those things that measure inflation such as Consumer Price Index (CPI). The CPI is a basket of goods and services designed to reflect the expenses of the average person. Changes in the CPI outline how much more (or less) expensive those goods and services have become. Since inflation is the rate of change in price over time, the CPI provides us a reading on just that. The Producer Price Index (PPI) does essentially the same thing on the business side. There are other measures of inflation that may be better or worse than the CPI at measuring inflation, but we do not get into a discussion of them here. Suffice it to say that there are ways to estimate inflation over a given time frame.

However, it is not current (or rather near past) inflation the markets concern themselves with. The fixed income market is worried about the rate of future inflation. Therefore, fundamental analysis for the fixed income market focuses on those things that can give a reading on inflation rates down the road.

So from where does inflation come? Well, what makes prices increase? We have had this discussion in market terms already. It's a supply and demand situation. If there is a preponderance of demand, prices will tend to rise as the competition to purchase drives buyers to pay more. Where there is an excess supply, prices drop as the sellers cut their demands to unload their inventory. When demand increases in the face of supply shortages, prices move rapidly higher. If supply surges, but demand decreases, the rate of price decline is more rapid.

Since copper, oil, grains, and other commodities are the inputs to the products purchased by consumers and businesses, they are watched closely as potential indicators of inflation. After all, as we have seen, if oil prices are rising we are likely to see higher gasoline prices at the pump. We can also see an impact on competitive products. Sticking with our example, when oil prices rise, there can be a similar move higher in natural gas. This is the result of increased demand in that market as people shift away from oil.

Labor is another input to the cost of producing goods and services, so traders watch the employment data for signs of pressure on that market. Labor operates like any other market. When demand increases, wage demands increase. That is why economists and fixed income traders become nervous when the unemployment rates get very low. It suggests the potential for wage rate increases.

That said, however, higher input costs do not always translate into higher prices for the consumer or business. Modern technology has led to serious gains in efficiency. As a result, businesses have been able to cut costs in other areas to keep their own total expenses from rising. At the same time, we come back to supply and demand. If businesses are in a highly competitive situation with others, one where there is an excess supply (in some manner of speaking) or demand is pressured, prices will be held down. As such, one cannot just assume that higher input prices mean higher output prices and rises in the measures such as the CPI. It does not always work that way.

There is another supply/demand element involved in inflation. That is money supply. Some have legitimately defined inflation (in its negative, excessive sense) as too much money chasing too few goods. We have already addressed the goods (and inputs) side of that definition. The other side is the money. Just like anything else, too much money means a decrease in the value of it. So if the supply of money is rising while the supply of goods and/or services is falling and demand for them rising, devastating inflation can occur. (Germany between World War I and World War II is a very dramatic example.)

The money supply issue brings one directly into the realm of the central banks, the keepers of the money and the dominant forces in interest rates. As much as the fixed income markets, which determine rates, trade freely, they are heavily influenced by the actions and statements of the central banks.

Federal funds rate: The overnight interest rate at which banks lend or borrow reserve balances among each other.

Discount rate: The overnight interest rate the Federal Reserve charges banks to borrow reserve funds directly from the Fed.

The most overt form of central bank influence on interest rates is the raising or lowering of specific government interest rates. In the United States these are the federal funds and discount rates, which are used by banks to determine things like the prime rate, the rate banks use as the benchmark for determining their lending rates. Other countries have similar benchmarks.

The Fed also does what is known as open market operations in which they buy and sell Treasury securities to increase or decrease, respectively, the money supply. In other countries there are different systems in place, but the operations and intentions are the same among the central banks.

In many cases, the primary focus of the central bank is to guard against excess inflation. Some are more aggressive than others, and some also have mandates related to economic growth and the strength of the country's currency, but inflationary concerns dominate. Central banks use interest rates to control inflation. They tend to raise rates when they feel inflationary risks are starting to show, and allowing rates to drop when they recede. This is where economic growth comes back into the picture. And you thought GDP growth had been left behind. Not so!

Open Market Operations

By executing transactions in the fixed income market, a central bank can influence the money supply and thus move interest rates.

If the central bank (i.e., the Fed) is a buyer of government securities (such as T-bills), they are expanding the money supply. This is because they are putting money into the market by paying the sellers. At the same time, the purchases will tend to increase the price of the fixed income securities in question, lowering their yields.

When selling, the central is taking money out of the system by receiving payment for the securities they are selling. The selling will tend to put pressure on the price of those fixed income instruments, raising the yield.

From where does demand come? In the case of consumers and businesses, it comes from increased income and money to spend. This is generally a function of economic growth. As such, central bankers are always on the lookout during good times for signs that the economy is "overheating." Inflation does not tend to crop up when there is steady economic growth. It is when growth starts to accelerate beyond normal rates that inflation can creep in. At least that is the idea, anyway. There are many who would contest this view. We do not take sides in that particular argument.

The point being made here is that if central bankers think that rapid economic growth might lead to increased inflation, they will increase interest rates in order to put on the brakes and slow things down.

As a result of the central banker's ability to manipulate interest rates, a whole branch of fundamental analysis has evolved. In the United States it is referred to as Fed watching, indicative of how its proponents spend much time monitoring all the goings on with those who are members of the Federal Reserve Board, and of course the chairman of the Federal Reserve. These individuals make public statements (as noted in Chapter 3) that analysts attempt to decipher for their meaning vis-à-vis interest rate and money supply policy.

It must be noted, however, that as powerful as central banks are, they do not have complete control of interest rates, particularly at the longer maturities. The central banks do their operations in the short-term instruments, which leaves the longer-term ones to move around fairly freely. That means one can see times when traders and the central bank do not seem to be in agreement, such as when rates are increased but 10-year yields, for example, stay level or even fall.

This brings up the yield curve, as depicted in Figure 6.3.

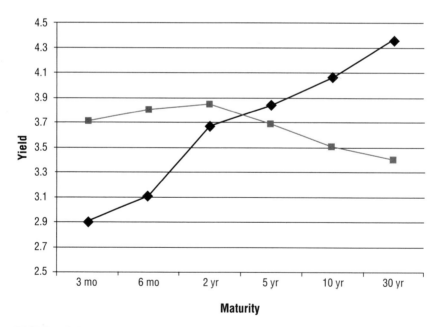

FIGURE 6.3 U.S. Yield Curve

The yield curve is a visual depiction of interest rates through the series of maturities. Through it one can see the spread between any two specific maturities. In Figure 6.3 there are two plots. The dark one is a normal yield curve with an upward slope from left to right. The light line is of the type referred to as an inverted curve because short-term rates are higher than long-term ones.

Recall that the yield curve (interest rate spread) is one of the leading indicators used to anticipate changes in GDP growth. It is so because an inverted, negatively sloping yield curve is oftentimes an indication of an economic downturn to come. Why? Because the higher short-term rates mean there is no incentive to make longer-term investments. Since business investment is a component of GDP, one that will be negatively impacted, an inverted yield curve can mean a decline in GDP, if not offset by one or more of the other components. So again we see the economic growth/interest rate linkage.

Foreign Exchange Rates

Like interest rates, foreign exchange rates (forex) are both a market unto themselves and a potential consideration in fundamental analysis. Forex rates are at the same time a reflection of economic strength or weakness (capital tends to flow toward strong currencies and away from weak ones) and an influence upon that condition. Recall that trade is a component of GDP, and forex rates are both the result of and an influence on trade flows. At the same time, interest rates both impact and are impacted by forex rates as capital moves in search of yield. It is a truly mind-spinning situation.

We are not spending a great deal of time here. As noted, forex shares common influences with all other markets. The same type of considerations as we have already mentioned so far apply, with a few added ones related to trade and capital flows. What we want to focus on instead is how forex impacts on the analysis of other markets.

On the macro level, foreign exchange rates come into play at several points. As already noted, they include GDP and interest rates through the functioning of trade and capital flows. The exchange rate between two currencies influences the relative cost of goods in trade, which can then lead to changes in the direction and/or scope of trade between two partners. That ties in with the export balance part of the GDP equation.

On the capital flow side forex is about investment. A strong or strengthening currency will attract investment. The additional supply of investment funds will tend to move interest rate lower (there's that supply and demand again!). This has long been the case in the United States where the relatively strong dollar has encouraged foreign investment. On the flip side, a weak currency can lead to higher interest rates. Consider concerns that foreign investors would begin pulling out of the U.S. market when the dollar suffered its sharp weakening against the euro. Had they in fact done so, there would have been sharp upward pressure in the U.S. interest rates arena.

On a more micro level, forex rates can directly influence company profitability. Many companies these days have an exposure to forex in some fashion or another, be it directly in terms of overseas operations or the purchase or sale of goods and services on the global trade market, or indirectly through the purchase of goods and services from other companies who have direct exposure. As such, the fundamental analyst often must take forex into consideration when evaluating a company's stock.

Commodities

We mentioned earlier the role of commodity prices in the inflation equation. They are obviously a tradable market unto themselves. Additionally, they are direct or indirect contributors to the profitability of companies. In fact, some stock prices are heavily dominated by a particular commodity, like gold mining shares or oil stocks.

So what does fundamental analysis mean for commodities? Well, start with supply and demand. One needs to evaluate those things that impact the two sides of that balance. What increases or decreases supply? What impacts demand?

The commodity market is diverse. There are agricultural goods. There are energy products. There are metals. Each has its own set of influences. For example, weather can factor quite heavily in the supply of corn or other crops, or in the demand for heating oil or natural gas. Labor strife and political unrest can impact the mining of metals and/or their transport to potential buyers. Changes in the demographics of a population alter the demand of things, in some cases specifically, in others across the board.

Additionally, as we have already noted, there are linkages between commodities that can impact supply and demand. The example we brought up before involved heating oil and natural gas, whereby increases in the price of the former can lead to increased demand for the latter. Corn could fall because wheat prices are falling, cutting into the demand for corn. It these relationships that often see general sectors (energy, grains, etc.) rise or fall in unison.

Stocks

We started off saying that it was in the stock market where fundamental analysis is most widely and overtly applied. After much discussion of things macro, we can now focus on how fundamentals are approached in regard to companies and their share prices. With that big-picture view of the external elements, we are ready to take a micro view of the company and the types of methods utilized to determine the value of a company's stock and/or project a path in prices for the future.

The process of determining a stock's value, or relative value, almost always involves some kind of forecast as to future earnings. Forecasts are arrived at through a process of projected financial statements. These projections combine expectations of the macroeconomic factors mentioned earlier in this section and company business plans to arrive at revenue growth figures. They then address the cost side through the forecast of expected input prices (also discussed earlier) to get a net profitability determination. It is often the case that five-year forecasts are used in this regard.

With those earnings and/or financial statement forecasts in hand, the analyst can then take one of two primary approaches.

Market Wisdom

"Discounted cash flow is only able to put a net present value on expected income flows discounted back to the present and cannot take into account the vagaries of alteration in price behavior due to fluctuations in imbalances between supply and demand functions. Therefore DCF can only show whether as rights to an income, the acquisition of those rights, in comparison to whatever else is available, when a yardstick for this is established, is expensive or cheap in comparison to this yardstick, which could be the income from a fixed interest instrument."

Posted at Trade2Win by SOCRATES

www.trade2win.com/boards/showthread.php?t=15679

Actual Value Analysis The application of actual value analysis takes two approaches, which can be combined in some circumstances. This first is determining the net present value (NPV) of the stock by discounting back the annual earnings. Here is where interest rates factor into the stock price. That gives one the value of the stock in terms of its future income.

The other path is in determining the option value of the company. This is something that would be done in the case, for example, of an oil drilling company where the value of the company will be very different depending on whether it strikes oil. Another example would be a company involved in a court battle, the outcome of which could have major implications to future earnings. As such, the fundamental analyst would determine the value of the company under any and all possible future scenarios, then combine them through option pricing methods to arrive at a stock value.

Regardless of how value is reached, its application is the same. If that value is higher than the current stock price, one would want to buy the undervalued shares. This is the classical financial model for evaluating stocks.

Comparative Analysis   This is the process by which one company's stock is compared to that of one or more others (such as a group or sector). Because companies often are not directly comparable on a straight up basis due to things such as differences in earnings per share, they must be compared on the basis of ratios. Among the most frequently used of these ratios are:

- Price to earnings (P/E): This is calculated as stock price divided by annual earnings per share (as measured on a trailing or historical basis, or in a projected forward fashion). Often referred to as the *multiple*, the P/E ratio can be used to judge a stock as compared to its peer group, or to the stock's own historical standard. For example, if a stock that normally has a P/E in the 10–15 range is currently trading such that is has a 20 P/E, one could take the view that on a relative basis, all else being approximately equal, the stock could be overvalued. (*Note:* Market analysts often calculate multiples for the market in general, usually based on one of the many indices, using them to get an overview of the relative value of the broad collection of stocks.)

- Book value: This is the company's net assets divided by the number of shares outstanding. It tells the analyst is if the company was to be liquidated, what each shareholder would receive. This can be a very complicated ratio to calculate, however, as the value of assets and liabilities on a company's balance sheet does not necessarily reflect its actual market value based on things such as depreciation. The analyst looking to make the book value a practical tool must be able to fairly accurately determine the value of the companies' various assets and liabilities. Otherwise, book value can be quite misleading.

- Dividend yield: This is calculated as annual dividends per share paid divided by stock price. In some market sectors—utility companies, for example—this can be a useful comparative measure. Unfortunately, there are a great many companies that do not even pay dividends (or at least meaningful ones), which limits the usefulness of this particular ratio.

P/E Ratios in Relation to Earnings Growth

Anyone observing the market will likely note that stocks of companies that are considered "growth" have higher P/E ratios. The reason for this is demonstrated quite clearly by Table 6.1.

This table compares the P/E ratios (at right) of a company with $5/share current (t0) earnings at three different growth rates. Given the same discount rate used to in all cases (4 percent) the NPV of stock is higher for higher earnings growth rates (leftmost column). That NPV, in theory, is the value of the stock and the price at which it should be trading. As such, progressively higher NPVs mean higher P/E ratios. Thus, higher earnings growth rates mean higher P/E ratios.

TABLE 6.1 Comparing P/E Ratios for Different Rates of Growth

Earnings Growth Rate (x)	Earnings per Share at Future Times Given Growth Rate x						NPV at 4% Discount Rate	P/E Ratio (at t0)
	t0	t1	t2	t3	t4	t5		
5%	$5.00	$5.25	$5.51	$5.79	$ 6.08	$ 6.38	$25.73	5.15
10%	$5.00	$5.50	$6.05	$6.66	$ 7.32	$ 8.05	$29.67	5.93
20%	$5.00	$6.00	$7.20	$8.64	$10.37	$12.44	$39.20	7.84

There are other accounting ratios such as profit margins, debt-equity, inventory turnover, and cash flow measures that also can be used by the fundamental equity analyst. These can be applied either individually in the analysis of a single company, or as part of a multistock comparison. Some will be important or valuable in their application in certain industries, but not in others, depending on the business in question. The fact of the matter is that one can go into as much detail as one likes in evaluating a company.

Market Wisdom

"PE ratios, dividend yields, cover, etc. . . . are the starting point when it comes to stock selection. The disparity that tends to exist between similar stocks can be down to any number of reasons—customer loyalty, brand recognition, growth prospects, management, product pipeline, geographic location etc. The companies in a sector cannot be exactly the same and the market will price them differently. Some shares will be chased aggressively and thus have higher PE ratios while others might not be the flavor of the month. The fundamental trader/investor is looking to exploit these inefficiencies."

Posted at Trade2Win by Lion63

www.trade2win.com/boards/showthread.php?t=15679

Before jumping forward, it is worth taking a more in-depth look at P/E, as the topic of low P/E stocks is a common one among market participants. First, a low P/E stock is generally one that is trading at a single digit multiple, but in reality could easily be defined as one that has a multiple significantly lower than that of some benchmark such as a market index or industry sector. Regardless, one must approach low P/E stocks cautiously. There are reasons for the depressed multiple. Some of the bigger ones are:

- Poor earnings growth prospects.
- Boring industry or business (e.g., funeral homes, garbage removal).
- Low institutional coverage (few analysts writing about it).
- Fear over a negative development.

As demonstrated earlier, P/E ratios and growth rates are linked. A stock with slow growth prospects will generally not see expansion of its multiple. Stocks in the middle two categories in the preceding list (boring, lack of coverage), however, can see multiple expansion. It can be very slow in coming, however, as it requires an upgrade in the company's market awareness and profile. In short, the stock needs to become more popular.

Multiple Expansion

Multiple expansion is when a stock price rises faster than the rate of earnings growth would indicate. For example, consider a $10 stock with $1/share earnings. That is a P/E of 10. If earnings were to rise to $1.50 and the stock move up to $18, the P/E would expand to 12. When the opposite occurs, it is multiple contraction.

The last category is the potentially most interesting one. As noted previously in this book, psychology can play a major role in the markets. Stocks can sometimes become victim to an overly pessimistic scenario and end up with low P/Es. In such a case, the fundamental trader can do quite well with a multiple expansion trade.

The problem, however, is in determining whether the selling that caused the low P/E was excessive, or if there is a very good reason for the P/E to be that low. Remember, a low P/E may not look so low when new earnings figures are applied. If a stock's earnings per share figures are halved, the P/E doubles. That is why one should not automatically assume a low P/E means a cheap stock ready to roar higher. Just as is the case when one goes shopping, low prices can mean lower quality. Sad is the trader who buys the stock because of the low P/E, then watches the P/E rise as the stock price falls.

Final Thoughts

Fundamental analysis can be applied in any market, though some are a bit more challenging than others. In fact, the top-down stock market analyst, if being very thorough, can incorporate analysis of several other markets into their assessment of a particular company's shares. Fundamentals are excellent for developing an overall picture of the markets, a long-term view, if you will, of where prices are heading.

There is a limitation to fundamental analysis, though. Even the supporters and active users of fundamentals will admit that it is nearly useless in terms of short-term trading. While fundamental influences will tend to win out over time (if a company's earnings are rising the stock price *will* tend to rise), in the near-term there are a great many other forces at play in the movement of prices. Back in Chapter 3 we documented some of those things. As such, one needs to consider trading time frame when determining whether fundamental analysis will be part of one's trade decision-making process. In the longer time frames, fundamentals can be quite useful.

There is a great deal of written material available for those interested in learning more. Check out this book's support web site for an updated list: www.andurilonline.com/book.

TECHNICAL ANALYSIS

On the surface, one could define technical analysis as the use of historical information (certainly price, in many cases volume, and some other data as well) to forecast the future. As such, thanks to the efficient market hypothesis (recall the weak form of EMH, which states that all historical information is already priced in), many in the markets, and even more in academia, have considered practitioners of technical analysis quacks. This point of view is changing rapidly, however. A big part of the reason is a revision in the definition of technical analysis.

Behavioral Finance

Behavioral finance combines psychology with financial theory. This is done by applying scientific research on individual and social cognitive and emotional biases to help understand economic decisions and how they affect market prices, with a focus on the rationality (or lack thereof) of market participants.

Technical analysis is now defined more in terms of measuring and predicting human behavior. This has led to a kinder view in academic circles, though the term Behavioral finance is more often the one used. Regardless, it is still historical information that is being applied, with the goal of attempting to predict the behavior of the markets (inasmuch as they are a collection of individuals) in the future. Even the Federal Reserve is interested in technical analysis, as can be read in some of its own research: www.ny.frb.org/research/epr/00v06n2/0007osle.html.

To be quite blunt, technical analysis does not care a bit about all the fundamental information and analysis presented in the previous section. It takes the view that it is all accounted for in price and/or the movement of price over time. The technician instead focuses on price as the market determined measure of value, since any given transaction is an agreement between buyer and seller as to value at a given point in time. To take it all a step further, the technical analyst is concerned with price movement, or the lack thereof. A technician, through the application of one or more methods, attempts to determine future direction. In this section we explore some of those methods.

Charting

The foundations of technical analysis are in price charts and the interpretation of them. Charts, of course, are simply price plotted over time. The so-called "chartist" believes that patterns can be identified in the price action depicted by the charts, which repeat with a measure of predictability. As such, they provide the opportunity for profit, and, of course, that is the name of the game.

Japanese Candlestick Charts

Candlesticks charts (originated in Japan) are akin to bar charts in that they use Open, High, Low, and Close prices to plot a period. The difference is that the area between the open and close is widened out to more clearly show the movement of price during the time period depicted. When Close > Open, this "body" is empty like the right image in Figure 6.4; else it is filled. See www.andurilonline.com/book for more on candlestick charting.

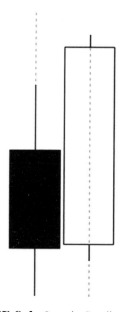

FIGURE 6.4 Sample Candlesticks

These price charts come in many varieties from the very simple line charts in which price is plotted at given intervals, usually from the end of one period (the close) to the end of the next, to bar charts, to Japanese candlesticks, and others. Each technician has his or her own preference, and some styles of charting, such as candlesticks, actually come with their own set of terminology and analytic rules. The charting packages of most trading platforms these days offer a variety of chart types from which to choose.

Market Profile

Market Profile (a registered trademark of the Chicago Board of Trade) is a charting method with which many market participants are unfamiliar because it was developed for use in the commodity futures arena. Its use has expanded, but it is still primarily a futures tool. The Market Profile chart is essentially a compressed bar chart as one can see in Table 6.2.

The vertical single-letter plots are 30 minute "bars." They depict a half hour of action just like a high/low bar would, except that they are plotted with letters rather than lines. Each letter represents a time period. To get the Market Profile plot at left each "bar" is kind of squashed together. Notice, for example, that at 102.10 in the Market Profile there is "ejk." This indicates that price reached that level during periods e, j, and k. If we look lower, at say 101.30, we can see more letters plotted, indicating more action at that price point.

The idea behind Market Profile is that price action builds distributions and that one can trade based on the development of these distributions.

See www.andurilonline.com/book for more on Market Profile.

Chart patterns are the starting point of analysis for the chartist. This is where the idea of technical analysis as an attempt to observe and anticipate behavior begins. We humans tend to fall into patterns of behavior, especially when considered in the group context (mass behavior). Charts show how the collection of market participants have acted in the past. The chartist looks for the kinds of price patterns this creates and attempts to profit by identifying the direction those patterns suggest for future market action.

There is not the space for an exhaustive study of chart patterns here. We will, however, cover a few key points, concepts that even the nontechnician can come across as part of normal involvement in the markets. The biggest of these ideas is that of *support* and *resistance*. In short, it is be-

TABLE 6.2 Sample Market Profile Plot

Market Profile Plot						Hour Bars								
	a	b	c	d	e	f	g	h	i	j	k	l	m	n
102.10 ejk					e					j	k			
102.00 ejk					e					j	k			
101.90 dejk				d	e					j	k			
101.80 adefijk	a			d	e	f			i	j	k			
101.70 adefijk	a			d	e	f			i	j	k			
101.60 abcdfik	a	b	c	d		f			i		k			
101.50 abcdfikln	a	b	c	d		f			i		k	l		n
101.40 abcdfikln	a	b	c	d		f			i		k	l		n
101.30 abcfhikln	a	b	c			f		h	i		k	l		n
101.20 abcfhiln	a	b	c			f		h	i			l		n
101.10 abfhilmn	a	b				f		h	i			l	m	n
101.00 abfhlmn	a	b				f		h				l	m	n
100.90 bfghlmn		b				f	g	h				l	m	n
100.80 bfghlmn		b				f	g	h				l	m	n
100.70 bfghlm		b				f	g	h				l	m	
100.60 bfghlm		b				f	g	h				l	m	
100.50 ghlm							g	h				l	m	
100.40 ghlm							g	h				l	m	
100.30 gm							g						m	
100.20 g							g							

lieved that specific prices or price regions can be barriers to future price movement. Support is a point below the current level at which it is expected price will cease to decline. Resistance is a point above the current price where an advance is expected to stall. Refer to the GBP/USD chart in Figure 6.5.

Consider the decline on the left side of the chart which eventually bottomed at 1.85–1.86. The market then rallied up to 1.93–1.94. When GBP/USD turned over again in March it found *support* near where the previous low was set. It then rebounded, but ran into *resistance* at the peak near 1.93. In this case, the support and resistance was not a single price point, but rather an area of congestion where prices had stalled out and traded for a period of time. This is often how support and resistance levels come into existence. The explanation proffered by the technical analyst is that there must be some underlying reason why so much trade took place at a given point. For this reason, it is often the case that support once broken becomes resistance, and vice versa.

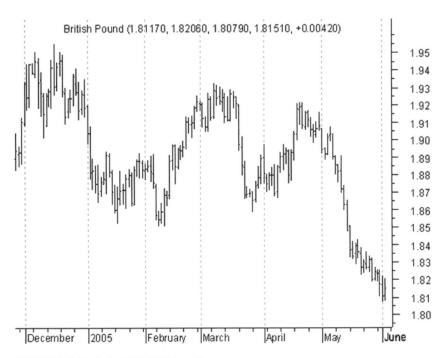

FIGURE 6.5　Daily GDP/USD Bar Chart
Source: Metastock.

Option Strike Prices as Support and Resistance

It is well understood in the market that option strike prices can turn into major support or resistance points. This is a function of the hedging action of option sellers—delta hedges. Specifically, this activity tends to create a kind of attraction to a nearby strike price, especially as option expiration approaches. It also keeps price from moving far away from the strike on the other side.

Although not the case in the GBP/USD example presented, support and resistance can also be a single price point if it holds some significance. An example could be a recent low or high, or a psychological number such at 1.00 in EUR/USD (parity between the euro and U.S. dollar).

The breach of a support or resistance point is considered significant. In general terms, two things increase the significance of a given support or resistance level or area. One is the time frame. A weekly resistance point is thought to be more significant than a daily one, for example. The second is touches. The more a level has been tested (approached, but not broken) the stronger it is thought to be. The more important the support or resistance level (time frame and touches), the more significant the break when it happens. As can be seen in the GBP/USD chart, when the 1.85–1.86 level was broken (an area twice touched) the market proceeded lower without pause or hesitation.

There are two ways traders use support and resistance levels in their methods. One is the range trade, in which one sells as the market approaches resistance or buys as price reaches support expecting a turnaround. Users of these methods take the view that the markets spend more time moving in ranges than they do in trends; thus it makes sense to trade with the expectation of range persistence.

The opposite is a breakout trader, which is a go-with approach where trades are taken in the direction of a break through important support or resistance. As we noted before, breaks are considered significant. The breakout trader, then, is making the play for the development of a trend in the direction of the break. (See Figure 6.6.)

Since much support and resistance is based on consolidation, it is worth touching on that notion quickly. A consolidation is a period of rela-

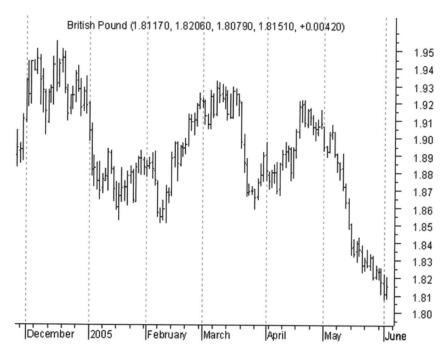

FIGURE 6.6 Daily GBP/USD Bar Chart
Source: Metastock.

tively narrow price action following a directional trend. On our GBP/USD chart, we can see a couple of consolidations. After the February rally from near 1.85–1.93, the market moved sideways in about a 2-point range. That is a consolidation.

In the GBP/USD example, the consolidation was the end of a move. The market rallied, then stalled out. This is not always the case, though, as one can see in the USD/CAD chart shown in Figure 6.7.

In Figure 6.7 (featuring candlestick charting) we can see that USD/CAD was in a long, fairly significant decline. This is about as close to a one-way market as can be seen. Even still, at several stages the market stopped falling and moved in a primarily sideways direction for a spell. It then continued lower again. This is an example of consolidations as breaks in a sustained trend rather than turning points as in the GBP/USD example.

Along with support and resistance, and in conjunction with the idea of consolidation, is the *continuation pattern*. As its name suggests, a continuation pattern is one in which it is expected that the market will recommence a given move. Continuation patterns are visible formations that

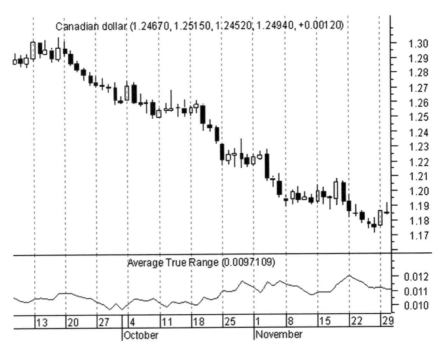

FIGURE 6.7 Daily USD/CAD Candlestick Chart
Source: Metastock.

appear on the charts. They have names like flag and pennant—basic descriptions of their appearance.

At the same time there are *reversal patterns*. As you can easily guess, a reversal pattern is a visual formation on a chart that indicates that one trend has ended and another started. They have names like head-and-shoulders. Both continuation and reversal patterns are far from exact things. History rarely repeats exactly, so no two chart patterns are going to look identical. This is why chart analysis is often considered fairly subjective, more art than science.

Getting away from patterns, but keeping in the charting theme, we come to the *trend line*. A trend line is an attempt to describe a directional move (a trend). Down trend lines follow a set of declining peaks, as in our USD/CAD example (see Figure 6.8). Up trend lines follow rising peaks. There can be quite specific rules as to how they get drawn, but the final analysis is the same. The trend line is intended to give the analyst an indication of direction. If a trend line is broken it suggests a change in the market, either to consolidation or to a slower (less steep) trend. As such, trend lines are not dissimilar to the idea of support and resistance.

Before leaving the idea of charting to move on to other technical analysis methods, we have to first address the important topic of volume.

FIGURE 6.8   Daily USD/CAD Candlestick Chart with Trend Line
Source: Metastock.

Volume is how trading activity is measured. For an exchange traded instrument this is presented in terms of shares (for stocks) or contracts (futures and options) traded during a given time frame. In nonexchange markets like forex, there is no real volume measure because there is no centralized point. Analysts will sometimes use the number of changes in the bid–offer rate as a proxy.

The chart of the December 2005 Eurodollar contract in Figure 6.9 shows how volume is most often presented.

The vertical bars at the bottom indicate the number of contracts traded on a given day. Notice how the amount rises and falls from day to day. Also notice how high volume often matches up with high volatility. The rightmost volume bar is an example. *Note:* Volume for the last trading day—the small range bar following the larger bar—is not plotted in this instance. Technical analysts consider volume an important supportive measure. For example, if a market rises and there is high volume, it is considered a good thing. Were the volume low, such a move might be considered suspect.

A topic related in some ways to volume is *open interest*. Open interest is a reading provided in the futures and options markets that indicates

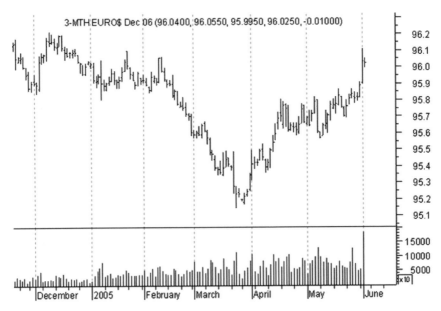

FIGURE 6.9   Weekly Eurodollar Futures with Volume
Source: Metastock.

how many active (open) contracts there are at a given time. Like volume, it is a figure published (normally daily) by the exchanges.

To explain further, imagine that you take a long position in a gold futures contract. You have initiated a new open position. That adds to the open interest. If you were to offset that long position by shorting the same gold contract, you would no longer have an open position and would reduce the total open interest by one. It must be noted that this does not apply only to long positions. Open interest measures how many longs there are with opposing shorts. Remember that in futures and options (unlike stocks), for each open long there must be an open short somewhere. The same applies to spot forex, but because there is no exchange, no open interest figures are available.

Indicators

Moving Average

A moving average is an n-period calculation based on the last n trading periods, usually using the close. It is called moving because at each new period it is recalculated.

A simple moving average (SMA) is a standard mean: $(P0 + P - 1 + \cdots + P - n - 1)/n$.

Other kinds of moving averages are the exponential (EMA) and weighted (WMA) versions.

An indicator is a tool employed by the technical analyst to make certain kinds of market assessments. Indicators come in a wide range of varieties from very simple to very complex. They run the gamut of intentions from trying to measure volatility, to determining trend, to getting a read on how powerfully the market is moving in a given direction.

An indicator is derived from price and/or volume, calculated on a running basis, and plotted along with price on a chart. Some indicators, such as moving averages, are plotted in an overlay fashion right on top of price. Others have their own scales, and thus require a separate plot, generally positioned below the main price section. The daily 10-year note futures chart in Figure 6.10 shows examples of both kinds.

We have several different things going on. First, the price chart is in candlestick format. Second, there is an overlay plot on the price chart. This is the Bollinger band study, which measures price volatility. The central line is a 20-day moving average. The two wider lines (the upper and lower bands) are plotted two standard deviations away from the average (using the same 20-day look-back of daily closes as the moving average). The lower plot is the Relative Strength Index (RSI). RSI uses

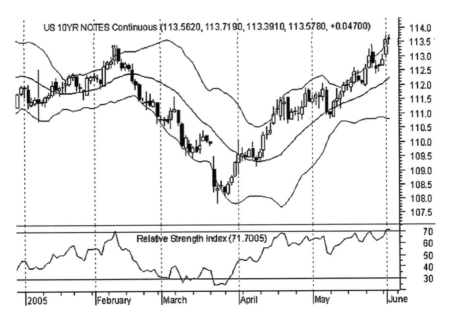

FIGURE 6.10   Daily 10-Year Note Futures with Bollinger Bands and RSI
Source: Metastock.

a price-based calculation to create an oscillator type of plot with a
0–100 scale.

That brings us to an important technical concept—*overbought/over-
sold.* In short, overbought means the market has rallied too much or too
rapidly in a given period of time. As such, it requires some time to settle
down. This could either mean retracing (pulling back part of the rally) or
consolidating. Oversold means the market has moved lower too far
and/or too fast. The aforementioned RSI indicator is one of a number of
so-called overbought/oversold indicators that are intended to point out
such conditions.

Oscillators

Many technical indicators are forced into a fixed scale (often 0–100). Their
readings fluctuate between the upper and lower bounds, in what can be
considered an oscillating fashion. Thus, the name. For the most part, they
have little to do with oscillation as would be defined scientifically.

Oscillators are most often associated with overbought/oversold
indicators.

Bollinger bands fall into the category of volatility-based indicators. The more volatile a market has been during the measurement period, the further apart the bands will be. Markets move from periods of relative calm to those of intense activity. Indicators that focus on that are intended to either point out likely changes in volatility or to use it as a way to make directional interpretation (i.e., trend or consolidation continuation).

We noted that part of the Bollinger band plot in Figure 6.10 was the 20-day moving average. Moving averages are not used by analysts to forecast, but rather fall into the category of trend indicators. This group tries to identify the current trend so that the trader can take the proper directional positions. In the case of a moving average, the trend is considered to be up when price is above the average and down when it is below. There are also momentum indicators. This group is designed to measure how strongly the market is moving. The idea there is that markets with high momentum will tend to continue in their current direction, while those with lower momentum are more likely to change course.

A very simple momentum indicator is rate of change (ROC). An n-period ROC is calculated by taking the most recent period close and subtracting the close from n-periods ago. For example, a 5-day ROC would be calculated as $C_0 - C_{-5}$ where C is the daily closing price. Obviously, a high positive ROC means the market has been moving aggressively higher, just as a high negative one indicates a market moving sharply lower. The ROC is about as simple as it gets. Other momentum indicators are significantly more complex, with some incorporating volume as well as price.

The collection of technical indicators is enormous. We can hardly even scratch the surface here. The reader is encouraged to do their own exploration if the interest is there.

Contrarian

A contrarian is one who seeks to profit by trading against what is considered to be the dominant trend or market bias. This is done either by identifying times when the market has moved too aggressively in one direction (overbought/oversold), or when the trend has run its course (reversal patterns).

Before moving on, however, it is worth mentioning sentiment indicators. This is a collection of measures that are used in assessing the overall market tone and/or bias. In most cases, this analysis is done in a contrary way. This is done by *fading* (going against) a strong bias. If the market is very bullish, the technician using a sentiment indicator might start looking for opportunities to get out of long positions and/or sell short. Were the market to get very bearish, he or she would look for buying opportunities.

This speaks directly to our earlier discussion of technical analysis as a method for evaluating and anticipating collective behavior.

Unlike most other indicators, which in some way involve a price measure, sentiment indicators use other data available in the markets. Volume is often utilized, but not in the fashion we discussed earlier. This can be demonstrated by looking at one of the better known in the collection called the put/call ratio.

The put/call ratio is calculated by dividing the total volume of put option trades by the total volume of call option trades for a given market over a certain time frame. The idea is that put buying is an indication of bearishness If put volume exceeds call volume, especially if it does so by a large margin, it suggests the market has become perhaps overly bearish and could change course.

There are sentiment indicators based on several other bits of available information. The recommendation patterns of trading newsletter authors is one. The volume of odd-lot sales in the stock market is another. (An odd lot in the stock market is a trade of less than 100 shares. Odd-lot trades are done by small investors lacking the funds to make larger trades). The pattern of headlines and/or stories in certain business publications is another.

The point behind all this measurement, though, is to find out if things have just gone too far. If everyone is bullish, there comes a point at which all the buying has been done. Since buying is what drives price higher, no buying means there is only one direction the market can go. Alternatively, the indicators are used to show the bias of what is considered the uneducated public, who is thought to always be wrong at important points.

This brings up a very important point in the discussion of indicators—the idea of *leading versus lagging* indicators. Any indicator that uses historical data, by definition has a lagging element to it. The further the indicator looks back in its calculation, the greater the lag. One could get into a mathematical discussion of how to compute lag, but suffice it to say that a 10-day moving average has more lag than does a 5-day moving average, and a 14-day RSI has more lag than a 9-day RSI. This lag means the trader basing decision making on such indicators will always be late.

This lag effect can most readily be seen in trend indicators such as moving averages. Because they require the market to actually start moving in a certain direction for some period of time to establish that a trend is in place, they will always be late jumping on board. Likewise, they will always be late exiting the trend at the end when the market has stopped moving in that direction. The chart of crude oil in Figure 6.11 provides an example.

LIGHT CRUDE Continuous (54.5400, 55.4000, 53.5000, 53.6300, -0.97000)

FIGURE 6.11   Daily Crude Oil with Moving Average and Volume
Source: Metastock.

The smooth line on the chart is a 14-day simple moving average (SMA) based on the daily closing price. Notice how nicely it outlines the trends in the price of oil during this time span. On the face it looks quite good. Take a look, however, at the middle of the chart in August when price crossed below the moving average. The up trend ended at a bit below 50, but the moving average did not tell us until the market was nearly 5 points lower that the trend was over.

The solution, one might be thinking, is to use a shorter time frame for the SMA. That could work, but it opens the door to what are commonly referred to as whipsaws. A whipsaw is when the market makes quick contrary moves that have the trader flipping positions long to short and vice versa, generally with losses incurred. One can be seen on the right side of the chart. Prices had been declining from the peak near 55. They rallied in late November, and moved up above the moving average—indicating an up trend. The trader who bought that move, however, would have lost money when the market turned back around only a few sessions later, and returned to a downward trend.

Late entries and exits, and whipsaws are the price for using lagging indicators. Those who use the overbought/oversold type of indicators and the sentiment measures will claim them to not be lagging, but rather leading indicators. As we commented just a few moments ago, any calculated indicator using historical information is by definition lagging. The argument for these so-called leading indicators, however, is that they are anticipatory in nature. As such, the lag is not of any concern, as long as it is not too large.

The problem with this point of view, however, is that overbought and oversold conditions and extremes in sentiment can persist. The trader who takes a black-and-white approach to such indicators (overbought—sell, oversold—buy) may do well for periods, but eventually will get hurt badly.

We can return to the crude oil example to demonstrate. In Figure 6.12 we have replaced volume with the stochastic oscillator, a popular overbought/oversold indicator. When the reading exceeds 80 (the upper horizontal line on the plot), the market is overbought. When below 20 (lower horizontal line), the market is oversold.

Refer to the triangles placed on both the price and indicator plots in September. You will note that crude started a strong trend. At the same time the stochastic oscillator read overbought. The rally continued for nearly 10 points from that date. Nearly the whole time the indicator was in overbought territory. That is a clear example of what we just mentioned,

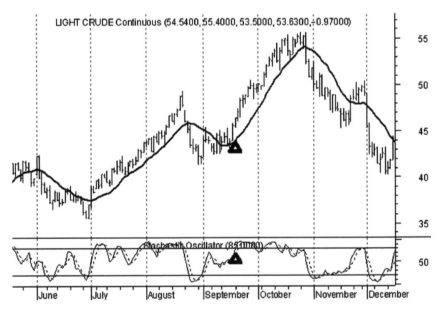

FIGURE 6.12   Daily Crude Oil with Moving Average and Stochastics
Source: Metastock.

the fact that these so-called overbought/oversold indicators have their limitations.

The argument those who use indicators like stochastics will make is that although they have obvious drawbacks in strong directional trending markets, they can be quite effective in choppier markets. As an example, look at Figure 6.13, again using crude oil, but from a later time period.

In this case the oscillator looks quite good. The indicator and the market both seem to be moving in sync. Stochastics do indeed seem to be effectively picking out the tops and bottoms. This is a bit of an illusion, though. If we take a closer look, we can see that not all is as neat as we might like.

We have dropped a vertical line on the chart. It shows where the indicator crossed into overbought territory in late April. Unfortunately, the market was still a couple of points away from peaking (a bit hard to see on the chart). So we still have the problems of timing our entry. The indicator was right that the market was going to turn; it just did not give us a good fix on exactly when that was going to happen.

It should be noted that overbought/oversold indicators hardly are alone in suffering the kind of idealized reading that can occur. The human eye will tend to find patterns and make associations, especially if one is

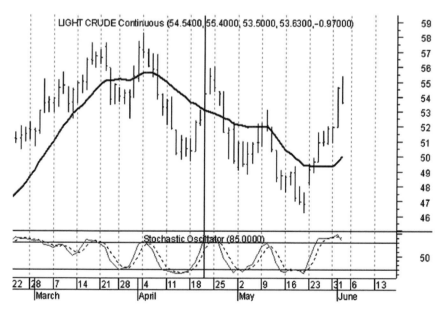

FIGURE 6.13 Daily Crude Oil with Moving Average and Stochastics
Source: Metastock.

looking for them. That is why the user of indicators must be careful not to rely solely on the visual.

Cycle Analysis

In reviewing Figure 6.13, one might take note of the cyclical appearance of the up and down action (one of those patterns the eye will pick up). There is a whole school of technical analysis that focuses on the use of market cycles for the sake of forecasting. The underlying assumption is that markets move in a wave type pattern, rising and falling in somewhat predictable fashion. Cycle analysts attempt to identify these patterns and use them to forecast future market movement. Their methods run from simple "wave" counting methods to highly complex signal filtering techniques brought over from other scientific and mathematic disciplines. There is a wealth of writing on the subject.

Other Technical Methods

While chart reading and the use of indicators are the two biggest focal points in technical analysis, they are not the only forms used. There are techniques that can be said to be variations and/or combinations of the primary, two. Examples include

- *Elliott wave Theory:* This is a method of chart analysis that is founded on the belief that markets move in certain very specific and definable waves. These waves are not the same as the ones defined by cycle analysis, though there are some parallels.
- *Gann theory:* Another charting technique, this particular method uses certain types of lines and angles to predict market turning points.
- *Inter-Market analysis:* This is a sort of composite method whereby the analysis of one market is applied to another market. For example, one could use the analysis of bonds to contribute to the analysis of the stock market. It is based on the interrelations between markets.

The Time Consideration

The strong advantage of technical analysis when used to trade and/ or analyze the financial markets is that it can be applied in any time frame. It was noted in the section on fundamental analysis that the results thereof are not readily applicable in short-term trading. The same is not true of technical analysis. This is referred to as a fractal observation.

Regardless of whether one is operating in a time frame measured in minutes or months, the same tools and techniques can be applied. It all comes back to patterns of behavior. They are not time frame dependent.

Refer to the two USD/JPY charts, which are shown in Figures 6.14 and 6.15. One cannot tell just by glancing that one of them is a daily chart and the other a weekly graph.

Markets can become overbought or oversold just as easily in the course of an hour as they can in a week. They can develop trends and trading ranges in minutes just as readily as in months. It is just a matter of scope. As such, one can use the charts and indicators in all time frames and across all markets (with the obvious exception of indicators, which have specialized requirements available only in certain markets or time frames). This is one of the big reasons so many traders, especially those with a short-term time frame, have flocked to technical analysis in recent years.

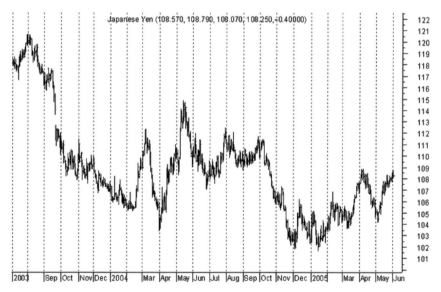

FIGURE 6.14 Daily USD/JPY
Source: Metastock.

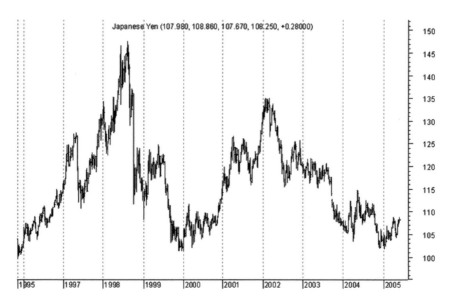

FIGURE 6.15 Weekly USD/JPY
Source: Metastock.

Criticisms of Technical Analysis

Those who oppose technical analysis point to several problems with the application of its methods.

- *Subjectivity:* Certain elements of technical analysis, like chart reading, do not necessarily have objective interpretation. This is often where technical analysis is referred to as more art than science. It is also where individual trader biases can come into play. This is certainly true in some regards, but there are plenty of objective technical methods.
- *Self-Fulfilling:* Technical analysis is said to be self-fulfilling in that the more people applying its methods, the more likely the expectation of the analysis is to come to pass. While it would be true that if everyone used the same or similar techniques such a thing could occur (and it has been known to happen in short time spans in the absence of other influences), the subjectivity of some methods, the diversity of techniques used (nontechnical included), and the fact that traders operate in different time frames mean a lack of unified approach.
- *Unreliable:* Since the past (upon which technical methods are based) does not often repeat exactly, meaning sometimes the product of the

analysis turns out not to be correct, the methods can be considered inconsistent. The question that must be asked, however, is whether that matters if the trader is able to make money.

A very legitimate additional criticism of technical analysis is the ease with which it can be applied. Because technical methods are so readily used in any time frame with seemingly little effort, new traders often gravitate to them as the easy solution. After all, most trading platforms these days come replete with numerous technical tools.

In some ways, however, this is a bit like giving a loaded gun to a child. The kid can certainly fire the weapon, but is at least as likely to hurt himself or herself, or someone else, as to hit the target. That isn't to say technical analysis cannot be effectively and safely employed, though. Like any other risk-taking venture, it requires a thorough understanding of both the application of the methods and the risks involved. Just as there are many who have lost money using technical analysis, there are many who have made money doing so.

Conclusion

Like fundamental analysis, technical analysis can also be applied to any market and in any time frame. Despite the critics, including a great many academics, traders can and do make money with technical analysis. That is a given. Like anything else, though, it is done by selecting the right tool for the job. That means matching the technical method to both the knowledgeable user and to the task at hand.

There is a massive amount of written material available for those interested in learning more. Check out this book's support web site for an updated list:

www.andurilonline.com/book

QUANTITATIVE ANALYSIS

Technical analysis and fundamental analysis can be viewed as separate and distinct ways at looking at the markets. They are. Quantitative analysis, the third leg of the triangle, often operates in conjunction with one or both of the other two. One can apply quantitative methods to fundamental data, and one can apply them to technical data.

Quantitative analysis, as we define it, is the application of mathematical and/or statistical methods to market data. This is primarily done for one of two reasons:

- To compare two or more markets or securities.
- To develop a probabilistic construct of market behavior.

In this section, we go through some of the methods employed by the quantitative analyst and see how they can be applied to trading.

Comparison

The first area of exploration is market and/or instrument comparison. The easiest way to describe this approach is to use an example. *Investor's Business Daily* (IBD), the financial newspaper that competes with the *Wall Street Journal* in the United States, publishes two figures in its stock tables (among other things). They are the rankings for earnings per share (EPS) and relative strength (RS—not related to RSI, the Relative Strength Index mentioned in the technical analysis section). Even if you have never seen an issue of IBD, or heard of the paper, you could still be familiar with EPS and RS, as many stock broker screening systems include variations of them.

In brief, the EPS rank is a top to bottom assessment of all companies in terms of their rate of earnings per share growth over a given time frame (3–5 years normally). The companies are arranged in order of their growth rates and ranked. In the IBD version the ranking is done on a percentile basis, such that the top 1 percent of all companies would get a 99 (99th percentile), while the worst 1 percent would be 1 (1st percentile). Companies can thus be compared on an equal basis, without regard to size, industry, or anything else. This is an example of using quantitative methods in conjunction with fundamental data.

The RS ranking takes more of a technical analysis view. It ranks, in the same manner as EPS, how well a stock has performed in comparison to all other stocks. The evaluation is based on price appreciation/depreciation over a given time period, so a stock that rose 10 percent would outrank one that rose 9 percent. Likewise, a stock that fell 5 percent would rate higher than one which fell 7 percent.

The EPS and RS rankings are very obvious and intentional comparison statistics. They are not overly complex in their calculation, but they serve the purpose of taking a given set of data and applying them in a useful fashion. As noted, they allow a kind of normalized comparison that takes all other considerations out of play. That is good in that it lets the trader accomplish a specific analysis. At the same time, the trader needs to realize that it is only one part of the whole, and that basing one's decision on a single narrow figure has its shortcomings.

Market Behavior Constructs

Recall the charts and tables presented in Chapter 3 during the discussion of price movement. Those were very simple statistical studies of market behavior. There was no implied analysis in those particular results, as there is in the comparative studies just mentioned, but they have a usefulness nonetheless. They allow us to understand how the market tends to operate. Take note of the use of the word "tend." The form of quantitative analysis we are discussing now is about probabilistic behavior—defining or approximating odds and likelihoods.

As an example, we bring back Table 3.4, the one that outlines the frequency of the market going in the same direction from one day to the next. You will remember that the table shows the percentage of time for a given trading day. The market traded in the same direction that day as it had the previous trading day (up/up or down/down). Now see Table 6.3.

The data that underlies Table 6.3 was fairly simple to compile. It was a basic day-to-day comparison done in a spreadsheet with no heavy math. Even still, it provides us with worthwhile information. In this case we find out that the market does not generally have a tendency one way or another in regard to day-to-day directional continuation, though there are a few potential days and currency pairs worth reviewing further.

Even if every number were to be spot on 50 percent, meaning that the market is equally likely to go in the same direction as to go the opposite, that can still be worth knowing. If nothing else, it allows one to eliminate certain factors from one's eventual market understanding and/or allows one to avoid certain paths of inquiry. Beyond that, the knowledge that there is no bias in the figures, and the random behavior it implies, can become part of a larger model.

TABLE 6.3 Directional Movement of Prices

	Percent of time market continued in same direction day-to-day				
	Mon.	**Tue.**	**Wed.**	**Thu.**	**Fri.**
AUD/USD	52%	44%	52%	44%	47%
EUR/USD	49%	45%	48%	42%	44%
GBP/USD	50%	48%	46%	47%	47%
USD/CAD	50%	**38%**	43%	50%	53%
USD/CHF	45%	46%	48%	45%	45%
USD/JPY	51%	47%	49%	46%	50%

In this case, however, there is at least one figure that points toward the potential for further research. On Tuesdays USD/CAD tends to move in the opposite direction as it had done on Monday (since the 38 percent represents moving in the same direction, it would be 62 percent for going in the opposite direction). This would seem like tradable information. If we fade Monday's price move (go against it) on Tuesday, we are going to be right 62 percent of the time.

On the surface, that seems like a workable system. The problem is while we know one thing—the tendency in absolute price behavior from one day to the next—we do not know any more than that. For example, we do not know how much price movement takes place. That is an important piece of information. If one does not make sufficient profits on the winning trades to more than offset the losses suffered on losing trades, then it matters not one bit how often the winners happen. (This topic is discussed in detail in the next chapter.)

The point is that statistics such as the ones we have just shown are very useful, but the quantitative analyst must understand the limits. Every statistical determination is done so with certain constraints. In the previous example, all that was considered was absolute direction, not amplitude of the moves. Constraints mean limitations; that is why such a study as we have just shown is generally just the first cut—a lead on to more comprehensive studies.

Types of Quantitative Analysis

The comparative and market price behavior analysis we have just discussed can be accomplished in a variety of ways. Some are very simple. Others are highly complex. They tend to fall into one of the following categories:

Observation Counting   The table in the previous section was generated through observation counting, which is nothing more than seeing how often something occurs. With a large enough data set one can use the results to get an idea of the tendencies of a market. Examples of some of the types of things one can learn are:

- How often do 1 percent or greater moves occur?
- Does the market tend to move in one direction on a given day?
- Are high volatility periods clustered or randomly scattered?
- How long do trends and/or trading ranges persist?

Think of a question. Observation counting can probably answer it.

Beta

Beta is a measure of a stock price's relative volatility in comparison to the overall market (as defined by some index). It is used both to judge a portfolio risk and to compare stocks.

A positive beta means the stock tends to move in the same direction as the overall market. A negative one implies an inverse relationship between the stock and the market.

Thinking in absolute value terms, a beta of 1.0 (+ or –) indicates that the stock will experience similar volatility to the market. A lower number suggests less relative volatility, while a higher one more.

Because beta figures are historical in nature, however, they are not necessarily reliable, especially over shorter time frames.

Statistical Evaluation   This category of market exploration includes things like regression analysis and other measures right out of most statistics textbooks. The most prevalent example of this kind of work is the well-known beta figure, which is based on the regression model. There are also commonly applied measures such as covariance that come into play in portfolio composition assessments.

Artificial Intelligence   The cutting edge of quantitative analysis is in this area, which encompasses such things at neural nets and genetic algorithms. These are powerful tools for modeling and forecasting. Their use in the markets has been talked about for quite some time. Until recently, however, they were slow and unwieldy, making their application in actual trading difficult. Of late, however, performance improvements have begun to make them a more legitimate possibility for future use.

Words of Warning

Quantitative analysis can be a powerful tool, providing an array of avenues for research and market assessment. One thing must be kept in mind, however. The application of quantitative analysis to fundamental or technical data imparts the same limitations as seen in those methods. Using fundamental information means timing questions and lack of short-term applicability. Should technical studies be involved, lags can become a problem, among other things.

The bottom line is, as always, to know your tools, what exactly they are saying, and how best to apply them.

FINAL THOUGHTS

The starting point of every trading system is determining future market direction. This can be done in value terms through fundamental analysis. It can be done via technical analysis in the application of chart patterns. Quantitative methods can be used to determine tendencies under given scenarios. Regardless of the specific method, however, the trader is still trying to figure out where prices are headed so as to profit.

In deciding which type or types of analysis to use, the trader must keep in mind both the strengths and weaknesses of each method:

Fundamental analysis: Very powerful in terms of determining long-term direction, but lacks short-term applicability.

Technical analysis: Can be applied to any market and in any time frame fairly simply, but the tools use historical information and patterns that do not always repeat the same way, hindering consistency.

Quantitative analysis: Excellent for gaining the understanding of specific elements of market behavior and movement, but has limitations in terms of immediate applicability for buy/sell signals.

Because each of these methods has its own strengths and weaknesses, some of which can offset those of another, may traders seek to combine methods. The idea there is one of synergy, whereby using two or more methods together is more powerful than they could have been alone. It is up to each individual trader to make his or her own determination as to which of the three, or which combination of them, is best.

This chapter has hardly been a comprehensive study of the three analytic techniques. Its intent was not such, since there are vast numbers of books on the subjects. Rather the objective here has been to present the basic ideas and concepts to create the foundation for further exploration by the reader.

For the new trader, learning the ins and outs of all three methods is an unreasonable expectation. The better route to take is to start with the one that most relates to one's strengths and/or interests. Those with strong accounting backgrounds would find fundamental analysis of the stock market quite easy to do, since there is so much reading of financial statements and whatnot. Those who are very visually oriented might find the charting techniques of technical analysis appealing. Engineers and those with strong math and/or quantitative backgrounds would no doubt be very comfortable exploring that particular form of market analysis. There is something for everyone.

Homework

Decide on the analytic method(s) you will use going forward. Be sure to enter in your system research journal a record of your explorations as you make the decision, as well as what you finally choose and why. Remember, this is a critical part of building your trading system. The next chapter gets into the real meat of putting together and performance testing specific trading systems, so you need to know from what base (fundamental, technical, quantitative, or a combination) you will base the buy/sell decisions that drive the system.

CHAPTER 7

System Design and Testing

I n the previous chapter we discussed the methods by which one can make determinations (or at least estimations) of future market direction. It is now time to turn that analysis into a way to make profits.

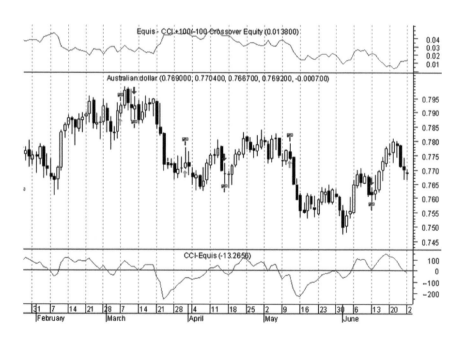

TRADING SYSTEMS DEFINED

We made the comment earlier that one must not confuse trading system with Trading Plan. The Plan was defined back in Chapter 4 as the all-encompassing definition of one's trading efforts. That includes the system, since without the information defined in the Plan, one cannot efficiently select a workable solution for an entry/exit methodology.

The easiest way to define a trading system is a set of predetermined rules by which one makes buy and sell decisions and executes them. One can think of a trading system as a series of statements:

Go Long if/when . . .

Exit Long if/when . . .

Go Short if/when . . .

Exit Short if/when . . .

There are some nuances involved, but one can go a long way toward building a usable trading system by simply filling in the blanks. This chapter is about doing just that. Before getting our hands dirty, though, there are some preliminary things to get out of the way first.

Mechanical versus Discretionary Systems

As would seem to be implied, a mechanical system is one in which the trader has little if any input. The system is set up in such a way that it takes some required data, does whatever manipulations are necessary, and spits out very clear buy and sell signals. These signals can then be applied in an automated fashion (some trading platforms allow for rule-based trading), or through manual entry by the trader.

The reverse of a mechanical system is a discretionary system. Where the former operates on a defined set of if . . . then rules, the latter is more free-form. A discretionary trader works with some general guidelines, but uses their judgment to make buy and sell decisions in light of circumstances, rather than always taking the same action given a specific cue. This sort of approach allows the experienced trader to be more adaptive to the market and use their feel for the market.

There is a great deal of debate in the markets over which type of system is better. Those claiming mechanical to be stronger tend to take the view that discretionary traders can fall victim to personal biases in their market assessment. There is also the issue of market breadth in some cases, since discretionary trading requires more work from the trader.

That means not being able to cover as many markets, as well as having to put more effort into trading.

Of course, those favoring discretionary trading would point to some significant drawbacks to mechanical trading, not the least of which is the boredom factor. A properly applied mechanical system requires little to no action from the trader, which can be frustrating to those who like a bit more stimulation. Moreover, a mechanical system generally is not very adaptive. If the market changes how it trades, a mechanical system will probably fail.

A new trader should start off leaning toward mechanical systems. They are easier to develop and apply than discretionary ones. As market knowledge and understanding increases, one can move away from mechanical trading if desired.

Trading System Objectives

Each trading system must have one or more objectives. Simply stated, what is the system expected to do? This question must be answered before one can even get started. After all, if we do not have a target in mind, how can we know if the system is going to do what we want?

Determination of the objective of a trading system should be based on one's Trading Plan. It is there that trading expectations in terms of returns are defined as well as what risk terms are acceptable. The Trading Plan also indicates how often one expects to trade. Those things come into play now in a statement of the parameters by which the system will be evaluated. For example:

The trading system should provide annualized returns in excess of 20 percent with no drawdown of more than 10 percent risking no more than 5 percent per trade with no restriction on number of trades or trade holding period.

This is a very simple objective that one might have for a stock portfolio. If one were day trading, however, the objective might look like this:

The trading system should generate at least one trade per day, with a weekly average return of 2 percent monthly, drawdowns of no more than 5 percent, and risking no more than 1 percent per trade.

The second objective statement takes into account some time-based measures, reflecting the trader's intended time frame. Other adjustments can be made as well, based on the individual's specific intent and desires. It should all come out of the Trading Plan.

Warning

In the pages that follow we go through the process of developing a trading system. It will be mechanical in nature for the sake of simplicity. The focus is on forex, continuing our use of that market for training purposes. *Do not get fixated on the market or the system!* They are used only to provide easy examples. Neither is necessarily recommended.

Homework

Develop a trading system objective statement based on your Trading Plan. Enter it in to your system research journal.

A SAMPLE SYSTEM

Always In System

This is a trading system that is never out of the market. One is always either long or short.

Before getting into the process of building a system of our own, as we do through these pages, it may first be helpful to demonstrate a very simple one, the moving average crossover system. Moving averages are considered trend indicators. It is held that if price is above the average, the trend is up. If price is below the average, the trend is down. As such, we have the following basic systems:

Go Long when Price is > Moving Average

Go Short when Price is < Moving Average

You will note that the exit rules are not included. This is because the moving average system is always in either long or short. One could actually reword the rules thus:

Exit Short and Go Long when Price is > Moving Average

Exit Long and Go Short when Price is < Moving Average

If you are saying to yourself that this system is not completely defined, you are right. We have to answer two questions to make it complete. The first is which Price will we use. In most systems it is the closing price, which is the basis for decision making. The other question is how long a moving average to use. We will use 10 for this particular example. That gives the following:

Exit Short and Go Long when Close is > 10-period Moving Average

Exit Long and Go Short when Close is < 10-period Moving Average

Now we have a complete trading system, excepting only the size of the trade. We can see it in action by taking a look at Figure 7.2.

The chart shows buy and sell signals based on the moving average system just outlined applied to daily EUR/USD. Notice that when the market closed below the smooth line of the average (the close being indicated by the right pointing tick mark on each price bar), a down arrow sell signal was generated. When the close was above the average, an up arrow buy signal occurred. The signals were as follows:

1. March 2: Short @ 1.3130.
2. March 4: Cover Short & Go Long @ 1.3238.
3. March 18: Cover Long & Go Short @ 1.3316.
4. April 8: Cover Short & Go Long @ 1.2936.

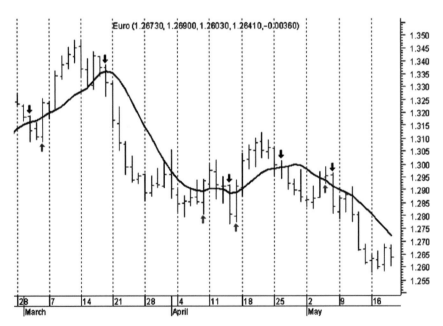

FIGURE 7.2 EUR/USD Moving Average System Trades
Source: Metastock.

5. April 14: Cover Long & Go Short @ 1.2806.
6. April 15: Cover Short & Go Long @ 1.2916.
7. April 26: Cover Long & Go Short @ 1.2988.
8. May 5: Cover Short & Go Long @ 1.2956.
9. May 6: Cover Long & Go Short @1.2835.

If we do a few simple calculations, we can find out how well each trade did (see Table 7.1).

Figure 7.3 shows the cumulative profits for the system over the 9 trades. The system resulted in 4 losers and 5 winners (counting the last open short position) for a total gain of 327 pips (1 pip = $^1/_{10,000}$ of a point in EUR/USD). Had a position of 100,000 EUR/USD been traded on each trade (which would require less than $2,700 maximum initial margin on any position), the system would have made $3,270. That is a return on margin of more than 121 percent over the course of less than three months' time. *Note:* This sample system was chosen for its simplicity, not its profitability. It should not be assumed that a 10-period moving average system will produce these kinds of results consistently.

Of course, return on margin is not necessarily the same as return on account or portfolio. Unless the trader applying this system used 100 percent of the portfolio to make the trades in question, the actual return would be lower. How much lower depends on the risk management portion of the Trading Plan, which was defined in Chapter 5.

For example, the trader's risk management plan might allow for applying only 10 percent of the account for margin on trades from this moving average crossover system. If that were the case, the trader taking

TABLE 7.1 System Results

Trade	L/S	In	Out	Profit
1	S	1.3130	1.3238	−108
2	L	1.3238	1.3316	78
3	S	1.3316	1.2936	380
4	L	1.2936	1.2806	−130
5	S	1.2806	1.2916	−110
6	L	1.2916	1.2988	72
7	S	1.2988	1.2956	32
8	L	1.2956	1.2855	−101
9	S	1.2855	1.2641*	214

*Close as of the last day on the graph.

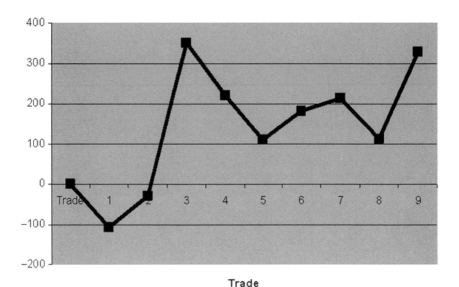

FIGURE 7.3 Simple Moving Average System Profits

positions of 100,000 EUR/USD would have an account size of around $25,000. The account return for the 9 trades would therefore be only about 13 percent.

Risk and position sizing will be integral parts of the discussions ahead in the next chapter. For now we focus on the entry and exit elements of a system.

DEFINING THE SYSTEM FOCUS

At the start of this chapter we noted that for the sake of clarity we were going to use a mechanical system to help demonstrate the process of developing a system. The system will be based on technical analysis, since it is the easiest for the new trader to replicate and readily applicable on the FXTrade platform. In an educational situation such as this, that is more important for practice purposes than individual suitability.

Analytic methodology aside for a moment, to create a good system one must first have some idea of the direction to be taken. System objectives were mentioned earlier. That is a sort of top level target. What needs to be done now is to sort out that path to be taken to reach those objectives.

Time Frame

As a starting point we must look to our Trading Plan to see what kind of time frame we are talking about. Is our system designed to be used in day trading? Or will it be used for swing, or some longer-term position taking? It does us no good to develop an awesome day trading system if we will be incapable of putting into use.

For the sake of the discussion, we assume that we require a system that is intermediate term in nature because we do not have the ability to spend much time watching the market day in and day out. Our focus will be on holding periods most often measured in weeks.

Market or Markets

Part of the Trading Plan discussion revolved around determining the "what?" part of trading. With a time frame in mind, we now shift down to the next sort of filter, which is the market and/or specific instruments we trade. This is based first on when we can trade, and then on our level of knowledge of and comfort with the potential alternatives. Just about any market can be traded in the intermediate to longer-term time frame we have selected. In fact, we could work with multiple markets (keeping in mind the warning of Chapter 5, of course). For the sake of our discussion here, though, we focus on foreign exchange. The forex market is definitely tradable in our time frame and by now we have a solid understanding of how it works. It is also very flexible in terms of allowing us to trade whatever size suits our financial situation and purpose.

Approach

There are two basic ways to approach trading, and thus defining a trading system. One is in term of trends. The other is in terms of ranges. In the former case one seeks to profit by capturing the directional moves (trends) that sometimes happen in the markets. The latter is based on the idea that markets tend to spend more time moving sideways in ranges than they do trending. It could be said that when a market carves out a range it does so by having a series of little, shorter time frame trends. For practical purposes, though, in a given time frame these are the two market conditions.

In order to successfully trade trends, one must have a way to enter them near their beginning and exit them near the end. It is not realistic to expect any system to hit the exact start and conclusion of a major directional move, but it is possible to catch a large portion of one and make good profits. The problem with trend systems, however, is that they tend to be wrong more often than right. If markets do not trend that frequently, this is to be expected. The result is that trend systems generally take many small losses. The good ones, though, make up for that by capturing the big moves.

On the range trading side it is all about defining a range and making trades near its boundaries. One wants to sell near the top of the range and buy near the bottom to capture profits when the market moves from one end to the other. These sorts of systems tend to be the opposite of trend systems in that their success rate is higher, but they make smaller gains and are subject to larger losses when the market shifts from ranging to trending.

The trading system we work to develop in this chapter is based on the trend trading idea. We make this selection because trend trading tends to be simpler to define and apply, especially for those just learning to use the analytic methods at our disposal.

Also, trading based on fundamentals could reasonably be considered trend trading. A fundamental trader is, after all, working in terms of trends in the economy and/or company earnings. As such, trend trading is likely to be easier for most readers to understand and apply in conceptual terms.

Our Starting Point

We have, at this stage, defined our framework. It tells us that we should look to develop a mechanical trend trading system based on technical analysis for the foreign exchange market, which has a holding period more likely to be measured in weeks than anything shorter. With that set, we can move forward into determining the specifics.

Homework

Using the same kind of progression as we just went through, determine your own trading system focus and starting point statement. Make note of it in your system research journal.

ENTRY AND EXIT RULES

At the core of every trading system are the entry and exit rules used to determine where and when to buy and sell. Using our trading system focus, as previously outlined, we can create a conceptual grid of these.

Go Long when . . .   A trend higher is identified.
Exit Long when . . .   The trend higher has ended.

Go Short when . . .   A trend lower is identified.

Exit Short when . . .   The trend lower has ended.

What this boils down to is that we need to find a way to recognize the early stages of new trends so we can jump on board. We also have to figure out a way to define when a trend has run its course. That leaves us with two questions to answer:

1. How do we identify new trends?
2. How do we know when a trend is over?

The process by which we answer these questions can be very involved. A great many traders (and would-be traders) have made the attempt. There is no other way than to test and evaluate.

Obviously, there is not the space here to go through an exhaustive trial process. The array of technical indicators and methods and variations on their application is enormous. We can, however, do a kind of abbreviated version here using the tools at hand.

In order to allow the reader easy duplication of the system we work with only those studies provided by the FXTrade platform. They include:

Bollinger bands	Momentum
Exponential moving average (EMA)	ROC
Parabolic SAR	RSI
Simple moving average (SMA)	Standard deviation
Weighted moving average (WMA)	Stochastic RSI
ADX	Fast stochastic
ATR	Full stochastic
CCI	Williams %R
MACD	Slow Stochastic

Please note that these technical studies from which we can choose do not represent either a comprehensive collection or necessarily the best ones. At this stage, however, the focus is on stepping through the trading system design process, not on determining which is the overall best technical indicator to use among the universe of available options. The latter determination is something that must be done by each trader for her or his own sake (assuming that technical analysis is even chosen as a focal point for market analysis).

We do not have the space here to define in full all of these indicators, especially since they are quite well handled in other places. Refer to this book's resource web site for direct links: www.andurilonline.com/book.

As we go along in our system development, we discuss them to the extent we need to for the sake of the objective.

Preparing to Develop and Test

At the core of the effort here, as indicated by our position taking rules outlined earlier, is identifying trends. As such, we need to take a look at the tools we have available to us in the FXTrade platform.

As noted earlier in the chapter, moving averages are often used as trend indicators. FXTrade provides the user with simple (SMA), exponential (EMA), and weighted (WMA) options for the moving average calculation. Parabolic SAR (stop and reverse) is another trend indicator. So too is Average Directional Index (ADX). The latter, however, is an indicator of only trend strength or persistence. It is not designed to provide buy/sell signals. As such, we will stick with the simple moving average (SMA) and parabolic SAR for our purposes here. Both can be used to signal entry, exit, or both.

Plotting an Indicator on the FXTrade Platform

Please see Figure 7.4. At the bottom left of the chart window is a dropdown labeled Add Study.

Clicking it brings up the list of studies (Figure 7.5). The first five are overlays drawn on the price plot. The remainder is plotted below as separate charts.

Clicking on one of the studies (SMA for example) provides one the opportunity to edit the settings for that particular indicator. As can be seen in Figure 7.5, the default for the SMA is 14 periods (never assume that the default option is the best).

Once the variable is set (or variables, as some studies have more than one), clicking on the + to the right will put the study on the graph. It is possible to plot multiple studies.

To delete a study, put the cursor on it and right click.

FIGURE 7.4 Study List Drop-Down
Source: Oanda.

FIGURE 7.5 Study Configuration
Source: Oanda.

For the sake of our simple little test, the SMA and SAR will provide a good basis for making comparisons. We thus have the following grid:

	I	II	III	IV
Enter	SMA	SMA	SAR	SAR
Exit	SMA	SAR	SAR	SMA

The approach we take in developing our trend system is to separately evaluate entry and exit rules. This is not always the way traders operate, but it is the most comprehensive way. There is a major problem among traders related to this. Every trader is concerned with finding good entry rules. Too few, however, spend as much time considering their exit strategy. As such, they do not develop optimal trading systems in terms of either per trade gains/losses or risk. We evaluate both sides of the system as we go forward.

TEST I—SMA ONLY FOR BUY AND SELL

For the sake of starting rather simply, we first evaluate the SMA only, and do so only for USD/JPY. That means taking Option I from the previous grid of system possibilities—SMA for entry and exit. Since we are looking at entry and exit separately, that means we have to find out which SMA is best suited for identifying a new trend and which is best for determining when a trend has ended. This means testing an array of look-back settings for the SMA.

Recall that the SMA is the average of the closing price for the last n periods. If $n = 1$, then the SMA is equal to the current period close. As n is increased, the SMA reflects longer time frames, meaning a low figure for n results in the SMA being quicker to adapt to price changes and likelier to capture shorter-term trends than a high n setting.

We use daily prices to develop this system as trend signals based on daily data tend to fit into the week or longer holding period we are after. A similar approach would be taken when using data from any other time frame.

The great advantage those developing systems in the modern day have over those who developed them years gone by is technology. There are some wonderful software packages out there with awesome tools for system testing. They can get a bit pricey, however, and mostly the same sort of research can be done using a spreadsheet. Actually, the author prefers to do a lot of his own testing in the latter fashion as it provides some additional flexibility and control.

In any case, a huge plus to the application of system testing in the modern day is that one can not only evaluate many variations quickly (read different time periods for our SMA), but can test entry and exit rules simultaneously to find optimal pairings. If we test look-back periods of 2 to 100 days for both entry and exit, that is nearly 10,000 combinations. Each test covers the period from 1999 through 2004, roughly 1,300 data points. That's a lot of data manipulation. After more than 45 minutes' worth of processing time, the following results are presented.

The report shown in Table 7.2 was produced using the Metastock software package (www.equis.com). It was set up to show the top results as ranked by total profit over the time period tested (Net Profit). The % Gain column is N/A in all cases because we did a points-only test.

ID	Net Profit	% Gain	Trades	Trade Profit/Loss	Avg. Profit/Avg. Loss	OPT1	OPT2
9	31.0700 Pts	N/A	79	23/56	4.20	91	51
1..	31.0500 Pts	N/A	83	23/60	4.41	95	51
5	30.8400 Pts	N/A	79	23/56	4.18	91	50
7	30.8200 Pts	N/A	83	23/60	4.39	95	50
1..	30.4700 Pts	N/A	85	23/62	4.49	96	51
2..	30.4000 Pts	N/A	173	50/123	3.25	19	56
1..	30.2800 Pts	N/A	173	50/123	3.25	19	55
8	30.2400 Pts	N/A	85	23/62	4.47	96	50
1..	30.1300 Pts	N/A	77	23/54	3.96	92	51
1..	29.9900 Pts	N/A	79	22/57	4.37	91	52
1	29.9900 Pts	N/A	173	51/122	3.22	19	34
1..	29.9700 Pts	N/A	83	22/61	4.58	95	52
3	29.9700 Pts	N/A	173	51/122	3.20	19	36
6	29.9000 Pts	N/A	77	23/54	3.94	92	50
2..	29.6900 Pts	N/A	173	49/124	3.33	19	59
2..	29.5200 Pts	N/A	79	22/57	4.37	91	59
2..	29.5000 Pts	N/A	83	22/61	4.59	95	59
1..	29.3900 Pts	N/A	85	22/63	4.67	96	52
2..	29.3699 Pts	N/A	169	52/117	2.99	20	56
2..	29.2499 Pts	N/A	169	52/117	2.99	20	55
4	29.2000 Pts	N/A	173	55/118	2.82	19	45
1..	29.1000 Pts	N/A	79	22/57	4.28	91	53
1..	29.0800 Pts	N/A	83	22/61	4.50	95	53
2	29.0700 Pts	N/A	173	51/122	3.18	19	35
1..	29.0500 Pts	N/A	77	22/55	4.12	92	52

TABLE 7.2 SMA System Test Results
Source: Metastock.

Points-Only Test

A type of system evaluation that does not take into account returns, but instead measures only the amount of points made or lost.

Profit/Loss Ratio

The average profit for winning trades divided by the average loss for losing trades.

For each of the test results we can see the total number of trades executed (Trades), the split between winning and losing trades (Trade Profit/Loss), the profit/loss ratio (Avg. Profit/Avg. Loss), and the moving average look-back periods for the entry signal (OPT1) and the exit (OPT2).

One of the things that will stand out to the viewer is that there is a split between the tests. About half show a trade count between 75 and 85. The other is about twice that. By looking over at the OPT1 column, the reason becomes clear. The tests with higher trade counts used a look-back period of 19–20 periods, while for the others it was 90–96. Remember that a shorter time frame moving average will react more quickly, which will mean more signals. More signals, however, means more trades, and more trades means higher transaction costs. As such, all else being equal, it is better to trade a system with fewer signals for a given time frame than one with more. What's more, in this case, the longer time frame tests show a better per trade profit/loss ratio, as seen in Table 7.3.

Take a moment to look at the Trade Profit/Loss column. Note how the number of winning trades is far exceeded by the number of losing trades. The ratio is in the 1:2 to 1:3 range meaning the tests were profitable for only 25 percent to 30 percent of trades. The fact that the system was profitable despite the seemingly poor win/loss ratio is something very important. One of the serious pitfalls many new (and experienced) traders fall into is feeling the need to be right. Being right, as many see it, means having more winning trades than losing ones. This is something that needs to be overcome in order for truly successful trading to follow.

Slippage

This is the difference between where the system is expecting to execute a trade and where the trade actually gets filled. An example would be having a buy filled at 101 when the expectation was for a fill at 100. Although in theory this can be either positive or negative, in terms of system testing the conservative approach is taken with the assumption normally that slippage will go against the trader.

ID	Net Profit	% Gain	Trades	Trade Profit/Loss	Avg. Profit/Avg. Loss	OPT1	OPT2
1..	29.3900 Pts	N/A	85	22/63	4.67	96	52
2..	29.5000 Pts	N/A	83	22/61	4.59	95	59
1..	29.9700 Pts	N/A	83	22/61	4.58	95	52
1..	29.0800 Pts	N/A	83	22/61	4.50	95	53
1..	30.4700 Pts	N/A	85	23/62	4.49	96	51
8	30.2400 Pts	N/A	85	23/62	4.47	96	50
1..	31.0500 Pts	N/A	83	23/60	4.41	95	51
7	30.8200 Pts	N/A	83	23/60	4.39	95	50
2..	29.5200 Pts	N/A	79	22/57	4.37	91	59
1..	29.9900 Pts	N/A	79	22/57	4.37	91	52
1..	29.1000 Pts	N/A	79	22/57	4.28	91	53
9	31.0700 Pts	N/A	79	23/56	4.20	91	51
5	30.8400 Pts	N/A	79	23/56	4.18	91	50
1..	29.0500 Pts	N/A	77	22/55	4.12	92	52
1..	30.1300 Pts	N/A	77	23/54	3.96	92	51
6	29.9000 Pts	N/A	77	23/54	3.94	92	50
2..	29.6900 Pts	N/A	173	49/124	3.33	19	59
1..	30.2800 Pts	N/A	173	50/123	3.25	19	55
2..	30.4000 Pts	N/A	173	50/123	3.25	19	56
1	29.9900 Pts	N/A	173	51/122	3.22	19	34
3	29.9700 Pts	N/A	173	51/122	3.20	19	36
2	29.0700 Pts	N/A	173	51/122	3.18	19	35
2..	29.3699 Pts	N/A	169	52/117	2.99	20	56
2..	29.2499 Pts	N/A	169	52/117	2.99	20	55
4	29.2000 Pts	N/A	173	55/118	2.82	19	45

TABLE 7.3 SMA System Test Results Sorted by Profit/Loss
Source: Metastock.

Trading system profitability takes into account two things. One is the Win%. The other is the Profit/Loss ratio. The former is how often winning trades occur. The latter is how profitable each trade is. If multiplying the two together and subtracting 1 – Win% results in a value of greater than zero, the system is profitable (assuming that transaction costs and slippage are included in the Profit/Loss ratio). Consider this scenario:

Win% = 20%

Profit/Loss ratio = 6:1

In words, this means that for every 5 trades there is one winner and four losers. At the same time, if the average losing trade costs 1, then the average winner is worth 6. The system is profitable because even though it loses 4 out of every 5 times, the one winner more than makes up for the losses ($1 \times 6 - 4 \times 1 = 2$).

Now consider this alternative scenario:

Win% = 80%

Profit/Loss ratio = 1:6

This is a losing system. Even though it is right much more often than not, the losers outweigh the gainers ($4 \times 1 - 1 \times 6 = -2$). A system like this is why it does no good to get overly caught up in Win%. All things being equal, then naturally higher is better. The ideal scenario is to have a high Win% and a high Profit/Loss ratio. That is every trader's dream. The perfect system! Most often there is a tradeoff, however.

In the case of trend systems, low a Win% is the norm, with a relatively high Profit/Loss ratio. Why? Because the markets spend more time (for any given time frame) moving sideways than in extended directional moves. That back and forth range trading creates losses for trend systems. The good ones, however, make up for the frequent small losses with periodic large gains when the good trends are caught and ridden. Remember our EUR/USD 10-day moving average example from earlier?

Notice the back and forth action, in the middle of Figure 7.6. You may

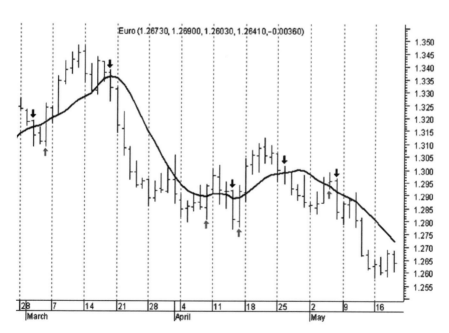

FIGURE 7.6 EUR/USD Moving Average System Trades
Source: Metastock.

recall that those trades were losers. A couple of nice trends were caught, too, though, especially the one from middle March until about middle April. That sort of move is where trend systems make their money. The trend trading system is patient in accepting the small losses to get those big gainers.

But why must a trend system suffer from these whipsaws? It comes down to the idea that a false positive reading is better than a false negative.

Trend trading systems are all about capturing large portions of major price moves. That means the system must be in the market when they are taking place. To be otherwise defeats the whole purpose. That means the system is going to be aggressive in terms of finding new trends. We have already established that markets move sideways more than directionally up or down. That means it is more often going to be the case that an indication of a potential new trend is wrong (false positive) than right. If it means catching the big trends, though, we accept that. If the system were to miss the trends (false negative), it would be rather useless, would it not?

We will see the same sort of split between whipsaw periods and profitable trend action occurring in our USD/JPY trend system. For the sake of conservatism, we select 92 days for our trade entry moving average and 50 days for our trade exit moving average. So our trading rules are:

Go Long when Close crosses above the 92-day moving average.

Exit Long when Close crosses below the 50-day moving average.

Go Short when Close crosses below the 92-day moving average.

Exit Short when Close crosses above the 50-day moving average.

Favorable Excursion

Movement of the market in the direction of the trade. This measure is used to determine how much profit was given back when the trade is exited. One wants to minimize the difference between the excursion of a trade and the actual profit made, as it represents money left on the table, so to speak.

These rules are based on a unified test (as run by Metastock) of both entry and exit signals together. It was done for the sake of speed and efficiency, and because we are operating with a limited number of tools for picking out trends and knowing when they are done. In actual practice one should take the time to review exit and entry strategies separately. In the case of a trend system, the entry method should be the one that best identifies trends of the length we require (a couple of weeks), while the exit strategy should be the one that best recognizes the end of the trends we trade and leaves the least amount of profit on the table. Keep this in mind. Traders too often get caught up in their entries and forget the fact that how they get out of the trade is at least as important as how they go in.

At this stage we have not incorporated in our system anything that indicates the size of the trades we are to make. That will get a lot of attention in the next chapter. For the moment we just focus on the buy/sell signals themselves.

We can see our SMA system in action in Figure 7.7 and Figure 7.8.

Figure 7.7 shows quite clearly the kind back and forth action that is the bane of the trend system. The 92-day moving average, our entry signal line, is the dark one. Notice how many times it is crossed in the period of this chart. Those back and forth moves whip the trader from long to short and back again (as shown by the up and down arrows), generally resulting in a string of relatively small losses.

Now consider the trend the system captured in Figure 7.8. This is a classic example of why one employs a trend trading system. The one trade that started in mid-August and ended in the latter part of February was worth something like 11 points. In account terms, had one traded $100,000 worth of USD/JPY, the profit would have been more than

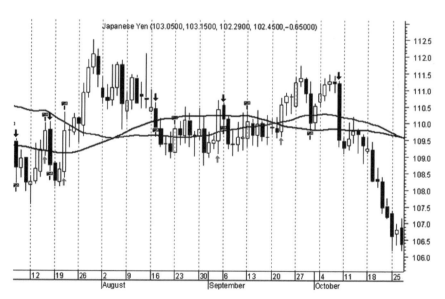

FIGURE 7.7   SMA System Trades: Nontrending Period
Source: Metastock.

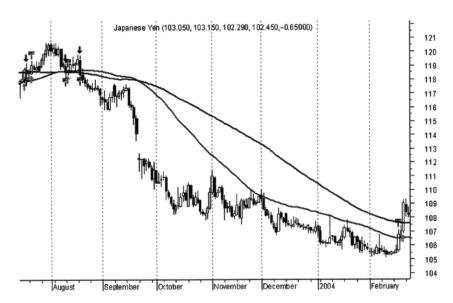

FIGURE 7.8　SMA System Trades: Trending Period
Source: Metastock.

$10,000. That's a heck of a return considering the margin for such a trade would be about $2,000.

Figure 7.9 shows the system equity line—the running point profit total. (Ignore the $s.) The equity line is rather jagged. One can see from the system statistics in Table 7.4 exactly why that is.

In the Unprofitable Trades section take a note of the Most Consecutive figure. It reads 13. That means at one point the system experienced 13 losses in a row. There were probably a number of other strings as well.

FIGURE 7.9　SMA System Equity Line
Source: Metastock.

Performance	
Profit	29.9000 Pts
Performance	N/A
Annualized Performance	N/A
Buy & Hold Profit	-9.4000 Pts
Buy & Hold Performance	N/A
Buy & Hold Annualized Performance	N/A

Trade Summary	
Total Trades	77
Trade Efficiency	-17.20 %
Average Profit/Average Loss	N/A

Profitable Trades	
Total	23
Long	12
Short	11
Average Profit	3.2148 Pts
Highest Profit	13.1500 Pts
Lowest Profit	0.0100 Pts
Most Consecutive	3

Unprofitable Trades	
Total	54
Long	26
Short	28
Average Loss	-0.8156 Pts
Highest Loss	-2.3800 Pts
Lowest Loss	-0.1100 Pts
Most Consecutive	13

Maximum Position Excursions	
Long Favorable	18.6700 Pts
Short Favorable	15.8200 Pts
Long Adverse	-2.7100 Pts
Short Adverse	-3.8000 Pts

Trade Efficiency	
Average Entry	47.64 %
Average Exit	33.86 %
Average Total	-17.20 %

Performance Indices	
Buy & Hold Index	418.09 %
Profit/Loss Index	40.44 %
Reward/Risk Index	88.75 %

Accounting	
Initial Equity	0.0000 Pts
Trade Profit	73.9400 Pts
Trade Loss	-44.0400 Pts
Commissions	0.0000 Pts
Interest Credited	0.0000 Pts
Interest Charged	0.0000 Pts
Final Equity	29.9000 Pts
Open Positions	7.0500 Pts

Account Variation	
Highest Account Balance	34.4700 Pts
Lowest Account Balance	-3.7900 Pts
Highest Portfolio Value	18.6700 Pts
Highest Open Drawdown	-3.7900 Pts
Highest Closed Drawdown	-3.5700 Pts

Account Events	
Margin Calls	0
Overdrafts	0

Profitable Timing	
Average Trade Length	38
Longest Trade Length	130
Shortest Trade Length	3
Total Trade Length	896

Unprofitable Timing	
Average Trade Length	5
Longest Trade Length	22
Shortest Trade Length	1
Total Trade Length	271

Out of Market Timing	
Average	16
Longest	111
Total	393

TABLE 7.4 SMA System Performance Statistics
Source: Metastock.

Those are a big reason for the sometimes substantial drawdowns in the equity line.

Winning trades did not bunch together as much. The most consecutive there was three. Given that losers happen more than twice as often as winners, this is no surprise. The reason the system is profitable is in the fact that while the average winning trade was worth 3.21 points (the biggest a whopping 13.15!), the average loser cost only 0.82 points.

On Data

Futures and Options Data

Because futures and options are fixed duration instruments that expire in a relatively short period of time, there is an additional consideration related to historical prices. How do you account for moving from one contract to the next to keep an unbroken price series?

The best method is to use the actual data specific to the contract the system is trading at a point in time. This is best for a truer set of results.

Many folks use continuous contract data series, however. These are series that incorporate a roll-over to switch from an expiring contract to the next active one in the series. This is done to provide a longer data set than would be possible if one just looks at one contract at a time.

The problem with continuous contract data is that either the adjustments in the price series create a kind of fabricated data set, or there are discontinuities in the prices that can actually cause inaccurate trading signals in a system.

At this point, however, it is well worth mentioning a couple of critical points in the assessment of a system. The first is data source. Not all data are the same, especially when one is using indicative data. The advantage of traded data is that they come from a centralized place and have specific parameters (time stamp, etc.). Indicative data, such as those coming from the forex market, are more variable in their presentation. The open/high/low/close data points for any given data set may not match those from another because of difference in quotes and time settings. For example, one supplier might consider 4:00 P.M. New York time to be the close of the forex trading day while another might use 5:00 P.M, and a third might run off GMT (Greenwich mean time). In order to effectively evaluate a system's profit potential, the trader must match up the data used with the data that will be traded. If one is trading via FXTrade, then one should use the data from the FXTrade platform to run tests.

Keeping with the data theme, if one is using indicative price quotes, it must be known whether the data are based on the bid, offer, or mid rate (midway between bid and offer), and along with that, have a good idea as to what the spread is. Why? Because the trader will sell at the bid and buy at the offer. The spread can substantially impact the profitability figures for a system. If, for example, one is testing a system on a market with a 10-pip spread, but only uses the bid in the testing, they are overestimating the per trade profits by those 10 pips because the purchases would all take place 10 pips higher than what the data indicate. This is an incredibly important consideration for systems with small per trade profits, which usually are those with higher trade frequency and shorter holding periods. For our intermediate trend system this is not that big an issue.

With all this talk of the issues surrounding indicative data, one might think it best to stick with traded figures (where possible). Keep in mind the discussion earlier in this text regarding the problem with traded price. One does not know necessarily how good that price is, especially in low volume instruments. What's more, the trade was executed at either the bid or offer price. The trader looking at a standard data set will not know which one, thus cannot know if that price is the one they should be using as an entry or exit point for a theoretical trade of the system. That is why forward testing of systems (which we address later) is important.

Many traders, when developing trading systems, attempt to account for the vagaries of their data by factoring a negative slippage into each trade. Most software packages allow for this, and of course it can easily be done as well if one is using a spreadsheet to do the testing. The same holds true here as with spreads. The longer holding periods and lower trade frequency tends to reduce the impact of slippage on the system profitability.

TEST II—SAR ONLY FOR BUY/SELL

With the SMA Only test done, it is time to make our next test, which is using only SAR to make buy and sell decisions. The parabolic SAR was originally intended to be a trailing stop of sorts based on the acceleration of price and continuation of a trend. It can be used for entry purposes as well, though (SAR stands for stop and reverse).

For our testing purposes, we need to determine the Acceleration settings for the SAR calculation (see the box for details on the calculation). The common default is to start the Acceleration step at 0.02 and have it capped at 0.20. For our testing we use a step range of 0.01 to 0.10 at intervals of 0.01, and set the cap range at 0.10 to 1.00 using intervals of 0.10.

As can be seen in Table 7.5, the SAR-Only system has some tests that show better results than our earlier SMA-Only test.

ID	Net Profit	% Gain	Trades	Trade Profit/Loss	Avg. Profit/Avg. Loss	OPT1	OPT2
4	41.2300 Pts	N/A	138	61/77	1.74	0.02	0.2
2..	37.9700 Pts	N/A	140	60/80	1.79	0.02	1
2..	37.9700 Pts	N/A	140	60/80	1.79	0.02	0.9
2..	37.9700 Pts	N/A	140	60/80	1.79	0.02	0.8
7	37.9700 Pts	N/A	140	60/80	1.79	0.02	0.3
1..	37.9700 Pts	N/A	140	60/80	1.79	0.02	0.7
9	37.9700 Pts	N/A	140	60/80	1.79	0.02	0.4
1..	37.9700 Pts	N/A	140	60/80	1.79	0.02	0.6
1..	37.9700 Pts	N/A	140	60/80	1.79	0.02	0.5
1..	30.1500 Pts	N/A	118	57/61	1.41	0.02	0.1
2	28.2300 Pts	N/A	160	68/92	1.70	0.05	0.1
1	18.3099 Pts	N/A	152	63/89	1.64	0.04	0.1
1..	16.5499 Pts	N/A	84	37/47	1.51	0.01	0.1
1..	11.8500 Pts	N/A	88	38/50	1.48	0.01	0.6
1..	11.8500 Pts	N/A	88	38/50	1.48	0.01	0.5
1..	11.8500 Pts	N/A	88	38/50	1.48	0.01	0.7
8	11.8500 Pts	N/A	88	38/50	1.48	0.01	0.4
6	11.8500 Pts	N/A	88	38/50	1.48	0.01	0.3
2..	11.8500 Pts	N/A	88	38/50	1.48	0.01	0.8
2..	11.8500 Pts	N/A	88	38/50	1.48	0.01	0.9
3	11.8500 Pts	N/A	88	38/50	1.48	0.01	0.2
2..	11.8500 Pts	N/A	88	38/50	1.48	0.01	1
5	9.9700 Pts	N/A	202	76/126	1.77	0.04	0.2
1..	9.7500 Pts	N/A	208	78/130	1.77	0.04	0.5
1..	9.7500 Pts	N/A	208	78/130	1.77	0.04	0.7

TABLE 7.5 SAR System Test Results
Source: Metastock.

Parabolic SAR

$$SAR(i) = SAR(i-1) + ACCELERATION * (EPRICE(i-1) - SAR(i-1))$$

where $SAR(i-1)$ = the value of the indicator on the previous bar

ACCELERATION = the acceleration factor

$EPRICE(i-1)$ = the highest (lowest) price for the previous period (EPRICE = HIGH for long positions and EPRICE = LOW for short positions)

The indicator value increases if the price of the current bar is higher than previous bullish and vice versa. The acceleration factor (ACCELERATION) will double at the same time, which would cause parabolic SAR and the price to come together. In other words, the faster the price rises or sinks, the faster the indicator approaches the current price.

One can see that the Win% percentage is higher with this method, much closer to 50% than was the case with the SMA system, though as is often the case the profit/loss ratio (Avg. Profit/Avg. Loss) is significantly lower across the board.

From our test, it does not seem as though the cap (OPT2) has a major impact on system performance. As a result, we stick with the standard default cap for the Accelerator of 0.20 for the sake of simplicity.

One can again see a split in the results between a longer and shorter bias in the testing. When the Acceleration step (OPT1) is at 0.02 or higher there are many more trades than in the case at a 0.01 setting. The Acceleration part of the calculation determines how quickly the SAR line converges toward price. A higher reading means faster convergence, which translates into more triggers in choppy markets. The chart in Figure 7.10 provides a very clear example of this in action.

The dotted line furthest above price on the chart when it starts on the left is SAR using a step of 0.02. The other is a step of 0.01. Notice how much more reactive the 0.02 line can be. It tends to more quickly hug price as trends accelerate.

The number of trades executed at the optimal setting of 0.2 for the Accelerator step and 0.20 as the cap for it produces a lot more trades than

FIGURE 7.10 SAR Plots with Different Parameter Settings
Source: Metastock.

was the case for the SMA-Only system. In this case, however, the
profit/loss ratios are also higher for the more active tests than for the less
active ones. That means if we were to apply slippage and/or transaction
costs, the 0.2 step results would still exceed the 0.1 step results. Using a
10-pip slippage (0.10 for USD/JPY), the 0.02/0.20 test shows a profit of
27.43 points, while the 0.01/0.10 test nets 8.15.

So our rules for the SAR-Only system are (note the always-in nature):

Exit Shorts and Go Long when the 0.02/0.20 setting SAR line moves
below the close

Exit Longs and Go Short when the 0.02/0.20 setting SAR line moves
above the close

Table 7.6 shows the analysis of the performance for our SAR-
Only system based on the rules we just listed. Notice that there was
actually a longer maximum string of profitable trades than was the
longest string of losing trades. One might not expect that to be the case
given that Win% is below 50 percent. In fact, the odds of seeing eight
winning trades in a row, based on the figures available, are only about
8 percent. It just goes to show that statistical improbabilities can certainly happen.

Figure 7.11 outlines what the system looks like in action during a segment of our test period. Notice that in some places rather nice trends
were captured, while in others the choppy trading caused some whipsaws. Like any other trend system, this SAR-Only system suffers during
nontrending periods, though decidedly less than we saw in the case of the
SMA-Only system.

In Figure 7.12 is the equity curve for the system. There are some significant drawdown periods, especially in the middle of the chart, but
there are also a few nice rapid advances as well. The character of the
graph is different from the case for the SMA-Only system. In the latter
case, most of the profit seemed to take place in the first half of the test,
with the latter part of the curve being fairly flat. In this case it looks to be
the opposite.

Trade Execution Consideration

Of important consideration in both the SAR and SMA systems we have
looked at so far, and in the combined ones to come, is the consideration of
entry and exit timing. These tests make certain assumptions as to when
trades get executed. Since both of these particular systems have signals

Performance		
Profit	41.2300 Pts	
Performance	N/A	
Annualized Performance	N/A	
Buy & Hold Profit	-7.0200 Pts	
Buy & Hold Performance	N/A	
Buy & Hold Annualized Performance	N/A	

Trade Summary		
Total Trades	138	
Trade Efficiency	-7.16 %	
Average Profit/Average Loss	N/A	

Profitable Trades		
Total	61	
Long	30	
Short	31	
Average Profit	2.4734 Pts	
Highest Profit	7.3300 Pts	
Lowest Profit	0.0300 Pts	
Most Consecutive	8	

Unprofitable Trades		
Total	77	
Long	39	
Short	38	
Average Loss	-1.4240 Pts	
Highest Loss	-4.2700 Pts	
Lowest Loss	-0.0400 Pts	
Most Consecutive	6	

Maximum Position Excursions		
Long Favorable	8.1600 Pts	
Short Favorable	8.4900 Pts	
Long Adverse	-4.6600 Pts	
Short Adverse	-4.7700 Pts	

Trade Efficiency		
Average Entry	53.29 %	
Average Exit	38.82 %	
Average Total	-7.16 %	

Performance Indices		
Buy & Hold Index	687.32 %	
Profit/Loss Index	27.33 %	
Reward/Risk Index	78.43 %	

Accounting		
Initial Equity	0.0000 Pts	
Trade Profit	150.8800 Pts	
Trade Loss	-109.6500 Pts	
Commissions	0.0000 Pts	
Interest Credited	0.0000 Pts	
Interest Charged	0.0000 Pts	
Final Equity	41.2300 Pts	
Open Positions	2.7700 Pts	

Account Variation		
Highest Account Balance	42.8600 Pts	
Lowest Account Balance	-11.3400 Pts	
Highest Portfolio Value	8.1600 Pts	
Highest Open Drawdown	-11.3400 Pts	
Highest Closed Drawdown	-9.9400 Pts	

Account Events		
Margin Calls	0	
Overdrafts	0	

Profitable Timing		
Average Trade Length	17	
Longest Trade Length	37	
Shortest Trade Length	1	
Total Trade Length	1038	

Unprofitable Timing		
Average Trade Length	6	
Longest Trade Length	19	
Shortest Trade Length	1	
Total Trade Length	507	

Out of Market Timing		
Average	0	
Longest	1	
Total	1	

TABLE 7.6 SMA System Performance Statistics
Source: Metastock.

based on closing price, they imply that one is executing trades at the close of the day, or the open of the next trading session.

In foreign exchange (with the exception of weekends) the market is continuous. One day's open is the previous day's close (except over the weekend), so one can be somewhat comfortable as to execution points, unless the market is very volatile at the time. In the case of exchange traded instruments, however, where there is a distinct time gap between one day's close and the next day's open, there can be substantial gaps. Here again is the issue of slippage.

FIGURE 7.11   SAR System Trades
Source: Metastock.

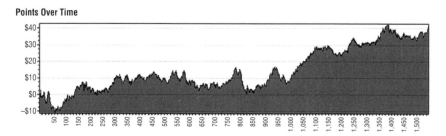

FIGURE 7.12   SAR System Equity Line
Source: Metastock.

TEST III—SMA ENTER/SAR EXIT

Now it is time to start combining our two entry/exit methods to see if using them in tandem produces better results then when they are applied individually. For this test we use our SMA as the entry signaler and the

SAR to determine when trades get closed. Our system rules will look like this:

Go Long when Close crosses above SMA

Exit Long when SAR moves above Close

Go Short when Close crosses below SMA

Exit Short when SAR moves below Close

Of course the list does not tell us what parameters we will use for either the SMA or the SAR. We test multiple settings for each, but just for the sake of an initial view, what if we just combine the rules from our previous two tests? That would give us the following rules:

Go Long when Close crosses above the 92-day moving average

Exit Long when the 0.02/0.20 setting SAR line moves above Close

Go Short when Close crosses below the 92-day moving average

Exit Short when the 0.02/0.20 setting SAR line moves below Close

The problem with combining the two systems, however, is that they tend to operate in different time scales. Remember that the SMA system had only 77 trades compared to 138 for the SAR system. This is an indication that the former is seeking out longer-term trends than is the case for the latter. As a result, the two systems do not synch up very well.

One can see this quite clearly in Table 7.7 where the results for the combined system are presented. There were 77 trades, which makes sense given that the SMA system, which is what is providing entry signals here, also had 77 trades.

The problem, however, is that the fast SAR exits (as compared to the SMA exits) caused trades to get cut short. The system caught less of the long trends, which severely reduced the profitability.

This means we have to go back to the drawing board and do a full test of the various parameter combinations to see if we can find a better option. This time around we cut down on the required iterations to speed up the testing. We use 0.01 to 0.10 for the SAR step (OPT2), and 0.1 to 0.9 for the cap (OPT3). That is not far off from what we used in our SAR-Only system testing. The real change we will make is go use SMAs from 5 to 100 periods, at intervals of five (OPT1). That gives us a test set of 1700, which takes only about 8 minutes to solve. The results are shown in Table 7.8.

Performance			Performance Indices	
Profit	5.8800 Pts		Buy & Hold Index	183.76 %
Performance	N/A		Profit/Loss Index	14.78 %
Annualized Performance	N/A		Reward/Risk Index	55.89 %
Buy & Hold Profit	-7.0200 Pts			
Buy & Hold Performance	N/A		Accounting	
Buy & Hold Annualized Performance	N/A		Initial Equity	0.0000 Pts
			Trade Profit	39.7900 Pts
Trade Summary			Trade Loss	-33.9100 Pts
Total Trades	77		Commissions	0.0000 Pts
Trade Efficiency	-8.68 %		Interest Credited	0.0000 Pts
Average Profit/Average Loss	N/A		Interest Charged	0.0000 Pts
			Final Equity	5.8800 Pts
Profitable Trades			Open Positions	0.0000 Pts
Total	30			
Long	16		Account Variation	
Short	14		Highest Account Balance	8.7200 Pts
			Lowest Account Balance	-4.6400 Pts
Average Profit	1.3263 Pts		Highest Portfolio Value	4.7100 Pts
Highest Profit	3.4400 Pts		Highest Open Drawdown	-4.6400 Pts
Lowest Profit	0.0300 Pts		Highest Closed Drawdown	-4.5900 Pts
Most Consecutive	5			
			Account Events	
Unprofitable Trades			Margin Calls	0
Total	47		Overdrafts	0
Long	22			
Short	25		Profitable Timing	
			Average Trade Length	11
Average Loss	-0.7215 Pts		Longest Trade Length	26
Highest Loss	-2.3800 Pts		Shortest Trade Length	1
Lowest Loss	-0.1000 Pts		Total Trade Length	337
Most Consecutive	8			
			Unprofitable Timing	
Maximum Position Excursions			Average Trade Length	4
Long Favorable	4.7100 Pts		Longest Trade Length	18
Short Favorable	4.5700 Pts		Shortest Trade Length	1
Long Adverse	-2.7100 Pts		Total Trade Length	201
Short Adverse	-3.8000 Pts			
			Out of Market Timing	
Trade Efficiency			Average	24
Average Entry	45.99 %		Longest	119
Average Exit	45.33 %		Total	1009
Average Total	-8.68 %			

TABLE 7.7 SMA/SAR System Performance Statistics
Source: Metastock.

The figures are dramatic. The best performing systems in terms of Net Profit were very active. The top systems, based on a 10-day moving average, had more than 275 trades. The Win% is comparable to the SMA-Only system—a bit better actually.

Notice again how time scope can impact trade frequency. The second best performing group was when the SMA was set at 20 days. Doubling the look-back of the moving average in that fashion resulted in 110 fewer trades. There is a modest dropoff in the net profit, but if one starts to factor in slippage and/or transaction costs, the longer-term time frame

ID	Net Profit	% Gain	Trades	Trade Profit/L...	Avg. Profit/Avg. Loss	OPT1	OPT2	OPT3
⊟ 2	28.8601 Pts	N/A	278	97/181	2.28	10	0.04	0.5
⊟ 2..	28.8601 Pts	N/A	278	97/181	2.28	10	0.04	0.4
⊟ 9	28.8601 Pts	N/A	278	97/181	2.28	10	0.04	0.8
⊟ 4	28.8601 Pts	N/A	278	97/181	2.28	10	0.04	0.6
⊟ 1..	28.8601 Pts	N/A	278	97/181	2.28	10	0.04	0.3
⊟ 7	28.8601 Pts	N/A	278	97/181	2.28	10	0.04	0.7
⊟ 1..	28.8601 Pts	N/A	278	97/181	2.28	10	0.04	0.9
⊟ 1..	28.0301 Pts	N/A	278	96/182	2.30	10	0.04	0.2
⊟ 1..	26.7099 Pts	N/A	168	61/107	2.38	20	0.1	0.2
⊟ 1..	26.5499 Pts	N/A	168	61/107	2.37	20	0.09	0.2
⊟ 8	23.7499 Pts	N/A	168	63/105	2.20	20	0.09	0.7
⊟ 3	23.7499 Pts	N/A	168	63/105	2.20	20	0.09	0.5
⊟ 6	23.7499 Pts	N/A	168	63/105	2.20	20	0.09	0.6
⊟ 1..	23.7499 Pts	N/A	168	63/105	2.20	20	0.09	0.9
⊟ 1..	23.7499 Pts	N/A	168	63/105	2.20	20	0.09	0.8
⊟ 1..	23.5500 Pts	N/A	200	75/125	2.07	15	0.1	0.2
⊟ 2..	23.5499 Pts	N/A	168	62/106	2.25	20	0.1	0.3
⊟ 1	23.4299 Pts	N/A	168	63/105	2.20	20	0.1	0.4
⊟ 2..	23.3899 Pts	N/A	168	62/106	2.25	20	0.09	0.3
⊟ 2..	23.2699 Pts	N/A	168	63/105	2.19	20	0.09	0.4
⊟ 1..	22.8000 Pts	N/A	200	75/125	2.05	15	0.09	0.2
⊟ 1..	22.1800 Pts	N/A	200	81/119	1.81	15	0.04	0.8
⊟ 5	22.1800 Pts	N/A	200	81/119	1.81	15	0.04	0.6
⊟ 2..	22.1800 Pts	N/A	200	81/119	1.81	15	0.04	0.3
⊟ 2..	22.1800 Pts	N/A	200	81/119	1.81	15	0.04	0.4

TABLE 7.8 SMA/SAR System Test Results
Source: Metastock.

tests would prove to be the winners. To demonstrate this, we will rerun the test using a 10-pip slippage for each trade.

Now if we look at the results in Table 7.9 there are no 10-period SMA tests shown among the best performers. The profits were all eaten up by slippage.

Going back to the original test, however, we need to select a fairly representative system for later comparison. If we use only the 20-day SMA test for the sake of overall performance we have a few options from which to choose. Interestingly, the SAR Acceleration step settings (OPT2) are quite high at 0.09 or 0.10. Those are very aggressive settings for that parameter.

Taking a conservative approach, we can select the test results based on the 0.09 step and 0.50 cap (OPT3) settings. It is not the optimal performance of all the 20-day SMA tests, but we do not want to put too fine a point on it at this stage. We are just looking to gain a basis for later system comparisons.

ID	Net Profit	% Gain	Trades	Trade Profit/Loss	Avg. Profit/Avg. Loss	OPT1	OPT2	OPT3
3	10.0099 Pts	N/A	168	56/112	2.23	20	0.1	0.2
2	9.8499 Pts	N/A	168	56/112	2.23	20	0.09	0.2
7	7.0499 Pts	N/A	168	59/109	2.00	20	0.09	0.7
22	7.0499 Pts	N/A	168	59/109	2.00	20	0.09	0.6
19	7.0499 Pts	N/A	168	59/109	2.00	20	0.09	0.5
11	7.0499 Pts	N/A	168	59/109	2.00	20	0.09	0.8
14	7.0499 Pts	N/A	168	59/109	2.00	20	0.09	0.9
6	6.8499 Pts	N/A	168	57/111	2.10	20	0.1	0.3
17	6.7299 Pts	N/A	168	58/110	2.05	20	0.1	0.4
5	6.6899 Pts	N/A	168	57/111	2.10	20	0.09	0.3
16	6.5699 Pts	N/A	168	58/110	2.04	20	0.09	0.4
8	4.9699 Pts	N/A	168	59/109	1.96	20	0.1	0.7
12	4.9699 Pts	N/A	168	59/109	1.96	20	0.1	0.8
15	4.9699 Pts	N/A	168	59/109	1.96	20	0.1	0.9
20	4.9699 Pts	N/A	168	59/109	1.96	20	0.1	0.5
23	4.9699 Pts	N/A	168	59/109	1.96	20	0.1	0.6
1	4.8199 Pts	N/A	168	55/113	2.17	20	0.04	0.2
4	4.7399 Pts	N/A	168	57/111	2.05	20	0.04	0.3
9	4.7399 Pts	N/A	168	57/111	2.05	20	0.04	0.4
10	4.7399 Pts	N/A	168	57/111	2.05	20	0.04	0.8
13	4.7399 Pts	N/A	168	57/111	2.05	20	0.04	0.9
18	4.7399 Pts	N/A	168	57/111	2.05	20	0.04	0.5
21	4.7399 Pts	N/A	168	57/111	2.05	20	0.04	0.6
24	4.7399 Pts	N/A	168	57/111	2.05	20	0.04	0.7
25	4.5899 Pts	N/A	168	56/112	2.11	20	0.08	0.7

TABLE 7.9 SMA/SAR System Test Results with Slippage
Source: Metastock.

That gives us the following system:

Go Long when Close crosses above the 20-day moving average
Exit Long when the 0.9/0.50 setting SAR line moves above Close
Go Short when Close crosses below the 20-day moving average
Exit Short when the 0.9/0.50 setting SAR line moves below Close

The results are shown in Table 7.10. In reviewing the numbers, there is nothing in particular that jumps out. The Win% is not quite as bad as the SMA-Only system, but not quite as good as the SAR-Only system. There is no real shock there since we are combining the two. The interesting thing is the equity graph in Figure 7.13. It shows essentially a break-even performance for the first half of the test period, but then very good results in the second half when basically all the gains were made. Figure 7.14 shows the system in action.

Performance			Performance Indices	
Profit	23.7499 Pts		Buy & Hold Index	438.32 %
Performance	N/A		Profit/Loss Index	24.32 %
Annualized Performance	N/A		Reward/Risk Index	78.28 %
Buy & Hold Profit	-7.0200 Pts			
Buy & Hold Performance	N/A		**Accounting**	
Buy & Hold Annualized Performance	N/A		Initial Equity	0.0000 Pts
			Trade Profit	97.6400 Pts
Trade Summary			Trade Loss	-73.8901 Pts
Total Trades	168		Commissions	0.0000 Pts
Trade Efficiency	-11.16 %		Interest Credited	0.0000 Pts
Average Profit/Average Loss	N/A		Interest Charged	0.0000 Pts
			Final Equity	23.7499 Pts
Profitable Trades			Open Positions	0.7900 Pts
Total	63			
Long	27		**Account Variation**	
Short	36		Highest Account Balance	24.0599 Pts
			Lowest Account Balance	-6.5900 Pts
Average Profit	1.5498 Pts		Highest Portfolio Value	7.0200 Pts
Highest Profit	6.1400 Pts		Highest Open Drawdown	-6.5900 Pts
Lowest Profit	0.0100 Pts		Highest Closed Drawdown	-6.5900 Pts
Most Consecutive	4			
			Account Events	
Unprofitable Trades			Margin Calls	0
Total	105		Overdrafts	0
Long	57			
Short	48		**Profitable Timing**	
			Average Trade Length	7
Average Loss	-0.7037 Pts		Longest Trade Length	19
Highest Loss	-2.4500 Pts		Shortest Trade Length	1
Lowest Loss	-0.0100 Pts		Total Trade Length	477
Most Consecutive	7			
			Unprofitable Timing	
Maximum Position Excursions			Average Trade Length	2
Long Favorable	7.0200 Pts		Longest Trade Length	8
Short Favorable	7.6500 Pts		Shortest Trade Length	1
Long Adverse	-2.5000 Pts		Total Trade Length	246
Short Adverse	-3.1800 Pts			
			Out of Market Timing	
Trade Efficiency			Average	10
Average Entry	43.80 %		Longest	47
Average Exit	44.45 %		Total	823
Average Total	-11.16 %			

TABLE 7.10 SMA/SAR System Performance Statistics
Source: Metastock.

Points Over Time

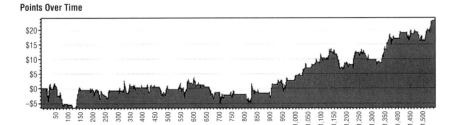

FIGURE 7.13 SMA/SAR System Equity Line
Source: Metastock.

FIGURE 7.14   SMA/SAR System Trades
Source: Metastock.

TEST IV—SAR ENTER/SMA EXIT

Now comes the final of our four testing scenarios. This is the one where we take a look at using SAR to determine our entries and exit trades based on the SMA. We showed already that joining the parameters from the SAR-Only and SMA-Only systems is not effective since they were widely diverged in terms of the time scopes in which they operated. As a result, we just dive right in with parameter testing.

We again use 0.01 to 0.10 for the SAR step (OPT2), and 0.1 to 0.9 for the cap (OPT3) and SMAs from 5 to 100 periods, at intervals of five (OPT1). It is just a question of flipping around the entry/exit rules in the following way:

Go Long when SAR moves below Close

Exit Long when Close crosses below SMA

Go Short when SAR moves above Close

Exit Short when Close crosses above SMA

Conditional Entry/Exit

Before looking at the results, it worth noting that in all cases of the systems we have tested, the Long/Short entry rules supersede the Exit ones. By that we mean if there is a long trade on and a short entry signal occurs, the long is exited regardless of whether or not the exit long rule indicated to do so. This might seem obvious on the face of it, but it does not necessarily have to be that way. All it takes is one little modifier to alter the situation. We could change our system rules to make them conditional in the following fashion:

If not Short, Go Long when SAR moves below Close

Exit Long when Close crosses below SMA

If not Long, Go Short when SAR moves above Close

Exit Short when Close crosses above SMA

In this case the entry rules have been modified to check to see if there is an active trade already. This is something that is done naturally when one is considering trade entries in the same direction. The actual rule for a short entry does not say "If not Short . . ." but it is implied. Likewise, the long entry rule.

For entry rules such as the ones we have been using there is only one discrete entry situation, with no wiggle room. That is why our entry rules are written in terms of crossing and moving above or below. The cross will occur once in a given direction. Before it can happen again there must first be a cross in the opposite direction.

If, however, we changed "moves above/below" or "crosses above/below" to "is above" or "is below" then there is no longer a discrete one-time signal. When price moves above the SMA, for example there will be a buy signal. If the next close was still above the moving average there would be another buy signal without an intervening exit long or sell short signal. That is why one must be very specific how one defines the trading rules, and the order of evaluation, too.

In a case such as the conditional entry rules we just described (if not short or if not long when considering a position in the opposite direction), there needs to be a clear order of signal checking. If one were to check for entry signals first before exit ones, it could be that signals are missed or ignored.

Imagine that one was long, but a short signal came about. If the system first looks at the entry rules it will see a long position and disregard the short signal ("If not Long"). What if, however, an exit signal occurs for that same point in time. The long will be exited, but because that processing happened after the processing of entry rules, it would be too late to allow for the short trade entry. One would have to flip the order of processing so that the exit rules were processed first to avoid such an occurrence.

All of this has been a somewhat long-winded way of saying be very clear and specific with your trading rules and make sure that your tests are equally so.

Now back to the system.

The results for the SAR entry/SMA exit testing are in Table 7.11. As was the case with the SAR-Only system, the default settings of 0.02 and 0.20 provided the best results, and the 0.02 step setting dominates the tests displayed. The trade frequency is on the higher end of what we have seen in the four tests, but then so, too, are the net profit figures.

Choosing the 60-day setting for the SMA and 0.02/0.20 for the SAR, we have the following rules:

Go Long when 0.02/0.20 setting SAR line moves below Close

Exit Long when Close crosses below the 60-day moving average

ID	Net Profit	% Gain	Trades	Trade Profit/Loss	Avg. Profit/Avg. Loss	OPT1	OPT2	OPT3
3	42.8600 Pts	N/A	137	59/78	1.89	55	0.02	0.2
5	42.8000 Pts	N/A	137	61/76	1.75	65	0.02	0.2
4	41.9200 Pts	N/A	137	61/76	1.74	60	0.02	0.2
23	39.6000 Pts	N/A	139	58/81	1.94	55	0.02	0.7
20	39.6000 Pts	N/A	139	58/81	1.94	55	0.02	0.6
6	39.6000 Pts	N/A	139	58/81	1.94	55	0.02	0.3
17	39.6000 Pts	N/A	139	58/81	1.94	55	0.02	0.9
9	39.6000 Pts	N/A	139	58/81	1.94	55	0.02	0.4
14	39.6000 Pts	N/A	139	58/81	1.94	55	0.02	0.8
11	39.6000 Pts	N/A	139	58/81	1.94	55	0.02	0.5
2	39.5800 Pts	N/A	159	69/90	1.81	95	0.05	0.1
8	39.5400 Pts	N/A	139	60/79	1.80	65	0.02	0.3
10	39.5400 Pts	N/A	139	60/79	1.80	65	0.02	0.4
13	39.5400 Pts	N/A	139	60/79	1.80	65	0.02	0.5
16	39.5400 Pts	N/A	139	60/79	1.80	65	0.02	0.8
19	39.5400 Pts	N/A	139	60/79	1.80	65	0.02	0.9
22	39.5400 Pts	N/A	139	60/79	1.80	65	0.02	0.6
25	39.5400 Pts	N/A	139	60/79	1.80	65	0.02	0.7
1	38.8000 Pts	N/A	159	68/91	1.84	90	0.05	0.1
12	38.6600 Pts	N/A	139	60/79	1.79	60	0.02	0.5
15	38.6600 Pts	N/A	139	60/79	1.79	60	0.02	0.8
18	38.6600 Pts	N/A	139	60/79	1.79	60	0.02	0.9
7	38.6600 Pts	N/A	139	60/79	1.79	60	0.02	0.3
21	38.6600 Pts	N/A	139	60/79	1.79	60	0.02	0.6
24	38.6600 Pts	N/A	139	60/79	1.79	60	0.02	0.7

TABLE 7.11 SAR/SMA Test Results
Source: Metastock.

Go Short when 0.02/0.20 setting SAR line moves above Close

Exit Short when Close crosses above the 60-day moving average

Table 7.12 contains the results for this particular set of system rules. Nothing in particular stands out as being surprising or all that different from what we have seen in the previous tests.

In considering the equity curve shown in Figure 7.15, however, one is a bit struck by how similar it looks to the one for the SAR-Only system. The indication there might be that the SMA exits are not coming into play very often. This should not be very surprising given our parameter set.

Performance			Performance Indices	
Profit		41.9200 Pts	Buy & Hold Index	697.15 %
Performance		N/A	Profit/Loss Index	28.49 %
Annualized Performance		N/A	Reward/Risk Index	81.29 %
Buy & Hold Profit		-7.0200 Pts		
Buy & Hold Performance		N/A	**Accounting**	
Buy & Hold Annualized Performance		N/A	Initial Equity	0.0000 Pts
			Trade Profit	147.1200 Pts
Trade Summary			Trade Loss	-105.2000 Pts
Total Trades		137	Commissions	0.0000 Pts
Trade Efficiency		-6.08 %	Interest Credited	0.0000 Pts
Average Profit/Average Loss		N/A	Interest Charged	0.0000 Pts
			Final Equity	41.9200 Pts
Profitable Trades			Open Positions	2.7700 Pts
Total	61			
Long	30		**Account Variation**	
Short	31		Highest Account Balance	47.1200 Pts
			Lowest Account Balance	-9.6500 Pts
Average Profit	2.4118 Pts		Highest Portfolio Value	8.1600 Pts
Highest Profit	7.3300 Pts		Highest Open Drawdown	-9.6500 Pts
Lowest Profit	0.0100 Pts		Highest Closed Drawdown	-8.2500 Pts
Most Consecutive	8			
			Account Events	
Unprofitable Trades			Margin Calls	0
Total	76		Overdrafts	0
Long	39			
Short	37		**Profitable Timing**	
Average Loss	-1.3842 Pts		Average Trade Length	15
Highest Loss	-4.2700 Pts		Longest Trade Length	37
Lowest Loss	-0.0400 Pts		Shortest Trade Length	1
Most Consecutive	6		Total Trade Length	933
Maximum Position Excursions			**Unprofitable Timing**	
Long Favorable	8.1600 Pts		Average Trade Length	5
Short Favorable	8.4900 Pts		Longest Trade Length	17
Long Adverse	-4.6600 Pts		Shortest Trade Length	1
Short Adverse	-4.7700 Pts		Total Trade Length	448
Trade Efficiency			**Out of Market Timing**	
Average Entry	52.53 %		Average	7
Average Exit	40.66 %		Longest	24
Average Total	-6.08 %		Total	165

TABLE 7.12 SAR/SMA System Performance Statistics
Source: Metastock.

Points Over Time

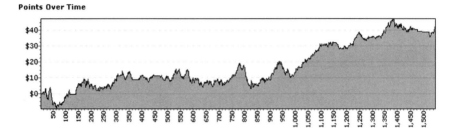

FIGURE 7.15　SAR/SMA System Equity Line
Source: Metastock.

The system is using a fairly slow SMA of 60 days, with a relatively quicker
SAR setup. The result is that in most instances the exit signals are not being triggered, but rather positions are closed out as the result of a reversing entry signal (long to short or short to long). Figure 7.16 shows out that
is likely the case. Notice how flat the solid SMA line is as compared to the
dotted SAR lines.

FIGURE 7.16　SAR/SMA System Trades
Source: Metastock.

ADDITIONAL CONSIDERATIONS

At this point we have completed testing of our four system alternatives. In the next chapter we take a look at them side-by-side to do a comparative analysis. Before that, however, there are a few more topics related to system design and development that need to be addressed.

Interest Credited/Earned

We previously mentioned slippage and transaction costs as they relate to trading system performance. Often one thinks only of broker's commissions when the term "transaction" cost comes up. For the spot forex trader that might lead to one excluding that consideration from system testing analysis.

Remember that when trading spot forex there is interest rate carry. The trader either pays or earns the interest spread. For the short-term trader this may not be an issue. The longer-term trader, however, can see performance significantly impacted, either positively or negatively. For example, a long position in USD/JPY generally means positive carry, so holding such a trade for weeks would actually be good. No so for a short trade.

Of course, interest costs are not exclusive to forex. In the stock market there are margin loan interest costs. They are charged when one trades stock on margin. Again, for short holding periods that is not a problem. For longer ones, though, there will be a negative impact.

Back-Testing Time Horizon

The question is often asked how far back to go when back-testing a trading system. The nonspecific answer is far enough back to take in at least one complete cycle of market activity.

What does that mean? It depends on your trading time frame. A stock trader who plans to take on longer-term positions (ones influenced by fundamental considerations) should be looking to test systems over a complete economic cycle, including both good and bad periods (growth and recession). A short-term trader will clearly look at a smaller time span, but should at least have enough data to cover periods of significant price increase and decrease, plus a range-bound spell to account for all the market's phases. *Note:* Our system testing time scope here began with the start of 1999 as that was the introduction of the euro, which had implications on the global currency markets.

Historical Data

Among the biggest challenges of the system testing the trader is getting good data, especially cheap data. While one can often find low cost daily data, intraday figures are not as readily available.

See this book's resource page for recommendations on places to look for the data you require:www.andurilonline.com/book.

Testing Entries and Exits Separately

When we did our testing we used software to evaluate entry and exit rules separately, but in conjunction with each other, testing them in pairs. As stated earlier, it is perfectly acceptable, and sometimes even preferable to test entries and exits separately and then combine them later. This is easily done.

One word of warning here, however. When testing one side of the equation, in order to get comparable results you must hold the other side constant. That means if one is testing exit rules, the exact same set of entries must be used (obviously, the same being true for entry rules and exit points). This is not just to say the same method of entry determination is used. Why? Because different exit strategies will presumably have different timings on when they exit positions. If one is using some kind of method to enter positions, it could be that the time discrepancy between the different exit methods produces different entry points as the entry method is applied.

By way of example, let us assume a random entry structure. A coin toss will determine long or short for each trade entry. One cannot set the exit testing up so that a new trade entry is made in the period immediately following the exiting of a trade. That would result in trade entries at varying times (and thus prices) for the different exit methods being tested. If, on the other hand, one were to not determine entry until it could be sure that all exit methods had closed their respective trade, such as doing the coin toss at the start of a new day when you know the exit methods will close out every trade by the end of the trading day, then the comparisons are valid and usable.

Trading Rules, Optimization, and Curve-Fitting

The rules we developed for our trading systems examples in this chapter were quite straightforward. Each had only one basic conditional element to them—if this, then that. We could quite easily have more conditions derived from any number of other sources. They could be values of other technical indicators, some kind of fundamental component (e.g. "if year-over-year earnings growth is +10% or better"), or even based on the system itself ("if the last trade was profitable"). Some conditions are fine. Too many are a problem.

What we did in the course of evaluating our four potential trading systems—running tests to see which variable settings performed best—is a form of optimization. Some optimization is reasonable, just like conditions. It helps one get pointed in the right direction and in some ways better understand the market. The problem comes, however, when the trader takes it too far, optimizes a whole array of variable parameters, and introduces a lot of conditional statements to the trading rules. When that happens, the trader is no longer trying to find a system with some likelihood of producing profits going forward, but rather finding a system that produced profits in the past. This is known as curve-fitting.

Everywhere you go in the financial arena there is the warning that past performance is not necessarily an indication of future results. Nowhere is that more true than in trading systems. Trading systems must be robust. The markets are changeable. A system must be able to deal with that. If a system's rules and parameters are too finely tuned, when the market changes character (and it will), the system falls apart.

You will note that when picking a specific set of trading rules for each of the tests in this chapter we never just took the best. Instead we took the ones that were a bit more middle-of-the-road in terms of having parameters that were in the middle area of the performance group (60-day SMA instead of the 55-day or the 65-day, which showed similar performance). This was done to try to favor a more robust set of trading rules rather than the absolute best.

Paper Testing to Real-World Trading

There is a huge difference between the results a trading system shows in back-testing (paper trading) and what they are in actual application. We mentioned things like slippage and the vagaries of data and prices. For that reason it is imperative that as soon as one has a system that comes out of a rigorous testing process looking good that it gets forward-tested.

Forward-testing is the process of using a trading system to make actual real-life trades over a testing period. This is where demo trading platforms like FXGame really show their value. One can take a system and trade it just as if it were actually in use with the same sort of price movement and trade execution considerations that come into play in regular trading. In this manner, the system can truly be put through its paces before being used with real money.

Homework

Develop three simple trading systems on the market you identified at the beginning of this chapter. Be sure that all are applied to the same market/instrument so they can be compared to one another later. Keep track in your system research journal of your research process as you evaluate the methods by which you will determine the exit and entry rules for each system.

CHAPTER 8

System Results and Position Size

In the previous chapter we went through the process of outlining a trading system. In this chapter we follow that up by comparing systems in several ways and talking about how to determine position size.

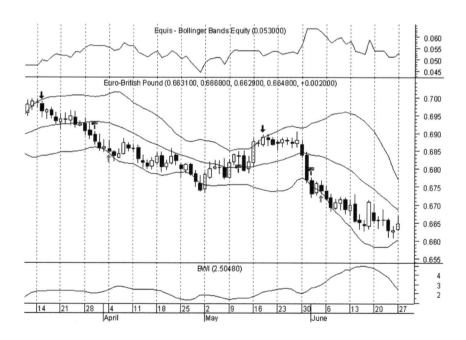

COMPARING PERFORMANCE

In Chapter 7 we worked through the process of defining individual trading systems as rule sets that determine entry and exit points. In this chapter, with our four systems in-hand, we shift our focus to comparisons. We will evaluate them side-by-side to see which is the best performer. Let's start the process by looking at Table 8.1.

The table figures are based on the raw results we looked at in the previous chapter, without considering slippage or other factors. (SMA/SAR = SMA entry, SAR exit; SAR/SMA = SAR entry, SMA exit). It is quite plain to see that the systems that use SAR for the entry show clearly superior net profit figures. Even if we were to include slippage, spread, or some other per transaction charge, that would still be the case. For example, a 10-pip per trade slippage would reduce the SMA net profit to 22.20, while the SAR result would be 27.43.

As we move down the table we can see some other comparisons, like the Win% and average and maximum profit and loss figures. The Profit/Loss Ratio, which is nothing more than the Average Profit divided by the Average Loss, shows a clear bias toward the SAR system with its reading of 3.91:1. This is well ahead of all three of the other systems.

TABLE 8.1 Comparison of the Four Test Systems

Base Comparison	SMA	SAR	SMA/SAR	SAR/SMA
Net Profit	29.90	41.23	23.75	41.92
Trades	77	138	168	137
Winners	23	61	63	61
Win %	30%	44%	38%	45%
Average Profit	3.21	2.47	1.55	2.41
Maximum Gain	13.15	7.33	6.14	7.33
Average Loss	0.82	1.42	0.70	1.38
Maximum Loss	2.38	4.27	2.45	4.27
Profit/Loss Ratio	3.91:1	1.74:1	2.21:1	1.75:1
Expected Per Trade Profit	0.38	0.30	0.14	0.31
Expected Per Quarter Profit	1.23	1.72	1.01	1.76
Quarterly Average Return	1.20%	1.63%	0.95%	1.64%
Standard Deviation	4.84%	6.19%	3.45%	5.93%
Sharpe Ratio (Quarterly)	0.25	0.26	0.27	0.28

Expectancy

The next section of the table is, in many cases, the real comparison. The idea of expectancy is simply an expression of what, given the system's performance statistics, one can anticipate happening. The first part of this equation is the Expected Per Trade Profit. The calculation there is:

$$\text{Win\%} \times \text{Average Profit} - (1 - \text{Win\%}) \times \text{Average Loss}$$

In many circumstances (but not all as we demonstrate later), that is the same as saying Average Per Trade Profit. This reading gives us an idea of what kind of result we should expect on the average trade (measured as points in this case). At first glance, this may seem like a pretty good comparative measure to evaluate trading systems. If each system has the same time trade density (trades per give period of time), then it is.

If, however, the systems do not have a similar trade frequency (as is our case with the SMA-Only system having many fewer trades), then one needs to take things a step further and determine Expected Per Quarter Profit (substitute any reasonable Period for Quarter as needed). This is calculated by multiplying the Expected Per Trade Profit times Trades per Quarter (Trades/24 quarters). In doing this we get an estimate as to the kind of profits to be anticipated for each quarter by the systems in question. In our particular case, because all four systems were tested over the same time period, this works out to be nothing more than Net Profit divided by the 24 quarters of the test period. Later in the chapter, though, we demonstrate the real usefulness of this measure.

Why is this important? Put bluntly, expectancy tells the trader how much profit a given system is likely to produce over a specific time frame. This allows systems that are not tested over the same time frame or do not have the same instrument in common to be evaluated side-by-side.

In our simple example, Expected Per Quarter Profit does not really tell us any more than Net Profit because the systems are measured over identical time frames. Had we used different time frames for the systems, or tested on multiple currency pairs, the expectancy measure would have been very important. Please see Table 8.2.

Risk Adjusted Results

A couple of additional studies have been included in the grid shown in Table 8.2. The Quarterly Average Return (again based on points) has been calculated for each trading system, along with the Standard Deviation of those returns. Both use a baseline of 100 points as a start value, to provide a unified calculation point and reference for comparison. These sorts of

TABLE 8.2 Standardized Comparison of the Four Test Systems

Base Comparison	SMA	SAR	SMA/SAR	SAR/SMA
Net Profit	29.90	41.23	23.75	41.92
Expected Per Trade Profit	0.38	0.30	0.14	0.31
Expected Per Quarter Profit	1.23	1.72	1.01	1.76
Quarterly Average Return	1.20%	1.63%	0.95%	1.64%
Standard Deviation	4.84%	6.19%	3.45%	5.93%
Sharpe Ratio (Quarterly)	0.25	0.26	0.27	0.28

measures allow one to take a more risk/return oriented view of the systems. The returns, as would be expected, go along with the Net Profit readings. It is the volatility figures that are the focus here, as they represent the risk side of the equation. Notice that the Standard Deviation readings are higher for the higher profit systems, and lower for the others.

Sharpe Ratio

This is a measure of risk-adjusted performance of an investment or trading strategy. It is calculated thus:

$$S = \frac{<R> - R_f}{\sigma}$$

where R = Expected Return

R_f = the Risk Free Rate of return

σ = the Standard Deviation of returns

Of course we have a way to judge risk-adjusted returns—the Sharpe ratio. In this case we have done so on a quarterly basis to match up with our other figures by using our average quarterly return and standard deviation. In this instance, since we are using a consistent set of trading parameters, we have taken the Risk Free Rate out of the equation for simplicity's sake and just done the calculation by dividing Quarterly Average Return by the Standard Deviation.

The Sharpe ratio readings are quite interesting. They serve first to highlight the fact that on an all-around basis the SAR entry/SMA exit system is the best performer (highest Expected Quarter Return, highest Sharpe Ratio). Importantly, however, the Sharpe readings also show that the SMA entry/SAR exit system, which shows the poorest results in a purely return basis, is very competitively positioned in comparison to the other systems when one is considering risk.

Return Measures

Up to this point we have used average returns as a point of comparison. That means we simply summed up all the quarterly returns and divided them by the 24 quarters of the test period. This is a useful measure, but the trader needs to be very aware of the limitation of doing so.

Consider this example.

A system has annual returns of +10%, −4%, +5%, +7%, and −10%. That is an average of 1.6%. If one trades the exact same account size each year by withdrawing profits at the end of the year or adding funds to make up for losses, then at the end of the five years the result is an 8% gain.

Compound Return

This is the effective period discount rate for a return. It is calculated as:

$$\wedge 1/n - 1$$

Where n = the number of periods

If, on the other hand, the account is handled on a compounding basis, as most are, the final return would be about 6.78 percent. Why is this? Because the losses the system experienced were on a larger account size than was the case in the previous average calculation. This is something to keep in mind. It will come up again later when we talk about position size.

Taking a Closer Look

Getting back to the idea of expectancy, though, with a set of trading results in hand (actual or hypothetical) one need not use averages to get an idea of how a system performs. Delving deeper into the actual profits and losses on a trade-by-trade basis can improve one's calculation of expectancy figures. After all, the expected result of any given trade is the sum of each potential outcome times the probability of that outcome.

Figure 8.2 takes a look at the distribution of our SAR/SMA system. It shows the frequency of certain outcomes.

The graph is based on the 137 trades, which we put into 25 bins of

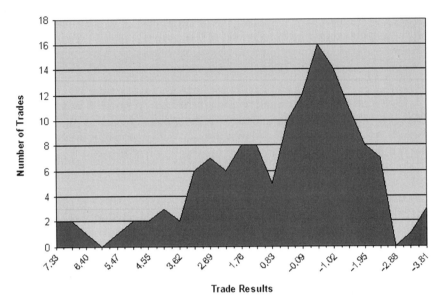

FIGURE 8.2   USD/JPY SAR Entry/SMA Exit System Results

about 0.46 points. Table 8.3 is a breakdown of those bins and how many trades posted results in each, as plotted in Figure 8.2.

By taking these figures and applying them, we can come up with a better reading for our expectancy of this system. To do so, we take the mean point of each of the bins, then multiply it through by its occurrence rate ($n/137$ where n is the number of trades that produced a result in that bin). Our bottom line figure of 0.31 is the same as our expected per trade profit as calculated before. Why? Because in this case we have done little more than calculated an average per trade result. The real test comes when one takes out the outliers.

In some systems there are clearly trades that fall outside the norm, either positively or negatively. For example, one could come across a system that generates 20 profitable trades all in the range of 1 to 5 points, but includes 1 trade that is a 15-point gainer. That outsized gain would be considered an "outlier" because it is so far away from the rest. Similarly, a huge loss that does not fit in with the rest of the losing trade results would be an outlier, too.

Since the trader involved in system evaluation must be thinking about performance going forward, outliers should be excluded. They do not represent what is most likely to occur in the future, so including them in determining a reasonable expected per trade result defeats the objective.

TABLE 8.3 Breakdown of System Trade Results

Range	Count	Range	Count	Range	Count	Range	Count	Range	Count
6.88 to 7.33	2	4.56 to 5.01	2	2.24 to 2.69	7	-0.08 to 0.37	10	-2.40 to -1.95	8
6.41 to 6.87	2	4.09 to 4.55	2	1.77 to 2.23	6	-0.55 to -0.09	12	-2.87 to -2.41	7
5.95 to 6.40	1	3.63 to 4.08	3	1.31 to 1.76	8	-1.01 to -0.56	16	-3.33 to -2.88	0
5.48 to 5.94	0	3.16 to 3.62	2	0.84 to 1.30	8	-1.48 to -1.02	14	-3.80 to -3.34	1
5.02 to 5.47	1	2.70 to 3.15	6	0.38 to 0.83	15	-1.94 to -1.49	11	-4.27 to -3.81	3

Please see Table 8.4.

Our SAR/SMA system does not have any blatant outliers, but we can stretch things for the sake of example. Let us assume that we consider any trades beyond the two empty bins (those trade result ranges with no occurrences) to be outliers. That means we consider results only in the range of –2.87 to +5.47, ruling out five of our most extreme bins. We then recalculate our expected trade result in the same fashion as before, but based only on 128 trades. The result is 0.19 points. This is a bit of an extreme example, though, as one would normally eliminate only the obviously unusual results.

Homework

Using the performance measures we have introduced in this section, compare the trading systems you designed as part of last chapter's homework.

TABLE 8.4 System Trade Expectancy

Bin Mid Pt.	Probability	Value
7.10	1.46%	0.10
6.63	1.46%	0.10
6.17	0.73%	0.05
5.71	0.00%	0.00
5.24	0.73%	0.04
4.78	1.46%	0.07
4.31	1.46%	0.06
3.85	2.19%	0.08
3.39	1.46%	0.05
2.92	4.38%	0.13
2.46	5.11%	0.13
1.99	4.38%	0.09
1.53	5.84%	0.09
1.07	5.84%	0.06
0.60	3.65%	0.02
0.14	7.30%	0.01
–0.33	8.76%	–0.03
–0.79	11.68%	–0.09
–1.25	10.22%	–0.13
–1.72	8.03%	–0.14
–2.18	5.84%	–0.13
–2.65	5.11%	–0.14
–3.11	0.00%	0.00
–3.57	0.73%	–0.03
–4.04	2.19%	–0.09
		0.31

Identify the one with the strongest performance or best risk profile, depending on your interests.

Record all of the results in your system research journal.

TRADE SIZE DETERMINATION

So far our trading system analysis has been handled in terms of points. It is time to move the discussion into account terms. By that we mean how much actual money a system is capable of making (or losing). The SAR entry/SMA exit system was the best performer out of our four test systems, so it will be the basis for our discussions going forward. To allow for further exploration of trading system comparisons, however, we will be adding GBP/USD to the mix. This will force us to look beyond points.

Before doing a system-to-system comparison, though, we take a closer look at our selected system, this time in monetary terms. In order to move in this direction, we must convert our point-based results to dollar ones. In the previous section we did our testing with the Metastock software package. While we could continue our testing in that fashion, it would cut down on the transparency and flexibility, so we switch over to a spreadsheet. (The actual spreadsheet used can be found on the Web at this book's resource page: www.andurilonline.com/book).

Fixed Unit Trading

There are two primary methods for determining trade size. The first of these, and the one we have used thus far, is to use a specific set trade size. For example, one employing a stock trading system might choose to buy or sell only 100 shares, no more or less, each trade. Regardless of how the profits or losses accrue, every trade is the same size.

Using this method, we can determine a dollar performance for our USD/JPY system. Assuming a $10,000 starting account value and a $100,000 trade size ($2,000 margin at a 50:1 margin setting on the account starting value), the system would have returned 401 percent or just a bit more than $40,000 in profits during the six years of the test period. That is an annualized compounded return of about 31 percent (not taking into account slippage or carry).

Variable Unit Trading

The other main method of selecting trade size is to do it based on some kind of formula—a variable method. The most common of these methods is to use account or portfolio balance as the determining factor. This is referred to as the fixed ratio approach. We can provide an example using our system.

Assume again that the starting account value is $10,000. If we use a margin setting of 50:1, that means applying 20 percent of our balance will allow for a trade of $100,000. We will use that 20 percent as our ratio; each trade will be sized as 50 times our margin, which will be 20 percent of the current account value. That will give us a sliding trade size as the profits and losses accrue. If we look at the first group of trades in Table 8.5, we can see clearly how it works.

Note how the result of the first trade for both tests is the same. After that, however, things change dramatically. The loss on the first trade reduces the second trade's size for the variable unit method. The result is a reduced loss on that one, though it also means a reduced gain on the third trade. That is the tradeoff that can take place. In the event of a string of losses, or a preponderance of them during a time span, the fixed trade size method will suffer more than will the variable size method. It will, however, also recover more quickly, as the example demonstrates. The variable size method has the advantage of doing extremely well when a system has a series of gains, because they compound. The problem, however, is that it can also take large losses when the system turns around and suffers losses. See Figure 8.3, especially on the right.

TABLE 8.5 Trading Size and Account Balance Performance

$ Profit (Fixed Trade Size)	Running Acc't Balance	Trade Size	$ Profit (Variable Trade Size)	Running Acc't Balance
	$10,000.00			**$10,000.00**
$ (875.41)	$ 9,124.59	$ 100,000	$ (875.41)	$ 9,124.59
$ (2,027.62)	$ 7,096.97	$ 91,246	$ (1,850.12)	$ 7,274.47
$ 3,959.10	$ 11,056.07	$ 72,745	$ 2,880.04	$ 10,154.51
$ (3,465.35)	$ 7,590.73	$ 101,545	$ (3,518.89)	$ 6,635.62
$ (3,335.50)	$ 4,255.23	$ 66,356	$ (2,213.31)	$ 4,422.31
$ (906.82)	$ 3,348.41	$ 44,223	$ (401.02)	$ 4,021.29
$ 116.47	$ 3,464.88	$ 40,213	$ 46.84	$ 4,068.12
$ 1,185.57	$ 4,650.45	$ 40,681	$ 482.30	$ 4,550.43
$ 3,106.16	$ 7,756.61	$ 45,504	$ 1,413.44	$ 5,963.86
$ 2,148.31	$ 9,904.92	$ 59,639	$ 1,281.22	$ 7,245.09
$ (149.30)	$ 9,755.62	$ 72,451	$ (108.17)	$ 7,136.91
$ 5,334.96	$ 15,090.57	$ 71,369	$ 3,807.51	$ 10,944.43

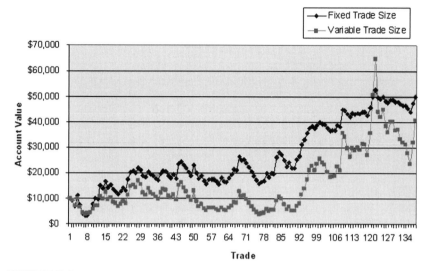

FIGURE 8.3 Fixed versus Variable Trade Size Equity Performance

	Avg. Return	Std Dev
Fixed	$292.38	$2,053.39
Variable	$223.52	$3,711.49

The difference between the two methods can be expressed in terms of comparing the per trade returns and standard deviation. Notice in the sidebar how the fixed size method has both a higher per trade return and a lower standard deviation of those returns. One can alter the settings of the variable size method to reduce the volatility, but doing so reduces the returns significantly. Likewise, attempting to increase the return by raising the ratio increases the standard deviation. In fact, there is no variable setting that outperforms the fixed size method for this system (you can make your own analysis with the sample).

Blended Approach

It should be noted that it is not always the case that the fixed position size system outperforms a variable one. It depends a lot on the trading system being used and the distribution of results. Also, there is a limitation inherent in the fixed trade size scheme. The longer one applies it, the lower will be the relative returns over time. Imagine, for example, a forex trading system that produces a 10 percent rate of annual return on the trade size used (e.g., $10,000 profit when trading $100,000). If the position sizes were never changed, the system would produce a series of diminishing returns, as Table 8.6 demonstrates.

The way traders get around this limitation of the fixed trade size scheme is to introduce a step process to the equation to combine the fixed and variable methods. This is achieved by defining a mechanism by which the trade size is changed, not on a continuous basis, but rather as the result of achieving some kind of goal.

Creating such a position sizing method would require determining first the step point at which the trade size is changed, then how much that change would be. A very simple example of this would be to say that each time the account value doubles, the position sizes double. Essentially, one sets the mechanism so a gain of x dollars or percent means an increase in the number of units traded by y.

	Avg. Return	Std Dev
Fixed	$292.38	$2,053.39
Variable	$439.95	$5,039.76

The advantage to this blended method is that it combines the recovery ability of the fixed size method with the ability to maintain a rate of return going forward. In the case of our SAR entry/SMA exit system, the step method (increase the trade size by $100,000 for each $10,000 of account value gain) actually shows a better final return than the fixed method does, though there is a cost on the volatility side, which can be seen on the right side of Figure 8.4. The step trade size method results get very choppy as the increased trade size comes to the fore.

TABLE 8.6 Diminishing Returns

Year Start	Year Profits	Return
$ 10,000	$10,000	100%
$ 20,000	$10,000	50%
$ 30,000	$10,000	33%
$ 40,000	$10,000	25%
$ 50,000	$10,000	20%
$ 60,000	$10,000	17%
$ 70,000	$10,000	14%
$ 80,000	$10,000	13%
$ 90,000	$10,000	11%
$100,000	$10,000	10%

Actually, the performance shown in Figure 8.4 is tame compared to what could be seen had we used different settings, or had we opted to make the step locked. By that we mean once the trade size is increased, it is never decreased. In this example we actually allowed trade size to decrease if losses drop account value below the threshold points. (The reader is encouraged to play with the spreadsheet to see what happens at different settings.)

Risk-Based Trade Sizing

Another variation on the trade sizing model is to use trade risk to determine the position size. The system we have put together does not lend itself to this particular technique, but others do. A risk-based method can be applied when one can define or closely approximate the risk for each given trade and that risk varies from trade to trade. If it doesn't vary, then it can be assumed that would be accounted for in determining the fixed, variable, or step approach settings. This sort of approach is most often taken by the discretionary trader, for example a chartist, who can identify the point risk for a given trade. By translating that into a dollar amount in relation to a given position size (for example $1,000 per $100,000 traded), the trader can set the trade size accordingly.

The risk-based approach is actually combined with one of the three previously mentioned methods. The other method used (fixed, variable, or

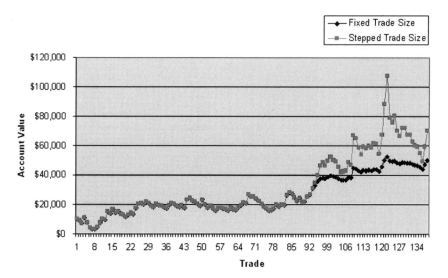

FIGURE 8.4 Fixed versus Stepped Trade Size

step) would define the amount of money available to trade while the risk would determine how many units would be traded.

Using our earlier example, a fixed scheme could say one is willing to risk 10 percent. That would mean $1,000 on a $10,000 account. If the trading system defines the risk per unit as $500, the trader can take on two units. Perhaps the risk on the next trade is $750 per unit. That would mean only a single unit traded (assuming no fractions). If the risk for a given position were $1,500, the trader would not make the trade. (The advantage to FXTrade, and one of our reasons for preferring it is that one can set the trading size to exactly match the risk they are willing to accept for a given trade.)

Clearly, the risk-based approach draws upon one's overall risk settings. We commented on how it would not be applied to a system such as the one we have designed herein. While that is true on a trade-by-trade basis since we do not have a mechanism for defining the risk on a trade-by-trade basis, a similar mechanism is used to determine the general position size settings. That is part of the next section.

Homework

If you have not already done so, convert the results of your trade system from the last section to a dollar (or other currency) basis. Apply the position sizing methods we have introduced here to see which makes the most sense.

MONETARY COMPARISON

We now combine the previous two sections and compare two systems in terms of a theoretical account change. One of those systems is the SAR entry/SMA exit trend system we chose as the best of the USD/JPY group. We compare that to a system for GBP/USD. This allows us the opportunity to look at systems that have both a different design approach, are back-tested over different time frames, and also are not equivalent in terms of quotes (one GBP/USD pip = 1/10,000 of a USD while a USD/JPY pip = 1/100 of a JPY).

The system we are using for GBP/USD is one based on the stochastic oscillator, which, as mentioned previously is available as part of the FXTrade platform. As such, you can replicate it just as you can our USD/JPY system. On the FXTrade platform select Fast Stochastic and make the settings 5 and 3. When you click the + button, the chart of the indicator will show up below the price chart showing two sets of lines.

Stochastic Oscillator

This indicator consists of two lines called the %K line and the %D line, and are controlled through two parameters, n and m, specifying a number of periods. Both the %K and %D lines are plotted on a scale of 0 to 100. They measure where the closing price is in relation to the total price range of the selected number of periods.

Calculation
The %K line is defined as follows:

$$(CP - Ln) / (Hn - Ln) * 100$$

where   CP = Latest Closing Price
Ln = the lowest price over the past n periods
Hn = the highest price over the past n periods

The %D line is an m-period simple moving average of the %K line.

Our GBP/USD system is defined as:

Go Long when 5-period Fast Stochastic %K rises above 40

Exit Long when 5-period Fast Stochastic %K falls below 40

Go Short when 5-period Fast Stochastic %K falls below 60

Exit Short when 5-period Fast Stochastic %K rises above 60

Results of the system are presented in Table 8.7.

The test was made on a points basis over the period of January 2002 through May 2004. The equity plot is shown in Figure 8.5.

If we do a point comparison of the USD/JPY and GBP/USD systems, we do not really learn much more than that they are both net profitable. Because they are quoted in different terms the results are not directly comparable. Table 8.8 demonstrates that. There are a couple of comparable measures based on ratios, such as Win% and Profit/Loss ratio. It is fine to use those as ways to view the two systems, but everything else is blurred by the differences in quotes.

By the way, the differences in quote method hamper the Quarterly Return and Sharpe Ratio figures. Recall that we used 100 as a base from which to start in our return figures previously. For GBP/USD, because it is quoted at two more decimal places, we opted for a base of 1.00. Even that, however, does not give us a real way to compare since the calculations are still based on points, which are different for the two systems in question. We therefore must shift everything over into monetary terms, meaning

Performance			Performance Indices	
Profit	0.2672 Pts		Buy & Hold Index	-30.71 %
Performance	N/A		Profit/Loss Index	32.87 %
Annualized Performance	N/A		Reward/Risk Index	81.61 %
Buy & Hold Profit	0.3856 Pts			
Buy & Hold Performance	N/A		**Accounting**	
Buy & Hold Annualized Performance	N/A		Initial Equity	0.0000 Pts
			Trade Profit	0.8129 Pts
Trade Summary			Trade Loss	-0.5457 Pts
Total Trades	84		Commissions	0.0000 Pts
Trade Efficiency	-7.56 %		Interest Credited	0.0000 Pts
Average Profit/Average Loss	N/A		Interest Charged	0.0000 Pts
			Final Equity	0.2672 Pts
Profitable Trades			Open Positions	0.0638 Pts
Total	37			
Long	20		**Account Variation**	
Short	17		Highest Account Balance	0.3128 Pts
			Lowest Account Balance	-0.0602 Pts
Average Profit	0.0220 Pts		Highest Portfolio Value	0.0957 Pts
Highest Profit	0.0802 Pts		Highest Open Drawdown	-0.0602 Pts
Lowest Profit	0.0002 Pts		Highest Closed Drawdown	-0.0559 Pts
Most Consecutive	5			
			Account Events	
Unprofitable Trades			Margin Calls	0
Total	47		Overdrafts	0
Long	18			
Short	29		**Profitable Timing**	
			Average Trade Length	9
Average Loss	-0.0116 Pts		Longest Trade Length	23
Highest Loss	-0.0453 Pts		Shortest Trade Length	1
Lowest Loss	-0.0005 Pts		Total Trade Length	352
Most Consecutive	5			
			Unprofitable Timing	
Maximum Position Excursions			Average Trade Length	3
Long Favorable	0.0957 Pts		Longest Trade Length	9
Short Favorable	0.0792 Pts		Shortest Trade Length	1
Long Adverse	-0.0536 Pts		Total Trade Length	146
Short Adverse	-0.0394 Pts			
			Out of Market Timing	
Trade Efficiency			Average	6
Average Entry	53.04 %		Longest	34
Average Exit	38.21 %		Total	128
Average Total	-7.56 %			

TABLE 8.7 System Test Results
Source: Metastock.

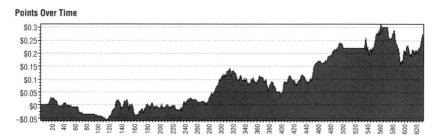

Points Over Time

FIGURE 8.5 System Test Equity Plot
Source: Metastock.

TABLE 8.8 Comparison of USD/JPY and GBP/USD Systems

	USD/JPY	GBP/USD
Net P/L	41.92	0.2672
Trades	137	84
Winners	61	37
Win %	45%	44%
Avg. Prof	2.41	0.0220
Max Gain	7.33	0.0802
Avg. Loss	−1.38	−0.0116
Max Loss	−4.27	−0.0453
Profit/Loss Ratio	1.75:1	1.90:1
Expected Per Trade Profit	0.31	0.0032
Expected Per Quarter Profit	1.76	0.0112
Quarterly Average Return	1.64%	2.22%
Standard Deviation	5.93%	5.07%
Sharpe Ratio (Quarterly)	0.28	0.44

dollars in our case. To accomplish this, we will again bring our spreadsheet into action.

Table 8.9 takes us through what is an interesting comparison. Before we delve into the numbers, though, we must highlight the absolute importance of using comparable figures. The table contains data based on the fixed trade size method we described previously. That means each trade was $100,000 worth. For USD/JPY that is very simple as the pair is based in dollars. With GBP/USD, however, the pair is based in pounds. That means a trade of 100,000 units would actually be worth 100,000 × (GBP/USD rate). The average trade entry rate for our GBP/USD system was 1.60, which means 100,000 units would be worth $160,000. We cannot effectively compare our two systems if they are making different size transactions (at least for this basic assessment), so each GBP/USD trade unit was calculated as $100,000/(GBP/USD rate).

Looking now to the table, our USD/JPY systems has the superior profits. They were generated more than 60 months while the test period was only 29 for the GBP/USD system, though. That being the case, we cannot use Net P/L to judge the two effectively.

The average profit and loss figures lower down are interesting. They, along with the max gain and loss readings, give us some idea of the comparative volatility of results. The USD/JPY system shows a tendency to

TABLE 8.9 Further Comparison of USD/JPY and GBP/USD Systems

	USD/JPY	GBP/USD
Net P/L	$40,055.83	$16,163.40
Trades	137	84
Winners	61	37
Win %	45%	44%
Avg. Prof	$ 2,115.90	$ 1,344.40
Max. Gain	$ 6,686.87	$ 5,069.53
Avg. Loss	−$1,171.24	−$714.45
Max Loss	−$3,465.35	−$2,449.44
Profit/Loss Ratio	1.81:1	1.88:1
Expected Per Trade Profit	$ 307.97	$191.44
Expected Per Quarter Profit	$ 1,758.02	$ 1,662.98
Quarterly Average Return	15.89%	15.45%
Standard Deviation	48.39%	33.61%
Sharpe Ratio (Quarterly)	0.33	0.46

be choppier. Interestingly, the GBP/USD system has a slightly higher Profit/Loss ratio, if only just.

The real telling bit is lower, though (see Table 8.10). That is where we get into expectancy and see that the USD/JPY system far exceeds the GBP/USD system on a per trade basis, although it is a bit closer when extended out to a quarterly view. That is a sign of trade frequency.

Remember, expectancy is based on both a system's expected results and how often the system can generate those results. A system can have fantastic expected per trade figures, but not be of much value as compared to a system with much lower results if the latter system can be applied more often.

TABLE 8.10 Additional Comparison of USD/JPY and GBP/USD Systems

	USD/JPY	GBP/USD
Profit/Loss Ratio	1.81:1	1.88:1
Expected Per Trade Profit	$307.97	$191.44
Expected Per Quarter Profit	$1,758.02	$1,662.98
Quarterly Average Return	15.89%	15.45%
Standard Deviation	48.39%	33.61%
Sharpe Ratio (Quarterly)	0.33	0.46

For example, consider a system that is expected to generate $1,000 per trade and does an average of five trades each year. Now consider the system that has an expected profit of $200 per trade and produces 30 trades a year. Which is better? With the first system, we would make $5,000 per year, while the second would make us $6,000 each year. All else being equal, we would certainly favor the second system.

Now, in our particular example set, GBP/USD does have a higher per quarter trade frequency, but it is not enough to make up for the USD/JPY system's higher per trade performance. If both systems had a similar risk profile, we would certainly pick the USD/JPY system as the better of the two.

The two systems, however, do not have the same risk profile. We noted that earlier when looking at the per trade average and maximum gains and losses. That is extended out in the quarterly average return and standard deviation lines from the table. The two systems are quite close on the return side, but the GBP/USD system has a much lower standard deviation. The result is a significantly higher Sharpe ratio. This tells us that the GBP/USD system has a better profile in terms of risk taken to achieve a comparable level of return.

Who cares, though? The USD/JPY system is more profitable when trading equal dollar amounts. Isn't that what it's all about? The answer is (or at least should be) no.

Why? Because we have not compared the systems based on risk, but only on raw profitability. Because the GBP/USD system is less volatile—which means less risky—we can take larger positions to get up to a comparable dollar risk level with the USD/JPY system.

If we increase the GBP/USD system transaction size up to $135,000 per trade, we can observe that the system's maximum loss is close to the maximum loss for the USD/JPY system, which we call a rough equivalent of taking the same size risk in dollar terms. Take a look at the comparison now in Table 8.11.

Our GBP/USD system still has a lower per trade profit expectancy, but the gap has narrowed to the point that its higher trade frequency makes for a higher per quarter profit expectancy. The quarterly average return figures are substantially higher for the GBP/USD system now, with a slightly lower standard deviation. When looked at this way, it is much more obvious that the GBP/USD system is a better performer than is the USD/JPY system.

Of course, all this testing was done using a fixed trade size method. We could quite easily extend our comparison by working with the other trade sizing techniques mentioned in the previous section. It would simply be a question of applying the different methods to GBP/USD to find the best performer, and then compare the result to the step method result we identified as the strongest for the USD/JPY system.

TABLE 8.11 Comparison of USD/JPY and GBP/USD Systems, Risk Adjusted

	USD/JPY	GBP/USD
Net P/L	$40,055.83	$21,820.58
Trades	137	84
Winners	61	37
Win %	45%	44%
Avg. Prof	$ 2,115.90	$ 1,814.40
Max. Gain	$ 6,686.87	$ 6,843.87
Avg. Loss	−$1,171.24	−$964.51
Max Loss	−$3,465.35	−$3,306.75
Profit/Loss Ratio	1.81:1	1.88:1
Expected Per Trade Profit	$ 307.97	$ 258.45
Expected Per Quarter Profit	$ 1,758.02	$ 2,245.03
Quarterly Average Return	15.89%	22.43%
Standard Deviation	48.39%	47.89%
Sharpe Ratio (Quarterly)	0.33	0.47

Point of Note

The GBP/USD system test data were determined without much consideration for suitability as they were merely for the purposes of developing an example. Keep in mind that the system results generated were based on a smaller data set that actually represented a time frame within the time frame of the larger data set used for our USD/JPY system testing. Given that in both cases the systems were based on daily data, it can be said that the USD/JPY test is probably more representative of that system's performance over various market conditions. If the data are available, it is always preferable to compare based on the same time frame. It is quite possible that over the same time frame (1/2002–5/2004) the USD/JPY system performed better than the GBP/USD system.

Homework

Compare at least two of your systems on a monetary basis using a standard fixed trade size method. If you can, use two systems that have differing point values as we did with USD/JPY and GBP/USD. Extend that comparison to account for risk by using the maximum loss. Adjust the trade sizes so as to match the two systems based on that risk measure and see which comes out stronger. Note all observations in your system research journal.

FINE TUNING

With a trading system we like in hand, there are things we can do in an effort to produce better results. Be warned, however. This is a process that requires some work. It involves taking a very close look at the trades the system generates to see if there are ways to trim back some of the losers.

The Maximum Adverse Excursion (MAE) is the largest amount a position goes negative. This is used to determine how far the market moves against trades that eventually turn profitable. For example, a long position taken on at 100 dips to 95, then rallies to 120. The MAE would be 5 (100 – 95).

The concept of MAE can be a valuable one in system development. Some trades go negative, then turn around. Others go negative and stay that way. The scatter diagram in Figure 8.6 shows the MAE for the trades of the GBP/USD system (in points). Notice the general slope of the dots up and to the left. It is natural for losing trades to have larger MAEs than winners.

The GBP/USD actually shows a rather loose pattern to the right side of the graph, which is where the profitable trades are depicted. Some systems are this way. Others show tighter patterns where the MAEs are relatively small for winning trades, especially for the more profitable ones.

The reason for looking at MAE in this fashion is to determine whether or not there is a kind of point of no return, an excursion beyond which

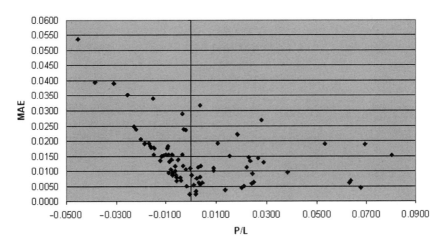

FIGURE 8.6 Maximum Adverse Excursion (MAE) versus Net Profit

trades do not come back and turn profitable. If one can be found—and it is not always the case that one can—then that point can be used to trim some of the losses the system suffers. Smaller losses mean better overall profitability.

In our GBP/USD system, it looks like we could use 0.0350 (350 pips) as a cutoff point. There are no trades that go positive after having an excursion that large, though there looks to be a couple of trades that ended at a loss of less than 350 pips. Whether that is a problem or not will come out in our testing.

Looking at the actual trades in Table 8.12, we can see there are four that went at least 350 pips in the wrong direction.

Remember that we can put stops into protect against adverse movement. In this case, we would have one set 350 pips away from our entry price on the assumption that if the market goes that far, it is not coming back. So what does that do for our profitability? It is a simple question of doing the math:

$$453 - 350 = 103 \text{ pips saved}$$
$$387 - 350 = 37 \text{ pips saved}$$
$$312 - 350 = 38 \text{ pips lost}$$
$$254 - 350 = 96 \text{ pips lost}$$

Add that all up and the 350-pips stop (system, not money management) would improve our overall system performance by a whole 6 pips. We would do better with a 400-pips stop, but only marginally so (40 pips). In this instance there is only relatively little to be gained by using a stop. This is the case for a lot of systems, but not all. It is always worth looking at MAE to see if there is a way to shave the losses effectively. Remember that we used maximum loss as a kind of risk indicator earlier to set our trade size. If the big losses can be cut down, it might be possible to trade larger and thereby make more profits.

TABLE 8.12 GBP/USD System Trades

Enter Date	Type	Enter Price	Exit Date	Exit Price	P&L	MAE
3/8/2004	Buy	1.8494	3/10/2004	1.8041	−0.0453	0.0536
3/25/2004	Sell Short	1.8067	3/31/2004	1.8454	−0.0387	0.0394
8/2/2002	Buy	1.5693	8/7/2002	1.5381	−0.0312	0.0390
3/31/2004	Buy	1.8454	4/5/2004	1.8200	−0.0254	0.0352

Positive Excursion

Remember that positive excursion is how much the market goes in favor of a trade before it is exited. It can be thought of as the amount of profit left on the table.

This should be considered when setting up exit rules as a trading system is developed.

Stops in Practice

While stops can be worthwhile, one must be very cautious when trying to incorporate stop or limit orders into a trading system. Why? It's a data issue. If one is testing using daily figures, it cannot be known, for example, if the high of the day was reached before the low, or the other way around. If one's trading rules are based on such information (or some manipulation of that data), the results of testing come into question.

Another thing one must be conscious of when doing system testing is the impact of stop orders in practice. Consider a trading system that includes the following rule:

Go Long if price is higher than 10-day moving average

Exit Long if price is lower than 10-day moving average or if prices fall 100 pips from the entry point (Stop-Loss)

This set of rules could see one get stopped out of a position, but then immediately reenter if the stop is hit, but the market does not break back below the 10-day moving average. In fact, the same sort of thing can happen with one's exit rules if the entry condition still holds. That is why one needs to be very specific when defining a trading system and why one needs to review the trades generated by a system closely to ensure it is doing exactly what is intended.

Time

Before we move on, it is worth noting that if one were so inclined, the MAE discussion could be expanded upon to include a time factor. Imagine that instead of thinking in terms of price, one were to think of time periods. The question then becomes how many periods will the trade be negative before it goes positive? Alternatively, after how many periods will it become clear that a trade is not going to turn positive? We have not done this specific analysis with our GBP/USD system, but it could be worth pursuing.

Experienced traders often have both time and price accounted for in their systems. This is many times expressed as a length of time by which if a certain objective has not been reached, the trade is seen to not be a good one. The idea is that the impetus that created the entry signal has faded away. This is sometimes referred to as a time stop.

Homework

Perform a MAE analysis of at least one of the systems you developed. Determine whether or not putting a stop into the system makes sense. Also do a time analysis to see if you can define any point at which trades show distinct characteristics that could be used to further refine your system(s). Record all of your findings in your system research journal.

RISK AND POSITION SIZE

Earlier we introduced the idea of varying trade size. The discussion at that time centered primarily around using account balance ratios such as percent of account size for margin application, but we also brought risk into the discussion. In comparing systems we again brought up risk as a consideration, but only in the most basic of fashion. Now we are going to take a much more thorough look at how it necessarily comes together with system development and assessment.

Everything in this part of the trading system definition process comes right out of the Trading Plan, specifically the part of it in which one's risk parameters are outlined. In the earlier chapter on risk management, the question of how much per trade exposure one is willing to take was posed. That now needs to become part of the trading system as an amendment to the entry rules that define trade size. That starts with determining a point risk for each trade, which comes from a few methods.

Stop Loss

Many traders opt to use stop orders to ensure that no loss exceeds their risk cutoff. This is a money management stop, rather than a system stop, though the two can be one and the same in practice. On the face of it, this would seem like a solid approach, but there are issues.

Blindly putting in stops can be self-defeating. Recall our discussion of the MAE. If a system often sees 300+ pip excursions, even for profitable trades, putting a stop at 100 pips is likely to hinder system performance. This is a mistake made by many inexperienced traders who think that using a close stop allows them to trade larger. While it is true that one using a 100-pip stop can take on positions three times the size of the case with a 300-pip stop and have the same net exposure, the risk is actually higher. Remember, risk for a trader incorporates both the probability of taking a loss and the size of the loss taken. Putting a stop at 100 pips when the system requires 300 pips of room to move means the odds of taking a loss are increased while the size of the loss taken (assuming equal account exposure) holds level. Thus, there can actually be more risk in using a tighter stop.

Stops also are not guarantees. This was remarked upon at several points. One cannot be 100 percent sure that a stop loss will result in a position being exited right at the order price, or sometimes even close to it. Thus, a stop loss as the risk defining element of a trading system can be problematic.

Maximum Loss

When comparing our trading systems we used the maximum loss figure as a proxy for system risk. If a system is testing over a sufficiently large data set, then the maximum loss figure is probably a good basis for decision making. There is always the possibility of a larger one coming along at some point in the future, but the odds are likely slim.

Quantitative Analysis

One can use an analysis of the price data itself to get an idea of risk. If, for example, one had a trading system with an expected holding period of one week, one could look to a breakdown of one week price changes. Those data could be a guide in terms of possible volatility and expected price moves. As with the maximum loss idea, one does have to keep in mind that there is always the potential out there for a larger than expected (or previously observed) move.

One can combine either the maximum loss or quantitative analysis with a stop loss scheme. For example, one can apply either of the former to get a feel for how much risk there is in a given trade and use a stop to protect against a worst case scenario type of occurrence (keeping in mind the stop order's limitations).

Turning from how to determine the point risk, it is time to once more think in monetary terms. Using our GBP/USD system to provide a working example we can evaluate our options.

Fixed Risk

The idea of fixed risk is that the system makes position size decisions based on a preset account exposure. For example, a 5 percent risk level on a $10,000 account means a trade exposure of $500. This dollar figure, of course, will vary with changes in the account balance.

At a $100,000 per trade position size the maximum loss of any trade for the GBP/USD system was about $2,450. If we were to declare our per trade risk to be 5 percent, that means in order to have our exposure where we want it, we would have to trade position sizes of about $20,000.

What if, however, we opted to use our MAE analysis (or a quantitative measure) and have a 400-pip stop. Since the largest point loss the system took without a stop was 453 points, one would suspect that we could take a larger position size than if we use the maximum loss figure. That is true. We could bump our position size up to about $23,000. This may not seem a lot, but the difference can add up over time.

Fixed risk, however, means variable trade size. After all, if our account suffered losses and fell below the $10,000 starting point, our per trade risk would dip, too. Similarly, if profits drove the account balance above that $10,000 level, the per trade dollar risk would similarly rise as well. That means a fixed risk position sizing scheme is actually a variable trade size method.

Variable Risk

The alternative to a fixed risk scheme is a variable risk one. The variability, however, is only one-sided. There is still the 5 percent per trade risk cap (using our example setting), but the risk could actually be lower than that.

Applying this sort of scheme would be done by combining fixed and variable trade size methods. If one's account balance is below its starting point, then the positions' sizes would be variable because the 5 percent risk cap would force them to become smaller. On the flip side, as the account value rises above the starting point ($10,000), the per trade percent risk would actually fall.

By way of example, using a fixed position size method one would trade as much at an account value of $30,000 as at $15,000, which means the per trade risk is half as much. Of course that lower risk means lower returns over time, the drawback to a fixed trade size scheme. As mentioned earlier in the chapter, this can be overcome by using a step method to essentially reset the account size in terms of what is used to calculate per trade exposure.

Drawdowns

Per trade is not the only way to look at the risk question, nor is it necessarily the best one. In some cases it makes more sense to think in terms of peak-to-trough drawdowns in equity. Doing so requires tracking the changes in account value over the course of a system and seeing how it matches up with the parameters that have been set in the Trading Plan.

Please see Table 8.13.

Assume that we have set our maximum permissible drawdown at 20 percent. We can take a look at the GBP/USD results in Table 8.13 to see how it matches up. Using our fixed trade size of $100,000, we can see that there is actually a drawdown of more than 50 percent during the early part of the data from the peak balance of $11,391.40 after the first trade to $6,087.96 after trade 16. Clearly this far exceeds our 20 percent cutoff point, meaning we need to trim back the trade size to get in compliance. In fact, to meet our requirement, the trade size would have to be $40,000.

Whether the drawdown method is better than the per trade risk limit depends on the system in question. Trading systems with low Win%s are more prone to the strings of losses that create big drawdowns. Also, variable trade size methods can create larger drawdowns when they occur than fixed size ones, especially further out in time from the start point if the system has been profitable.

TABLE 8.13 System Equity Performance

Trade	$ Profit	Balance
		$10,000
1	$ 1,391.40	$ 11,391.40
2	$ (232.82)	$ 11,158.58
3	$(1,421.40)	$ 9,737.18
4	$ 154.19	$ 9,891.37
5	$ (308.86)	$ 9,582.51
6	$ (288.69)	$ 9,293.82
7	$ 77.23	$ 9,371.05
8	$(1,024.27)	$ 8,346.78
9	$ (520.83)	$ 7,825.95
10	$ (411.87)	$ 7,414.08
11	$ (34.34)	$ 7,379.74
12	$ (446.24)	$ 6,933.50
13	$ 137.36	$ 7,070.86
14	$ (116.60)	$ 6,954.26
15	$ (515.50)	$ 6,438.76
16	$ (350.80)	$ 6,087.96

Risk of Ruin

Keeping that Win% in mind, we can also take a second big picture approach to determining our trade position size, one based on the idea of risk of ruin (RoR). Ruin is a concept we discussed earlier in regard to risk management and trader risk tolerance. Now we want to take that and apply it in an objective fashion.

We can estimate the risk of ruin in a number of ways. The tool on this book's support web site (www.andurilonline.com/book/calculator.aspx) uses the Monte Carlo method, which means a series of essentially random tests are done and the results aggregated to determine probabilities. In the case of RoR, we are looking to determine the chance the system would blow out our account. Since we have a decent estimate of Win% and the Win/Loss ratio, we can get to work.

Figure 8.7 shows the result of using the figures from our SMA/SAR system, which had a Win% of 45% and a Win/Loss Ratio of 1.75. Doing a points-only test with our trade size set at 1, meaning each loss is 1 point, over 100 trades we can see that our Ruin Rate is 0%. That means in none of the 500 tests run did the hypothetical account drop below 50 (from a starting level of 100).

The results show the most extreme drawdowns, both in terms of percentage decline from peak to trough and length of time to a new equity high. There are also the data on strings of losing trades. Both sets of information can come in handy in determining position size and in assessing a system's performance over time.

Those last results probably seem a bit unspectacular, though. After all, the best performer made only 62 points over about five years' worth of trades (the SMA/SAR system average a bit over 20 trades a year). What if

FIGURE 8.7 Monte Carlo Test Results
Source: www.andurilonline.com.

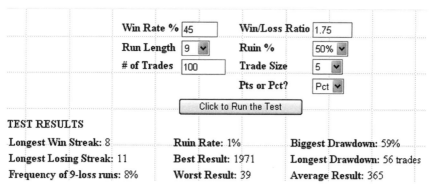

Win Rate % 45		Win/Loss Ratio 1.75
Run Length 9 ⌄		Ruin % 50% ⌄
# of Trades 100		Trade Size 5 ⌄
		Pts or Pct? Pts ⌄

Click to Run the Test

TEST RESULTS

Longest Win Streak: 8	Ruin Rate: 1%	Biggest Drawdown: 95%
Longest Losing Streak: 11	Best Result: 411	Longest Drawdown: 56 trades
Frequency of 9-loss runs: 9%	Worst Result: 12	Average Result: 215

FIGURE 8.8 Monte Carlo Test Results
Source: www.andurilonline.com.

we bump the risk up to 5 points per trade? See Figure 8.8. That certainly changes things! The system now averages more than doubling over the course of 100 trades and the RoR is a puny 1 percent.

It comes at a cost, though. The largest drawdown has jumped dramatically to 95 percent and at least one sample trade period lost more than 85 percent of the account. This is a fixed points-only test, though. What about a fixed percent test instead? See Figure 8.9.

Shifting to the fixed percentage text proved better on all fronts. The biggest drawdown has dropped sharply and returns have jumped considerably. This reflects two things that we touched on earlier. The fixed percentage system tends to suffer less during strings of losing trades because less and less risk is taken, at least when one is looking at similar account

Win Rate % 45		Win/Loss Ratio 1.75
Run Length 9 ⌄		Ruin % 50% ⌄
# of Trades 100		Trade Size 5 ⌄
		Pts or Pct? Pct ⌄

Click to Run the Test

TEST RESULTS

Longest Win Streak: 8	Ruin Rate: 1%	Biggest Drawdown: 59%
Longest Losing Streak: 11	Best Result: 1971	Longest Drawdown: 56 trades
Frequency of 9-loss runs: 8%	Worst Result: 39	Average Result: 365

FIGURE 8.9 Monte Carlo Test Results
Source: www.andurilonline.com.

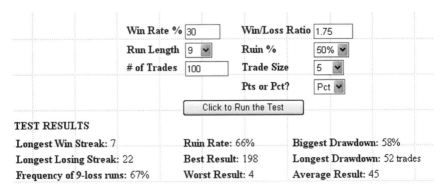

Win Rate %	30	Win/Loss Ratio	1.75
Run Length	9	Ruin %	50%
# of Trades	100	Trade Size	5
		Pts or Pct?	Pct

Click to Run the Test

TEST RESULTS

Longest Win Streak: 7	Ruin Rate: 66%	Biggest Drawdown: 58%
Longest Losing Streak: 22	Best Result: 198	Longest Drawdown: 52 trades
Frequency of 9-loss runs: 67%	Worst Result: 4	Average Result: 45

FIGURE 8.10   Monte Carlo Test Results
Source: www.andurilonline.com.

values. At the same time, it takes larger positions as the account grows, which can mean much larger profits.

We may still not like the size of the drawdowns, but the SMA/SAR system has a quite small RoR, even at a larger risk setting, thanks to a good Win% and Win/Loss Ratio pairing. A drop of either one, however, can mean a major rise in the RoR, as witnessed in Figure 8.10 when the Win% was cut to 30 percent.

These figures are not very nice at all. Given the size of our test period, it is unlikely that our Win% is off by 15 percent, so we need not fear its having an RoR that says that our chance of sinking an account is 2 in 3. We include this example for dramatic effect. It is worth, however, taking a look at what could happen in the future if the system's Win% and/or Win/Loss Ratio deteriorates.

Monte Carlo

As noted, the technique used to derive the results just displayed was Monte Carlo. This is a method whereby one creates a series of simulated results. In our case here we ran 500 simulations based on the statistics of our USD/JPY trading system. Each simulation was the result of a random set of trades defined by the Win% and Win/Loss Ratio. By making so many passes through, the expectation is that we can produce a good approximation of what the future is likely to bring. Figure 8.11 shows the dispersion of the results (final account balance) from the first test we ran with the trade size set at 1.

The advantage of reviewing the individual results of a Monte Carlo

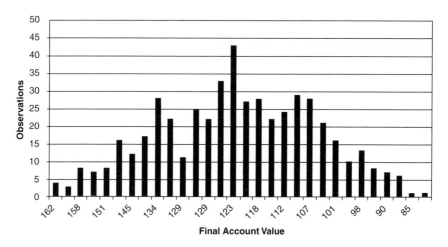

FIGURE 8.11 System Results Distribution

situation is that we can get a handle on just how often the worst case situations come to pass. The data we looked at before for this test showed that the worst performance was a decline to 79. The graph shows, though, that such an occurrence is quite unlikely. In fact, the odds of showing a net loss seem to be only about 15 percent. That does not mean the results will be spectacular, of course, but at least it gives us something we can use in determining how to size our trades, which is the point of this whole discussion.

Homework

Using the tool on the web site and the statistics you have for Win% and Win/Loss ratio for your system, do an analysis of RoR, maximum drawdown, and so on. Record the results in your system research journal.

THE FINAL SYSTEM

The definition of a trading system is a set of rules by which buy and sell decisions are made. We have gone through the process of determining the entry and exit rules and comparing them across systems. We have also wrapped risk into the equation. It is now time to bring the two together.

An entry rule, in all its glory looks like this:

Go Long/Short n units when x occurs

where n is either a fixed number, or the formula for determining that number (based on risk, of course), and x is the signal criteria. In the latter case, it could be expressed as either a single event:

The Close crosses above the 10-day moving average

or as a series of happenings:

The Close crosses above the 10-day moving average
and
The 10-day moving average is above the 20-day moving average

or even a conditional set:

The Close crosses above the 10-day moving average
and
The 10-day moving average is above the 20-day moving average
or
The Close crosses above the 10-day moving average
and
The Fast Stochastic %K is below 70

An exit rule can be structured the same way, even to the extent of incorporating whether to exit all or just part of an open position:

Exit n% of Short/Long when x occurs

If we elect a fixed percentage method of trade sizing based on a risk level of 5 percent for our USD/JPY SAR-entry/SMA-exit system our rules would be:

Exit 100% of an Open Short and Go Long .05A/G units of GBP/USD when 0.02/0.20 setting SAR line moves below Close

Exit 100% of an Open Long position when Close crosses below the 60-day moving average

Exit 100% of an Open Long and Go Short .05A/G units of GBP/USD when 0.02/0.20 setting SAR line moves above Close

Exit 100% of an Open Short position when Close crosses above the 60-day moving average

where

A = the current Account Balance

G = the current rate for GBP/USD

We were probably overly specific in the rules we finally laid out here, but it is always better to be more specific rather than less. Remember the earlier discussion about what can happen if trading rules are ill defined or applied. In both testing and application (especially in regard to mechanical systems) the result can be something very different from what is intended.

With further testing, we could make the system a bit more refined and complex in terms of perhaps scaling into or out of trades (adding or subtracting fractional positions rather than all at once), or identifying conditions to trade. Just remember, though, one should not get carried away with the rules. Simpler systems tend to be better performers in the long run. The trader should not fall into the curve fitting trap and design the perfect system for the past. Chances are, it will not work for the future, which is when it will be applied.

Along similar lines, beware of systems that have extremely high probability but have a low trade count. Keep in mind our discussion of expectancy. A system with relatively low profitability per trade can be better than one with a high per trade expectancy simply because it can be applied more frequently. It is not how right a system is that determines its worthiness, it is how much profit it churns out over a given time span.

Homework

Having identified at least one good system and looked at the risk scenario, define the final set of rules for the system(s) for your Trading Plan and note them in your system research journal. Then start trading it in your demo account. Record all of your trades in your trading log.

CHAPTER 9

Application

T his final portion of the text brings all of the previous sections to-gether and ties them in with some additional final thoughts before setting the reader on the trading path.

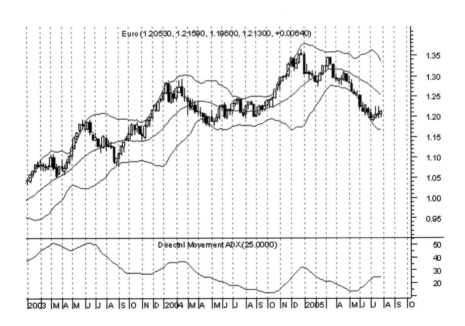

A FEW LAST PLAN/SYSTEM POINTS

Before launching you forward on the trading journey, there are a few final things we need to touch on.

Money Management, Again!

One can never spend too much time talking about risk and money management. We have discussed methods for identifying risk and how to reduce or avoid it. We have also gone over the idea of risk tolerance and how it ties in with trading and system design. We have not spent a great deal of time on the risk mindset, though, so we will take some time to do that here.

There is a common way of presenting the risk/reward/expectancy triumvirate in relation to taking losses. This is often done through example. Assume two potential trading options in which the trader is down $100 on an open position. One can either exit immediately and take the sure $100 loss, or one can employ a strategy that gives the trader a 10 percent chance at breaking even on the position, but a 90 percent chance of losing $1,000. Which would you chose?

Now imagine a second scenario. In this case you are up $100 on a trade. You can get out and take the guaranteed gain of $100. Alternatively, you can hold on and have a 90 percent chance of making $1,000 and a 10 percent chance of ending up with no profit at all. Which way do you go?

If looking strictly at expectancy, one would choose to exit the losing position at a loss of $100 and hold the winner. If one holds the loser, the expected return is −$900 (10% × $0 − 90% × $1,000), much worse than the $100 guaranteed loss. At the same time, holding the winner provides an expected return of +$900 (10% × $0 + 90% × $1,000), far better than a sure gain of $100.

All this seems quite simple when presented in such a rational fashion, but it is often not so in application. Many, many traders fall into the hope and fear trap when they have positions on. They hope their losers turn around and they fear the winners will reverse and wipe out their profits. The result is the opposite of the cut losses short, let winners run philosophy often espoused by experienced traders. This is one more reason why having a Trading Plan and *sticking to it* is so important. The Trading Plan helps to take the emotional aspect out of trade decision making, avoiding the hope and fear scenario.

It goes deeper than that, however. Money management is an obsession among the most successful traders. Some go into each trade assuming that it will be a loser. All know and embrace the fact that there will be ups and downs. No system or trading method is perfect. There are going to be losing trades, and probably strings of them. Each trader must be aware of this and prepare for it to happen, as it inevitably will.

Trader Quotes

Here are some nightmare situations taken from the Trade2Win boards:

Trading when 48 sheets to the wind is a sure way to doom and disaster. I accidentally managed to enter a trade with 10 times my normal size.—FetteredChinos

One of my friends . . . got confused about their leverage and lot size and ended up risking $100 a pip instead of $10 a pip. It was just before NFP (the non-farm payrolls report) and within a few minutes they were down $10,000.—adrianallen99

Trading risk management is also tied into preventing silly things like making avoidable mistakes or trading when one should not be doing so. Refer to the sidebar for a couple of examples. Imagine the mental and physical state of the trader who figured out too late that he was risking $100 per pip instead of $10 going into perhaps the most influential data release on the calendar. Even if the loss had not happened, the heart would have been fluttering pretty well. The worst part is that it could so easily have been avoided with some attention to detail.

It may sound obvious, but errors in order entry are a big problem, and not just for new traders. The quickest way to lose money in the markets is to make mistakes when you place your orders. Fortunately, this is something very easy to fix. PAY ATTENTION! It's as simple as that. Every trade entry system you could use has some kind of order confirmation mechanism. Take the extra two seconds and check to make sure everything is correct.

Analysis Pitfalls

Back in the chapter on market analysis methods we mentioned the representation bias, which is the tendency to view the portrayal of something as the thing itself. The example we used was a map, which shows the terrain, but is not the terrain itself. As such, it presents a limitation on one's ability to use it in the decision making process.

There are other biases as well.

The *lotto bias* relates to control. Its name comes from those who play the lottery and their belief that picking numbers somehow improves their chances of winning. If the odds of winning are one in a million for a given set of numbers to come up, it does not matter a bit whether those numbers are picked at random or by some kind of system.

Lotto bias relates to trading in regard to entry signals. Traders often spend enormous amounts of time trying to find the perfect system for getting into the market when the fact of the matter is that for any given trade the likelihood of profiting is essentially dictated by chance. That is why we have said a few times that at least as much effort must go into determining the exit strategy, to include money management. It is also why the trader must listen to the markets and not succumb to the idea that imposing one's will on them is possible.

Closely tied to the lotto bias is something known as the *gambler's fallacy*, which is the belief that a string of losses increases the chance of experiencing a winner. If one were to roll a standard six-sided die, the chance of getting a five is 1/6, or about 17 percent. It does not matter how many times in a row the die comes up with something other than five, the odds of the next roll being a five are 1/6.

The problem many people have is in thinking of the odds of a specific run happening and then extrapolating that into some kind of odds for a single event. For example, there is about a 1/3 chance of getting 20 non-five rolls in a row on our six-sided die if we roll it 100 times. Does that mean that if we see 19 non-five rolls in a row that there is a 2/3 chance of getting a five on the next roll? No! Why? Because each roll is an independent event. The 1/3 odds were for seeing a run of 20 consecutive non-five rolls, not the odds of getting a non-five if there had already been 19 non-fives in a row.

This discussion is all based on discrete, independent events assuming no memory and a fair die. One is likely to find that a trading system operates in the same fashion. Even if it does not, however, the point still stands. One must ask the right question of the statistics, and avoid using them to prove something, to get useful results.

Shifting back to biases, the *conservatism bias* essentially means being hard-headed. It is when one refuses to consider elements that do not mesh with one's existing opinion or belief, or to change one's position as circumstances dictate (or to do so only slowly). We have all seen this sort of thing happen, such as the case where someone refuses to accept a fact contrary to their belief until the evidence is incontrovertible. This kind of bias is particularly problematic when someone has expressed a view publicly, meaning they have to admit to being wrong. The point is not to trade with a set notion, and to be ready, willing, and able to make adjustments to one's view quickly

Biases such as the ones we have mentioned are serious pitfalls for those trading the markets. It is hard to accept that one is going to be wrong a lot and that one has no control over the markets, but both are the case. The trader that can overcome these hurdles is moving in the right direction.

Another thing to worry about in one's analysis, especially as it relates to system design and testing is *postdictive error*. This occurs when one uses information that would not have been available at the time to make decisions. Clearly, this is not something generally done on purpose. It can happen, however, as the result of incorrect referencing when one is doing calculations in spreadsheets and charting packages. Attention to detail is all that is required to avoid postdictive error creeping into one's work.

Do Your Own Work

It is highly unlikely that you will ever trade successfully by listening to the recommendations of others. This is something well-known among experienced traders, but a lesson often learned the hard way by newcomers. Trading is primarily an individual venture.

Think about the assessments done earlier in this book when you were making the Trading Plan. It is unlikely for any two people to have the same combination of market interest/knowledge, trading time frame, available capital, risk tolerance, and so on. They are things related to the individual's background and situation in life. That means trading tips and recommendations are out of context.

Consider the common tipster who tells you XYZ stock is a surefire winner. Well, in what time frame? How much risk is involved? Do you even have an interest in trading stocks? What's the exit strategy? What is the tip based on? This last one is important because one is highly unlikely to stick with a trade based on an analysis contrary to one's personal beliefs. The author, for example, would have a very hard time holding a stock that has negative earnings, and would probably be looking for the slightest sign of weakness in the price to bail out, even though it might cost loads of profits down the line. It is just a question of personal philosophy and style.

We use the tipster as an example here, but the same applies to anyone who provides trading recommendations. That includes market professionals. They have their own considerations, which may or may not match yours.

The point here is that one must do their homework. It is fine to get trading ideas from sources other than your own work, but you have to then make them yours by doing whatever due-diligence is necessary to put them in line with your own trading style. To do otherwise is to contradict your own nature, which can only lead to trouble in the long run.

Also note that doing your own work applies to Trading Plans. Just as a trading system often will not be as effective for people other than the originator, so, too, is the case with Trading Plans. You have to create your own Plan based on your own interests, circumstances, and strengths and weaknesses.

Risk/Reward

The risk/reward ratio is simply the expected gain (reward) on a given trade divided by the amount of loss (risk) one is exposing oneself to on that trade. It is a common comparative statistic for trades and trading systems.

Market Parlance

While the term risk/reward is commonly used in the market, it is most often done so backward. A trader, for example, may be heard to say his risk/reward is 3 to 1, meaning the expected gain is three times the size of the loss that could occur. Technically speaking, this should be stated as 1 to 3 (1:3), but for some reason traders like to think of profit first.

A mechanical system such as the ones we demonstrated as examples in the previous two chapters have well defined profit/loss ratios calculated. The trader of such systems, having done the research and testing, therefore has a pretty good idea of the risk/reward ratio for a given trade, at least on an average basis.

Discretionary traders do not have such nice clean figures from which to work. The discretionary trader has two ways to approach the risk/reward determination. One is to look back on their trading record and determine an average. That assumes a fairly standard approach to all trades, though. Otherwise the figures are not very comparable.

The other way a discretionary trader can approach risk/reward is to work from a predetermined figure. A trader could, as an example, state as part of her Trading Plan that she will take only trades with a 1:2 risk/reward profile. That means for every 1 unit of risk ($100), the trade is be expected to produce 2 units of profit ($200). The trader then looks for trades with that kind of prospect. If the success rate is high enough (greater than 33 percent), then the trader can be profitable over time. Of course, one needs to have an idea of the success rate.

Discretionary Trading Systems

The mention of discretionary traders and success rates brings us back to trading system development and testing. In many cases one cannot easily back-test a discretionary system by its very nature. That means the trader looking to develop a nonmechanical trading method lacks the ability to quickly and efficiently rate that method's performance.

There is a way, however, to produce a set of statistics, namely to actually trade the system in a demo environment (if it is a good approximation of real trading). Taking this particular route is not the fastest option, but in many ways it has big advantages. For one, the performance figures will be more representative of real trading. That gives them an added significance. They are most trustworthy.

At the same time, actual application of a trading system, even in a demo environment, is a good way to learn more about both the market(s) in question and the system. A great deal of extra value is created for the trader. This is one of the reasons why many feel that over the long run discretionary trading is better. In order to be successful over time, the discretionary trader must develop a good feel for the market. Failure to do so will result in the trader being cast aside like so many others.

It is also worth noting that you are more likely to have success with mechanical application of a discretionary system than by winging it, so to speak. Research indicates that traders who consistently apply a set of predetermined rules are more likely to achieve success than those who fly by the seat of their pants. You may not be able to define a discretionary system as precisely as you could a mechanical one, but that does not mean you cannot produce a set of rules based on whatever you use for the purpose. If not, do you really have a trading system?

GO LIVE

Early in this book it was strongly recommended that the reader not take the real money plunge into the markets at that stage. The reasoning then was that without a firm understanding of what it means to trade and how to actually do it, there is little sense in putting money at risk. It is like any other activity—one should practice before doing it for real.

Now we are going to shift gears.

Hopefully this book has at least gotten the reader to a reasonable level of comfort with the markets—how to execute transactions and how to develop a strategy to seek out profits. If the included exercises have been conscientiously worked through, then it is time to go live.

Making such a move early in one's trading development is something contrary to most market advice, which recommends new market participants spend a long time demo trading. There is much to be gained from making an early entry into actual trading, though.

Now before going any further, it should be *extremely* clear that no suggestion is even being hinted at that one dump their life's savings in a trading account and take positions in the market. That would be foolish. Rather, what we are talking about here is putting a *very* small amount of money into an account, an amount that is so insignificant as to make one wonder Why bother? Here is the advantage of Oanda's FXTrade system. One can use PayPal to put even just $10 into an account and trade single currency units.

Trader Quote

"Trading real money has brought much greater focus to my trading than I had in a demo account. Because I have real money on the line, I have improved my method substantially."—RM250 Oanda's FXMessage Board

---

Why do we suggest making the move to real money trading so early? To put it quite simply, it *is* because demo trading and real trading are very different. We are not talking about differences between demo trading platforms and live ones, which can be the case (not with FXTrade, but definitely with some other broker/dealer platforms), but instead the difference between trading phony money and your own real money. It *is* different, even if it does not seem like it should be. The transformation one goes through when making the jump from demo to real trading can be astonishing. Many traders report that as demo traders they were very relaxed and did not get too caught up in their positions. Once they started putting their own money on the table, though, things changed. Suddenly they were watching their open trades constantly, living and dying with each tick. This has some serious adverse side effects.

Trader Quote

"Since going live, I have rarely ever returned to the game. I still have a lot to learn, but I find some of the psychological aspects of trading some of the most difficult to overcome. If you have developed a trading system, but then break one of your rules in the game, there are not the same consequences as with breaking your rules with real money. Trading real money will insist upon discipline or you'll wipe yourself out."—osimprov Oanda's FXMessage Board

---

Overanalysis

Overanalysis is what often occurs when a trader spends too much time staring at price screens, as happens to many when they first move over to live trading. The fact of the matter is that most price moves are meaningless in the grand scheme of the markets, but this tends to get forgotten when one is watching each and every tick as if one's life depended on it. The result is using every little tick as an opportunity to reanalyze the market and/or one's position.

The other side of overanalysis is having too much information, which is a very real risk in today's information age. Modern traders have access to so much data. It can often be too much. There are analyst reports available to everyone. Business television is ubiquitous. There are loads of chat rooms. Recall our encouragement to do your own work. Most of the information out there is little more than the opinion of others, many of whom may have no better grasp of things than you do. In this regard, less can be a good thing.

The result of overanalysis is one of two things. One can become overwhelmed by it, which is referred to as analysis paralysis. This is a horrible situation in which one constantly second-guesses oneself to the point of not being able to pull the trigger. A trader who cannot execute trades is just a spectator.

Overtrading Part I

The other thing that can happen is overtrading. It is the opposite of analysis paralysis in that one is continually analyzing the markets afresh, and therefore making new buy/sell decisions frequently. The result is often a whipsaw type of situation in which one gets into a trade, second-guesses it, reverses in the other direction, second-guesses that, reverses again, and so on. As one might expect, this is unlikely to be a profitable situation. Spreads and/or transaction costs will eat into one's account balance very quickly. What's more, the trader will get into a very unhealthy frantic state in which good decision making is lost.

It should be noted that while new traders are often afflicted by overanalysis and overtrading, they are not the only ones at risk. Professional analysts (which the author once was) and commentators are also susceptible to it because their jobs require them to monitor the markets on an almost constant basis and either determine reasons for movements, which often do not have a reason, or predict the next movement. Activity of this sort draws one into the shortest of time frames. It is something to keep in mind if planning a career in the markets and/or when listening to the pundits.

Overtrading Part II

Overtrading does not always come about as the result of overanalysis, though. Often it is simply enthusiasm. It is a natural thing to feel a certain elation when one makes money on a trade, and to want to seek to have the same feeling again. In this manner, trading is like betting—an intermittent reward venture.

Trader Quote

"The biggest problem I found when I started with real money was going too hard too early."—Ozzy Joker, Oanda's FXMessage Board

The problem with this, however, is one's elation often clouds judgment. The pursuit of that next winning trade can lead one to take on trades that are not in line with one's system or plan. Suddenly rationalizations come into play: "it's okay if one of the criteria isn't met," "the market is going to generate a signal; I'll just jump in now in anticipation," "I can take a bit more risk on this trade," and so on. It is, in particular, that last one that gets so many traders in trouble. They make one profitable trade, but give it all back and then some by trading too large on the next position.

The point is that the trader goes through a change when shifting over to live trading. The earlier this can happen in the overall educational process, the better. One who has the experience of actually trading their own money can make better judgments as they work through developing and refining a Trading Plan. Understanding of the risks inherent in trading is increased dramatically when one realizes being cavalier about position size and order entry is likely to cost money. One can develop and test trading systems in demo accounts (highly recommended), but without having actually traded in the live money environment, it is not so easy to know what systems suit the individual.

Trader Quote

"I suppose the transition from demo to live account involved some pain and sweat at the beginning. Personally, I could sense the difference between throwing real hard cash and virtual dollars. It sorta affected my risk profile as well, became more conservative in my strategies."—scolaire Oanda's FXMessage Board

For all these reasons, it is advisable to make the plunge sooner rather than later, like dipping one's toe into the pool to test the water. Just be sure to do it with 100 percent play money, and a small amount of it at that. There is a cost to any education, but there is no need for it to be higher than necessary.

TAKING IT FORWARD

If you have followed along the intended path of this text and completed the suggested homework assignments, you are well on your way at this stage. You should have a feel for what it means to be a trader and how to put together an effective plan of action for your trading as a whole and on a transaction-by-transaction basis with a system.

Trading can be thought of like just any other endeavor. There is a base of knowledge and understanding that presents the first hurdle—the sorts of things that can be learned from books and other sources. After that, however, application and experience take over. One can certainly receive guidance and inspiration along the way, but the path to success is by necessity a singular one. It requires dedication to the purpose and willingness to make the requisite sacrifices along the way, just as with anything else worth doing.

Hopefully this book has you pointed in the right direction, or has helped you decide that trading is not for you, which is just as important. The author welcomes questions and comments from readers of this text. A special forum has been created on the Anduril Analytics web site, which can be accessed through this book's resource page at www.andurilonline.com/book. Feel free to stop by and share your thoughts or to pose queries.

Remember, create the right Trading Plan for you and stick to it!

Best of luck in your trading and life endeavors!

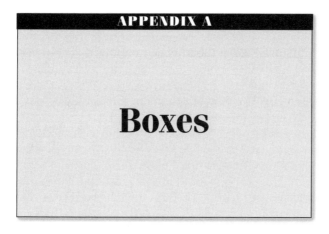

APPENDIX A

Boxes

Early in the text we noted the Boxes tab on the FXGame screen. It was not important to our discussion at the time, so it was essentially skipped. For those with an interest, however, we dedicate some space to exploring this trading alternative. (Refer to the FxTrade web site for an explanation. (http://fxtrade.oanda.com/boxoption).

Boxes are called such because they are expressed in two dimensions—price and time—and when depicted visually have a square or rectangular shape to them. The boxes offered on the FXGame system combine an upper and lower price band with a start and end time period to define what is essentially a chart area in which the market either will or will not trade. We can explain further by example.

A new box can be initiated by clicking on the Price Box button below the chart on the FXTrade screen (See Figure A.1).

You will notice that the Price Box button turns blue. When we move our cursor on the chart, it shows a cross-hair (Figure A.2).

Clicking the left mouse button once sets one corner of the box on the chart at the location of the cross-hair (just click, not a click

247

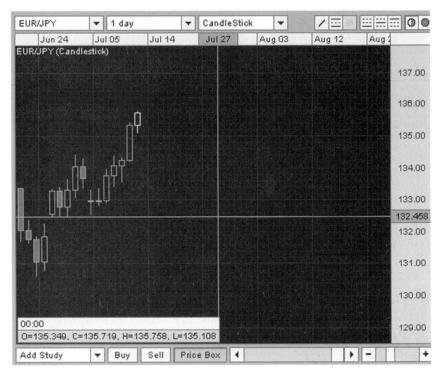

FIGURE A.2 Oanda FXTrade: Price Box Start
Source: Oanda.

and drag). Moving the mouse then creates a box on the screen (Figure A.3).

One more click of the left button sets the box. It also brings up the dialog box shown in Figure A.4 to allow fine-tuning of the price and/or time points.

The Start Time and End Time lines define the duration (width) of the box. The Maximum Level and Minimum Level set the price bands (height) of the box. The displayed box on the chart will change as you alter those values, creating a larger or smaller box as you make adjustments.

There are four other points of reference that must be reviewed as well. At the top of the dialog box are the Hit and Miss radial buttons. Choosing Hit means that the box is defined as being an area in which price is expected to trade. The Miss option means you are looking for price to not trade inside the box.

FIGURE A.3 Oanda FXTrade: Price Box Drawing
Source: Oanda.

The next line down is the Purchase Price where you set how much you are willing to spend to buy the box. It is editable. See Figure A.5.

The Payout line indicates how much the box will pay you if it is either hit or missed. This is a calculated amount that you cannot edit, but that will change if you alter the Purchase Price or any other variable, including switching from Hit to Miss, as you can see if you compare the example in Figure A.5 with the one in Figure A.4.

You can also set the Minimum Payout, though it is not critical to do so. When creating a box, however, one does want to make sure the Payout exceeds the Purchase Price. If not, then what is the point of the trade?

For the sake of example, let us assume that we do not think EUR/JPY (which is what this particular box is developed for) will not overcome resistance (see Chapter 6) at 136.00. We can use a Miss, as

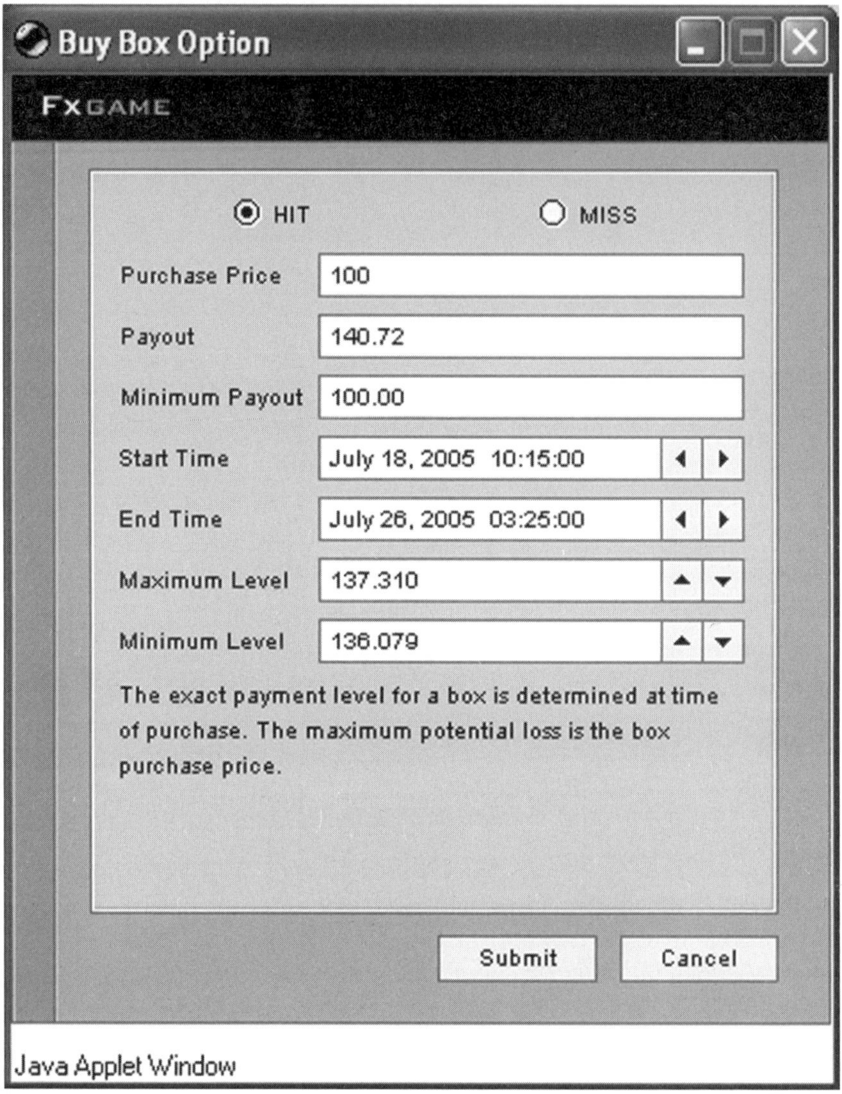

FIGURE A.4 Oanda FXTrade: Price Box Order Ticket
Source: Oanda.

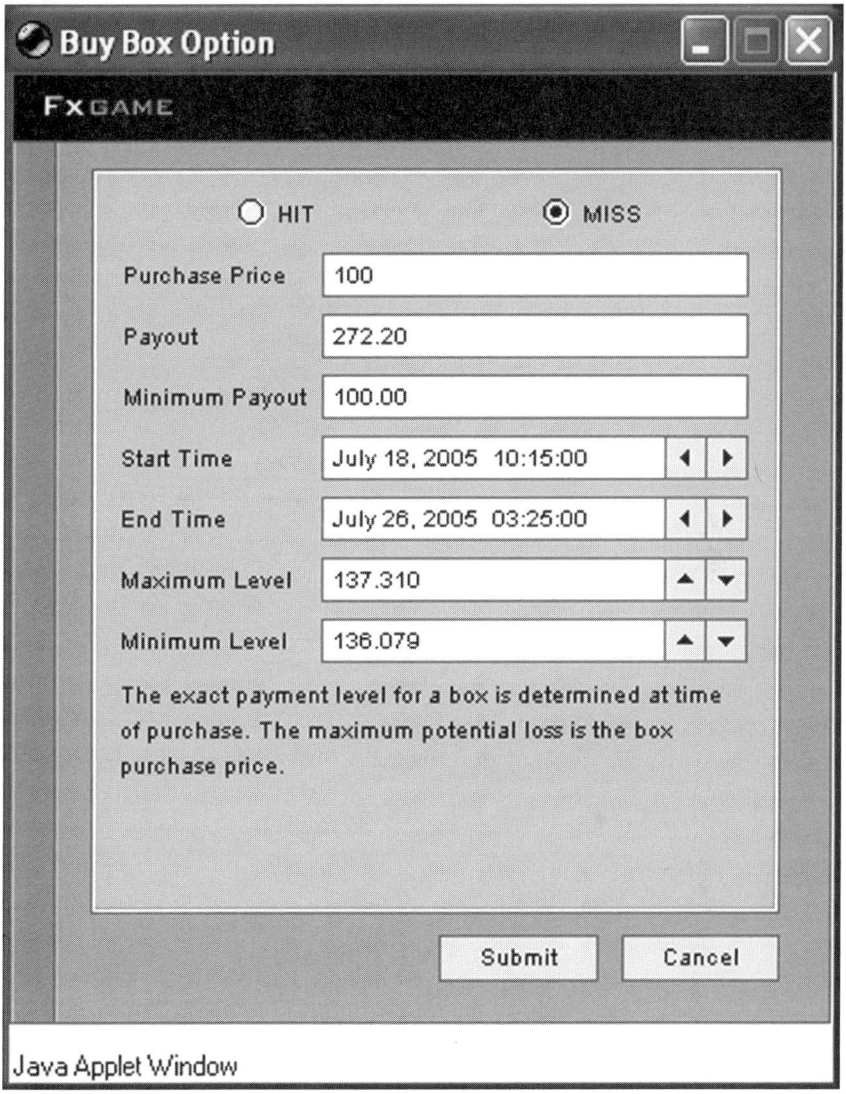

FIGURE A.5 Oanda FXTrade: Price Box Order Ticket
Source: Oanda.

shown in Figure A.6, to define our expectation. Setting the Minimum to 136.25 and Maximum to 137.25 gives us a 100-pip high box. We can then set the Start and End times to give us a weeklong window. The result will be a box that starts on July 18 at 10:00 (local 24-hour time) and ends on July 25 at 10:00. We are paying $100 for this box. If the market does not trade within its bounds we will be paid $231.00, for a profit of $131.00.

Notice on our confirmation (Figure A.7) that the Potential Payment (last line) is different from when we set up the order. That reflects a change in the market while we were setting up the trade. Our box now shows up in the Boxes tab, and on the chart (Figure A.8).

Our new box will also show up as a $100 expenditure on our activity log. Importantly, though, it will not show up under Positions or Exposure. Boxes are handled entirely separately from the spot trades.

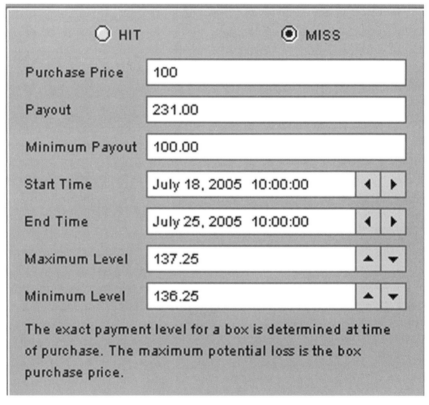

FIGURE A.6   Oanda FXTrade: Price Box Order Ticket
Source: Oanda.

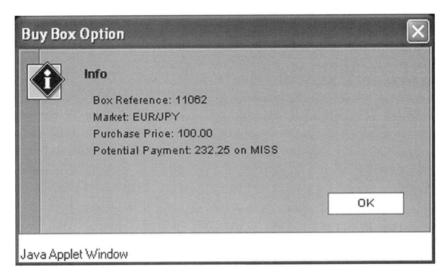

FIGURE A.7   Oanda FXTrade: Price Box Order Confirmation
Source: Oanda.

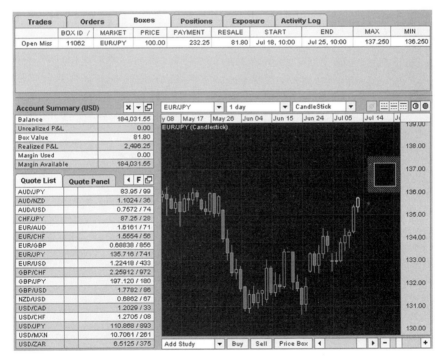

FIGURE A.8   Oanda FXTrade: Price Box Live
Source: Oanda.

Boxes, like other trades, will continue to show up on a chart even after they expire, unless you opt to hide the historical transactions. The chart in Figure A.9 shows some old box trades.

In this case we are looking at EUR/USD boxes. The two large ones paid off. (They show green on the FXTrade platform.) They were Hit boxes and as you can see, price did indeed trade inside the box. The third box was also a Hit. Price, however, did not trade inside it. As a result, the box did not pay off (and shows red).

We can see the results of a box by mousing over it (see the cross-hairs) and looking at the box that appears near the top of the chart screen. In this particular instance we had bought the box for $1,000 and it paid $0.00.

When a box expires, if there is a payout it will show up in the Activity Log. If not, nothing will appear. The box will just get cleared out of the Boxes tab.

It should be noted that boxes can be closed early, before completion.

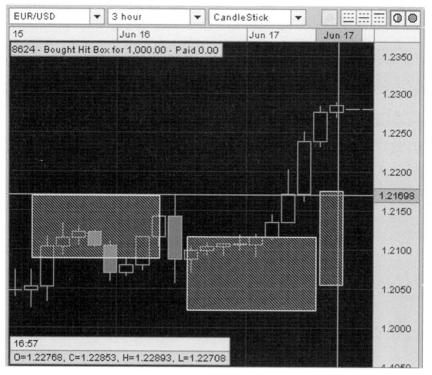

FIGURE A.9 Oanda FXTrade: Price Box Results
Source: Oanda.

You will note in the Boxes tab that there is a Resale column. That is the price at which you can sell the box. It will vary based on time and price movement. The more likely it is that the box will payoff, the higher the Resale, and vice versa. The Resale, however, will never exceed the Payment (Payout).

BOX TRADING STRATEGIES

Boxes may be used in a variety of ways by themselves, in combination, or in conjunction with spot positions. Let us start by taking a look at our earlier trade.

The premise behind the trade we developed in the example was that EUR/JPY would not trade in the 136.25 to 137.25 range between July 18 at 10:00 and July 25 at 10:00, a week's period. In this particular case, we basically took the view that the 136.25 chart resistance would keep prices from moving higher for a period of time, starting about a week out from when the trade was initiated. (The trade was done for example purposes, so do not get too caught up in the whys and wherefores of the analysis).

Figure A.10 shows the box payoff at various prices. The payoff is binomial in nature—either we lose $100 or we make $232.25—so both our

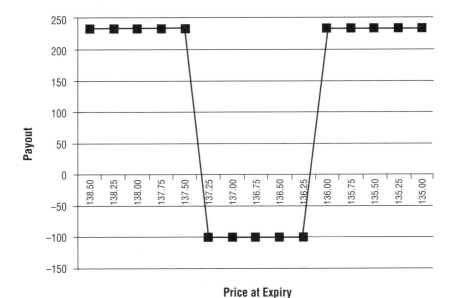

FIGURE A.10 Box Option Payoff

losses and our gains are capped. In fact, they are fixed. There is no middle ground. This is what makes boxes quite different from options, either outright or in terms of spreads. This binomial feature makes box pricing easier in one respect. Of course the fact that the hit/miss trigger time is not a discrete point, but rather a time span adds a layer of complexity. We are not about to get into a discussion of option pricing theory here. There is extensive material for those interested.

Getting back to our box trade, one could think of it as an outright bet. Either the market stays out of the price range we defined during the prescribed time, in which case we get $232.25 (making $132.25), or it does not and we lose the $100 we paid. It is rather cut and dried with no other possible outcomes.

In the case of our trade, the box was hit, as can be seen on the chart in Figure A.11. Since it was a Miss box, that is bad. We lost our money.

You can see that for a while the 136.25 resistance did hold. There was a quick breakout, though, which sank the position. Frustratingly, after a two-day trip into our box, the market fell right back out of it and has not been back since.

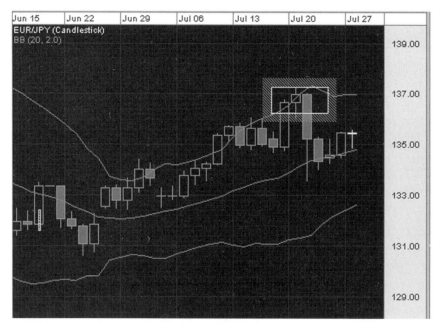

FIGURE A.11   Oanda FXTrade: Price Box Results
Source: Oanda.

This example demonstrates clearly the complexity of using boxes (like options). We can get almost everything right, but that one variable (in this case time) can still trip you up. This is not to say one cannot profitably use boxes to make money in this manner. It is just a question of having a sound trading system and sticking to one's Trading Plan. Boxes can be used for more than just making one very specific bet on market action. They can be combined with one another much like standard options to create a type of spread trade.

Let us consider the following scenario. EUR/USD has been trading mostly sideways for some time. Our analysis tells us that it will either continue to do so for the next week, or it will break out up or down (we can't be sure which). In such a situation, we can use boxes to construct and kind of spread trade to profit from the expected outcome.

Figure A.12 shows a visual of the strategy. It shows our three targets based on what we think will happen. We have made the boxes very thin (one hour wide as a matter of fact) for the sake of keeping a clean chart. They could easily have been larger without altering the basics of our intent. The point is that we expect to see, in one week's time, EUR/USD trading in one of those boxes. In Figure A.13 you can see the details.

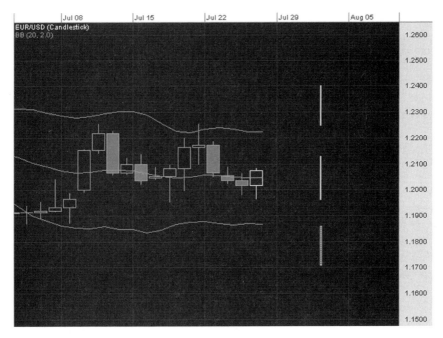

FIGURE A.12 Oanda FXTrade: Price Box Butterfly
Source: Oanda.

	BOX ID ▽	MARKET	PRICE	PAYMENT	RESALE	START	END	MAX	MIN
Open Hit	14854	EUR/USD	50.00	588.71	18.83	Aug 03, 00:00	Aug 03, 01:10	1.18600	1.17100
Open Hit	14853	EUR/USD	50.00	370.51	26.73	Aug 03, 00:00	Aug 03, 01:00	1.24000	1.22500
Open Hit	14852	EUR/USD	100.00	172.05	71.50	Aug 03, 00:00	Aug 03, 01:00	1.21280	1.19640

FIGURE A.13 Oanda FXTrade: Price Box Positions
Source: Oanda.

As you can see from the figure, we have our three positions arranged, such that we will profit if the market remains flat, or if it jumps into the expected ranges. The payoff scenario is portrayed in Figure A.14.

There are two clear periods when we would lose all our money, those between the boxes. If the market should be trading there at the box time, we will be out $200. Should EUR/USD rally, we expect to make a bit under $200. If it falls, we make nearly $400. But look, we lose if the market remains flat, too? Why is that? Because our middle box is too big in relation to our wing boxes, cost-wise.

This is an important lesson. You must remember that you are paying money out to buy the boxes. In this case we spent a total of $200. It is very easy to forget that when making your calculations. The PAYMENT amount is not pure profit. To determine the profit, one must subtract the cost of the box. Think of it in the same way as our discussion of trading profits.

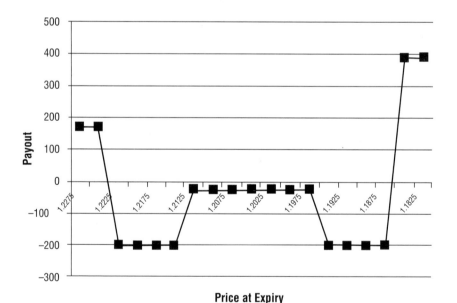

FIGURE A.14 Box Option Spread Payoff

The PRICE is the initial value of the box, while the PAYMENT is the end value. In this particular situation, we spent too much on the wing boxes, $100 total. Since we have to assume that the market is unlikely to hit multiple boxes in the time we have allotted (only one hour), then we have to figure that if the middle box is hit, we will lose our money on the other two. Unfortunately, we will only make about $70 if the middle box gets hit, meaning a net loss of about $30.

In order to make this particular spread trade profitable at the points we are targeting, we need to have smaller wings. If, for example, we cut the wing box sizes in half to $25 each, the profit picture would look like Figure A.15.

This figure is similar to a butterfly spread, with the difference that the wings do not offer unlimited upside. We can similarly make an approximation of a long strangle trade if we were to take out the middle box and just leave the two wings. That would give us a cost of $100 (using the trades we put in), and would result in a $270 profit if the upper box were hit, $538 if the lower box was.

The graph for that is in Figure A.16.

Again, the difference between the box version and a normal long strangle is that the former lacks the unlimited upside of the latter. At the same time, we have to define exactly where the payoff range is, rather

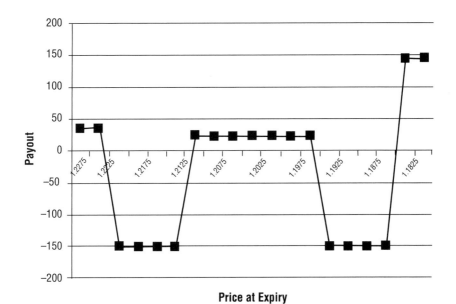

FIGURE A.15 Box Option Spread Payoff

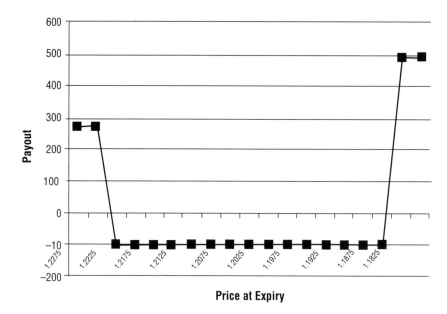

FIGURE A.16   Box Option Spread Payoff

than just having it based on being above or below a certain price. Practically speaking that can be worked around by making large boxes.

The point here is that boxes can be used in similar fashion to options as long as one is aware of the limitations. If a scenario can be outlined, there is most likely a way one could set up a box strategy to play it.

The real fun with boxes can come when working on expected returns for a given position. Consider our butterfly type spread. There is some probability (small though it may be) that more than one box is hit. Can you imagine how exciting it would be if all three of our boxes were? It would mean unbelievable market volatility, of course, but we would make out like bandits! That sort of occurrence, rare as it is, should be accounted for when putting together a trading strategy, just as one would factor in the chances of not hitting any box. Again, quantitative analysis can come in handy.

SYNTHETIC STOPS

One need not restrict oneself to using boxes for speculative purposes. They have application as money management tools as well when combined with outright positions in the spot forex market. Boxes, for example, can be used as a kind of stop to protect against adverse price movement.

Consider this. We have a long position in EUR/USD of 50,000 units and we want to limit our downside exposure. We buy a box to do so. For the sake of example, let us use the 1.1710 to 1.1860 box from our earlier butterfly. That means for a $50 payment we will receive $588.71 if the market is into our box area a week hence. This sounds great.

There is a catch, though, as Figure A.17 shows.

Since the box is a discrete fixed payment, it can provide only inefficient insurance against loss. The box is like a put option in this case in that when a certain price is reached we will get paid, but unlike the put, the amount of our payout does not increase as the market continues to fall. That is why we see a hook on the chart. The loss is reduced once the box is hit, but if EUR/USD keeps going lower, we are left unprotected. Sure, the net loss has been reduced. Once the box is paid off, though, there is no longer any further downside protection. Of course, one could set up a series of boxes to protect against further decline.

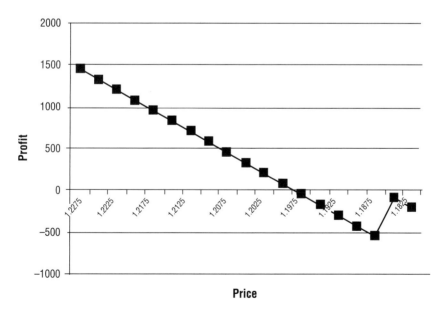

FIGURE A.17 Box Office Spot Long with Box Stop

ADDITIONAL COMBINATION STRATEGIES

Boxes are not limited to being used as protection against contrary price movement. They can also be employed to increase the profitability of another strategy. For example, a trader could be long USD/JPY in a position expected to be held for a considerable amount of time. Such long-term trades often require the trader sitting through periods of range trading and/or retracements in the overall trend. If one anticipates a price move, or lack thereof, which does not benefit the base position, boxes could be used to capture some additional profits.

As an example, think back to our EUR/JPY box. If we were long EUR/JPY and expecting the market to stall out below 136.25 for a while, as we were, the box trade we outlined could be a way for us to make a few bucks while keeping our long position intact. If the market fails to break the resistance, then the box makes us money. If the market breaks higher, we benefit from our long position. It is not such a bad scenario.

The reason boxes can be used so effectively in this fashion is that they do not create an offset in one's account. While a box position does have risk implications and does create an exposure to the market on which it is based, it can be held in parallel with a spot position without completely nullifying it. That gives the trader a great degree of flexibility in employ the box as part of a comprehensive trading strategy.

Sample System

The trading system outlined in this appendix is one the author has used with some considerable success. For example, it generated profits of more than 200 percent in 2004. It is based on work the author has done for nearly two decades, over which time the system has become modified and adapted to suit the author's personal trading style and time constraints. The system is presented here because it incorporates all three sides of the analytic triangle (see Chapter 6). As such, it should contain elements easily referenced by most readers.

Remember, past performance does not necessarily indicate future results. This applies to any trading system. That overarching warning can be extended further, though. The success of any trading system or method, no matter how brilliantly conceived and constructed, still comes down to its execution. The Trading Plan concept was harped on in this book, and this is the reason why. The author has had excellent success over the years trading the system presented in the pages that follow, but only by following it the way it is outlined and intended. That is the truth for any system.

A FEW ADVANCED WORDS

The stock market system that follows has as its backbone the CAN SLIM™ method taught by William J. O'Neil in his book, *How to Make Money in Stocks*. That system struck an immediate chord with the author, though he never traded exactly in the fashion of O'Neil. It was adapted to his own circumstances in terms of funds, free time, and information availability, and has continued in that manner over the years. This is something the author fully supports and encourages in anyone taking a look at this system and evaluating it in the context of their own style, personality, and situation.

At different points in this text the author refers to his broker. He has used Charles Schwab for many years and is very happy with the service and support received during that time. This is not a specific recommendation, as everyone has different needs. Most of the information obtained through Schwab is readily available from most online discount brokers these days. Use the one that makes the most sense for you and your situation.

There is included an accounting the author's actual trading performance in an section at the end of this appendix. Each trade done in 2004 is listed with its percent gain or loss. The results can be evaluated in two ways. First, if viewed in strict dollar figures—meaning starting balance to ending balance—the gains were about 135 percent.

The more realistic measure of account performance, however, is on a per share basis as one would do with a mutual fund. This is because the author made a high number of cash transactions in the account, adding funds and withdrawing them (especially withdrawing them). Using the per share measure, the gains were 227 percent. Stated another way, each share of the account valued at $1.00 to start 2004 ended the year at $3.27. With that said, let's get down to it!

PART I—IDENTIFYING THE STOCKS

Step 1—Filtering/Screening

There are thousands of stocks in the trading galaxy. One cannot possibly evaluate every single one of them. That's why we filter using a screening process—to narrow the field down a bit. Because of the sheer numbers involved, this filtering has to be done quantitatively. This can be handled automatically or manually. For example, the author is able to do his filtering for free through the online screening tools his broker provides.

The first filter is Relative Strength (RS), a measure of how a stock's price has performed in comparison to the rest of the market. The objective here is to identify stocks in the top 10 percent—an RS reading of 90 or better. The author applies an RS filter through his broker's online tools. If you don't have some kind of similar functionality at hand, you can find RS in a couple of places. One very easy place is *Investor's Business Daily*

(IBD). Each day IBD lists every stock's RS figure. There is also Daily Graphs, available by subscription online. These are essentially the backbone data for IBD's stock tables. You can get all the same information from Daily Graphs that you can from the paper itself, and then some. The Daily Graphs system has nice charting and screening capabilities as well. (*Note:* The author has no beneficial relationships with IBD or Daily Graphs)

Now that RS has cut 90 percent of the stocks out of the picture, there are still hundreds more to sort through. That means more filtering. We still have to take a couple of more passes through with a series of additional filters. There are several we can choose from. Depending on what is available by way of information, the trader can use one or more of the following:

EPS Rank Similar to RS, this ranks stocks by their earnings growth rate. You can find it in IBD and Daily Graphs. Although it is perfectly fine to accept any stock with an EPS above 80, the author generally works only with stocks having an EPS rank of 90 or higher, meaning those companies have had earnings growth in the top 10 percent.

Nearness to a New High This will be addressed later, but basically one is looking for stocks within approximately 10 percent of their 52-week high.

Current Price It is normally best to work with stocks that are trading at 20 or better. You can use a lower figure—just keep it in double digits—but for reasons outlined later, it is best to work with stocks trading above $20—the higher, the better.

Volume—Part I One wants to see rising volume. Recent volume figures should be above the longer-term average. The author currently runs a filter in which he looks for stocks whose 20-day average volume is greater than their 6-month average.

Volume—Part II It is also important to look to make sure that a stock is trading actively. That means an average of at least 10,000 shares per day. If the volume is light, the activity is less significant. Also, low volume can mean little price movement in the future. It takes trading activity (volume) to create sustainable price action.

You can see the output from one screener in Figure B.1. The first column after the stock symbol is RS. Then there is current price, followed by the difference between current price and the 52-week high (as a percentage). To the right of that you can see the 20-day average volume, the actual 52-week high, the P/E ratio, and the EPS figure. In this case, EPS is not the

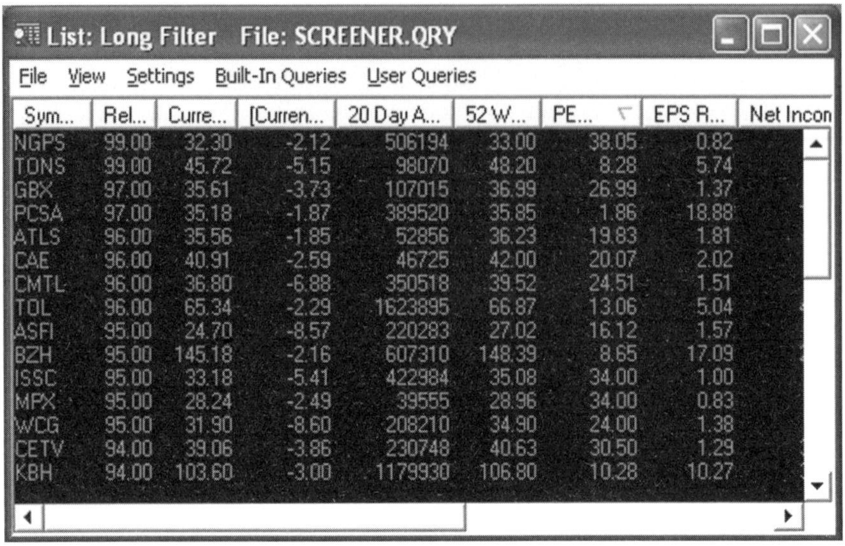

•⊞ List: Long Filter File: SCREENER.QRY									⊟ ◻ ⊠
File View Settings Built-In Queries User Queries									
Sym...	Rel...	Curre...	[Curren...	20 Day A...	52 W...	PE... ▽	EPS R...	Net Incon	
NGPS	99.00	32.30	-2.12	506194	33.00	38.05	0.82		▲
TONS	99.00	45.72	-5.15	98070	48.20	8.28	5.74		
GBX	97.00	35.61	-3.73	107015	36.99	26.99	1.37		
PCSA	97.00	35.18	-1.87	389520	35.85	1.86	18.88		
ATLS	96.00	35.56	-1.85	52856	36.23	19.83	1.81		
CAE	96.00	40.91	-2.59	46725	42.00	20.07	2.02		
CMTL	96.00	36.80	-6.88	350518	39.52	24.51	1.51		
TOL	96.00	65.34	-2.29	1623895	66.87	13.06	5.04		
ASFI	95.00	24.70	-8.57	220283	27.02	16.12	1.57		
BZH	95.00	145.18	-2.16	607310	148.39	8.65	17.09		
ISSC	95.00	33.18	-5.41	422984	35.08	34.00	1.00		
MPX	95.00	28.24	-2.49	39555	28.96	34.00	0.83		
WCG	95.00	31.90	-8.60	208210	34.90	24.00	1.38		
CETV	94.00	39.06	-3.86	230748	40.63	30.50	1.29		
KBH	94.00	103.60	-3.00	1179930	106.80	10.28	10.27		▼
◀								▶	

FIGURE B.1   Stock Screener
Source: Charles Schwab & Co.

rank mentioned previously, but rather the most recent annual earnings per share figure.

After running a screener to filter the market down, there are often 10 to 30 stocks remaining. When markets are generally moving higher, this number will be higher. Declining overall markets normally result in fewer stocks making it through the filtering process. This makes sense since one of the primary filters is nearness to the 52-week high.

Step 2—Stock Selection

With a group of stocks in place, it is time to look at each individually. This is still a filtering process to a large degree, though. When looking through the list of stocks that made it through the initial screening, one is still thinking in terms of cutting away as many as possible. The reasons for this are twofold. First, often the list is a couple of dozen long. One is hardly going to buy them all, so it is necessary to get the list down to a more manageable size. Secondly, the author does not have a lot of time. Each stock on his list of prospects means more work analyzing, comparing, and possibly trading. In order to spend as little time as possible on the analysis, the author tries to find any excuse to knock stocks off the list. This can often be done relatively quickly over three phases.

Phase I: Check the Earnings Outlook   Start with the fundamentals. One wants to see a pattern of earnings growth recently. What's more, there should be an expectation of earnings growth going forward that is at least double-digit percentages. There are plenty of modest and slow growers out there. One wants companies that are doing better than that. This gives us the fundamental justification behind the trade. This system is not looking for companies who are losing money or whose earnings expectations are for lower levels in the future. Stock prices may not always reflect the fundamentals in the short term, but they most certainly do in the long haul. The trader's objective here is to have that in their favor when entering a position.

You will notice that the P/E ratio was included in the previous screener, but not listed among the filters. While the P/E is not a major component of the process, it does get used when one is evaluating stocks where there are possible extreme situations. The author tries not to trade those with P/Es much above 30. This does rule out many high flyers, but it is a personal preference that lets him sleep better at night. The higher the P/E, the more risk there is in the stock, should adverse earnings-related news come out.

On the flip side, though, one loves to find those stocks with outstanding earnings trading at single-digit P/Es. This particular system is not value-based, but low P/E stocks can be some of the best performers because they add a potential value play into the mix via multiple expansion, providing even more upside.

Beazer Homes (BZH) was such an example. In November 2004, BZH appeared on the screener list with a P/E of below 7 when calculated against the most recent earnings ($116 price, $17/share earnings). What's more, expectations were for an increase in annual earnings by about 20 percent for the next fiscal year. That was very exciting. If one can get a stock with great earnings and excellent growth prospects trading at a P/E south of 10, do it.

Before you start thinking that you have to find stocks trading at less than 10 times earnings, though, it must be said that is not the case. Gems like BZH will show up periodically, but most of the time you will be looking at stocks with double-digit P/Es. You can still do very well trading these stocks, especially if you identify ones with strong double-digit earnings prospects.

Phase II: Check the Price Chart   This is where technical analysis comes in. Just as one wants the fundamentals on their side, the trader also wants the technicals in their favor. The author looks for stocks breaking out to new highs, thus the filter to find only stocks near their 52-week high. The more significant the breakout, the better. That means a 2-year high is more important than a 52-week high, which is more significant than a 6-month high. The author favors the weekly charts to see how the market appear from that longer-term perspective. See Figure B.2 for an example.

Figure B.2 is a weekly chart of BZH. The horizontal line is where the author got into the stock—around the $116 mark in early November 2004. As you can see, that is just above the high from earlier in the year, and after an extended period of primarily sideways action. This is exactly the kind of chart setup sought. In general terms, the longer the market moves sideways, and the more important the high it breaks, the better the upside potential. You can see how aggressively higher BZH went following its move to new highs.

If he were looking at BZH the way Figure B.2 is set up, however, the author would be quite cautious because the market has already run 20 percent to 30 percent from its breakout point in a very sharp fashion. This is what is referred to as being extended from a base. It says one should

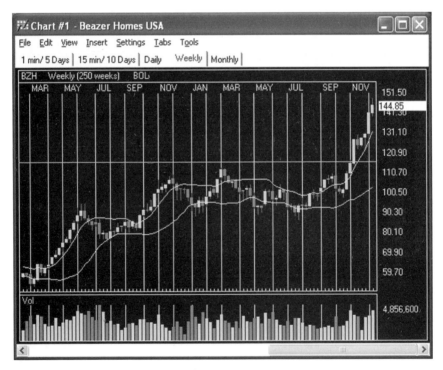

FIGURE B.2   Beazer Homes (BZH)—November 2004
Source: Charles Schwab & Co.

not be surprised if there is a period of consolidation, or perhaps a pull-back, coming soon.

By no means does an extended chart say the market has finished moving higher, though. If one has picked a good stock from a fundamental basis, and the prospects remain solid, it should eventually keep going. Having an extended chart just means possibly sitting through some choppiness. That said, however, any retracement or sideways action could very well provide a nice buying opportunity down the line.

If you look at the daily BZH chart in Figure B.3, you can see exactly the kind of setup that is referred. The stock rallied strongly up to about 131. It then spent a couple of weeks going sideways. Since nothing changed from a fundamental outlook, and the market had only moved up modestly from its longer-term breakout, the outlook remained decidedly strong.

It is exactly that sort of setup the author looks for as entries. One wants to be buying into a break to new highs following a significant consolidation. As can be seen from the chart, BZH jumped up another 15 to 20

FIGURE B.3 Beazer Homes (BZH)—December 2004
Source: Charles Schwab & Co.

points when it broke out of that range. All of this goes right back to the discussion of support and resistance in the technical analysis section of Chapter 6. Time and contact lead to significance of a resistance point.

Phase III: Do Some More Research   Checking the earnings and evaluating the charts will cut the list down more than you might think. Sometimes one is left with nothing. If so, then just walk away and look forward to going through the process again at a later time.

Should there be one or more stocks left on the list, then it's time for the last step, one that takes a bit more time and effort. At this stage there is one more important thing to do: Review the recent news headlines about the company. The goal is to evaluate what is happening with the company to see if it is generally positive or not. That means reading earnings reports and press releases. This information is readily available in many places. One of the sites the author uses is Yahoo! Finance (http://finance.yahoo.com), and his broker is another source. Most companies have web sites with investor sections that provide recent headlines and news. Regardless of the source, one is looking for positive news about the company and its business, or at least no negative developments.

With the news checked, the screening and analysis are done. If no good stocks to purchase are found, then it is just a question of coming back again in about a week, depending on how the overall market is trading. If the broad market is moving higher, then one should run through the screens and filters more frequently. When the market is in decline, or moving mostly sideways, wait longer.

If one or more stocks made it through the process, then there are some decisions to be made, depending on the situation. If the trader has plenty of funds to use, then they can probably buy several different stocks. There may, however, be a situation where one is forced to choose among different stocks. If so, this can be done by comparing the companies based on their fundamental outlook (earnings growth and prospects) and chart situations (more significant price action) as well as the news. The choice made is based on the stock that looks best overall. That done, it is time to move on to the next stage of the system.

Step 3—Trade Entry and Management

Once you have identified one or more stocks to buy, it is time to start thinking about your money management and portfolio allocations. This system tends to take a bottom-up approach, which means it does not give a ton of attention to the industries a company is in or the business the company does. If they are growing their earnings, the stock price is performing well, and everything else looks good, that's all it worries about.

That said, however, the author will normally try to avoid having multiple stocks from the same industry in his portfolio to avoid having too much exposure in one area. If a couple of stocks get through the screening process, it is a question of trying to buy the one that looks the strongest. That's just a little effort at diversification. You may decide to take a more focused look at your allocations.

What you do need to be conscious of, however, is how much of your portfolio you are putting at risk. The author's basic rule of thumb is to not risk more than 10 percent of his funds in any one position. Some people use lower numbers. That's perfectly fine. It is not recommended to go higher, though.

In determining risk, first a stop point is established. That is a price level below the current market price that, if reached, strongly indicates that the stock is not going to perform as well as expected. This trading system is based primarily on strong upward momentum. If it looks as though the momentum is fading, then one wants to be looking for other opportunities.

The main way the author selects a stop is to look at the daily chart and identify the most recent significant low. In the case of the BZH daily chart (refer back to Figure B.3), if one were buying the break to new highs in December, the low of that consolidation before the breakout is a good get-out point. That would be something in the $122 area. If the market were to go there, one could feel pretty confident that most of the upside momentum had dissipated, and that there may be no longer the really significant gains to be made in the stock in the immediate future.

Once a stop point is determined, it can be turned into a dollar value. If, in the case of BZH, one is buying at $130, with a $122 stop, that's an $8 risk per share. Determining the size of the trade put on is then just a matter of calculating 10 percent of the portfolio value, then dividing that by $8 to get a number of shares.

Of course if one is planning to buy, one must also have a plan of action to sell. There are several exit scenarios for each trade:

Stopped Out: The market fell to the predetermined stop.

Inactivity Exit: If, after eight weeks in the trade, the market just is not progressing with any purpose, exit. This can also take place further out in time when, for example, a stock rallies nicely, but then stalls out for a long time and goes nowhere. Then, too, a sell would be in order.

Divergence: Similar to the inactivity exit, one also should watch to see how the stock is doing compared to the overall market. The stocks one buys are expected to outperform. If the market is rallying and the stock is just going sideways (or even worse, moving lower), then the trader should probably dump it in favor of something better.

Negative News: Sometimes there are negative news items like earnings disappointments. If something of this sort comes out that alters the positive outlook for the stock, get out immediately. Keep in mind, however, that not all negative news is significant. Some items are just bumps in the road.

Trailing Stop: Once a stock starts moving in the right direction, start raising the stop. These new stops are determined similarly to the initial stop—a spot below the last significant low. These stops serve to both preserve profits and to get out of trades that have lost their upside impetus.

Target Reached: Sometimes one can determine a target when entering a new stock position. There are two instances when this will be the case.

1. When buying a stock that gets through the screening process, but does not really blow one's socks off. In these cases, identify a target about 20 percent above the entry point, and take at least partial profits (exit part of the position) when that price is reached, especially if the market action is lackluster.

2. When buying a low P/E stock. With these stocks one can determine a rough price point based on where the price would trade with a P/E of 10 (or the industry average P/E if that seems more appropriate). In the case of BZH, the author went into the trade looking for the market to move up into $170 ($17/share for 2004 × 10) to $200 ($20/share for 2005 × 10) based on that system. Because these are not technical points, however, do not look at these P/E based levels as absolute targets. Rather they are guidelines. The author's philosophy is to not immediately sell when they are hit, but rather to be more aggressive in setting his trailing stops.

It should be noted at this point that just because one exits a trade, this does not mean they are forever done with a particular stock. There are occasions when the system can have one in and out of a single stock multiple times. It is a function of how the stock trades. If the underlying fundamental situation remains good, and the technical picture says "buy," then do so. One cannot hold feelings toward any of the stocks traded.

So now you have it. There is the author's stock trading system. Well, that's the hard part, anyway. The next step is where thing get really fun!

PART II—GOING AFTER BIG RETURNS

Putting One's Foot on the Gas

By itself, the trading system just outlined is perfectly acceptable. With it one is quite capable of beating all of the major benchmarks fairly consistently. The author, however, just did not see that as good enough. He sought truly exceptional performance, and gets that by trading stock options. Options offer several major advantages over just trading the stocks outright:

> *Leverage:* With options one can control larger numbers of shares, which means higher profit potential. The author's experience with the system is that more than half of the stocks picked will rise at least 10 percent within a matter of a couple of weeks. This may seem like a decent gain for a stock, but it can mean a much, much bigger gain in the options.

> *Limited Downside:* One can absolutely define one's risk with options. As an option buyer, the trader knows that they can lose no more than the money put into them.

> *Increased Diversification:* Since one can control more shares with less money trading options, the trader can spread the money around better. This can mean better diversification.

There is one more very important advantage to options as well—increased trading opportunities. Trading options rather than stocks lets one have more simultaneous positions open for a given account size, even taking margin into account. This is key.

The outlined system is capable of producing buy signals for several stocks at one time, or in a short period of time. Based on the author's experience, he expects more than half of them to gain at least 10 percent in a couple of weeks. One cannot predict, however, which ones will or will not do so. This means the trader needs to trade as many of these stocks as possible to ensure the overall odds are in their favor. This is much more doable in the options market than in the stocks themselves.

So what we have is a strategy to identify stocks that are likely to move higher, a way to increase gains in any given position from double-digit to triple-digit percentage rates, and the opportunity to improve the overall expectancy of returns by allowing one to do more trades. That's a pretty good situation.

Before moving on, there is a point worth making. Remember it was said that stocks with a price in excess of $20 should be sought. Options are the reason. In many instances one is playing for moves of 10 percent to 20 percent. This is not much of a point move for a stock trading at $10. Also, many stocks that trade under $20 do not have liquid options, so we want to avoid them, anyway. Ideally, it is worth looking for stocks at $50 or better.

Selecting the Options to Buy

There are two rules the author uses for buying options with this strategy.

1. Trade only the at-the-money (ATM) options. That normally means the in-the-money strike price closest to the stock's trading price, although one can buy ATM calls that are out-of-the-money if the strike is closer to the stock price. This done for the liquidity, as ATM options tend to have the highest volume and open interest.

    We also use ATM calls because they give the best trade-off between risk and reward. Buying options that are well in-the-money is not advised because they cost more and thereby eat up trading funds while reducing profit potential. Conversely, well out-of-the-money options (so called "lottery tickets") are to be avoided because the odds of success are significantly reduced. They may be really cheap, and certainly offer huge profit potential, but it takes the market a lot to get them in-the-money, and there is no way of knowing whether that price will be reached before the option expires.

2. Buy options that have at least two months left until expiry. The decay in an option price accelerates as it gets closer to the end of its life. For that reason, one should buy calls that it is anticipated will be exited with at least four weeks left. Given that the system uses a base eight-week time frame for the trades, one should try to buy options with at least three months to go. Given that many move that 10 percent inside a month, though, two-month options are also acceptable. This is especially true of those stocks that make it through the selection process, but do not really excite.

Continuing with the BZH example from earlier, the author became a buyer when the stock was at about $116 in early November. The February 115 calls were selected, being slightly in-the-money with three months remaining to expiration.

Managing the Options Positions

Even though options afford a limited downside, one must still think in terms of risk and stops. When buying an option, the author does not go into it thinking of holding until expiry if the market goes against negative. Stops are still used in the manner discussed in the basic strategy. One does not want to be in a nonperforming option position any more than one wants to hold a stock that's going against him. The author almost always uses a 50 percent base stop on the option, but will get out if the market hits the stop on the stock regardless.

In order to establish position size, one can use that 50 percent stop out. Calculate what that is in points, then use it to determine how many options to buy within the 10 percent or lower risk parameter mentioned previously. Keep one thing in mind, however. Options do not trade as actively as the underlying stock, and prices can move very quickly. That means you cannot consider your 50 percent stop a sure thing. Be prepared for slippage, and account for that in your risk assessment.

In terms of exiting options positions, the same basic principles outlined earlier with stops, targets, and periods of relative inactivity or action contrary to the overall market are followed. There is one additional thing, though. It is sometimes worth rolling options positions up, and sometimes forward. To explain this, let us return to the BZH example.

As mentioned previously, the author bought February 115 calls in early November. The price was $9.10. By mid-November BZH had risen to about $130 and the calls were trading at $18. That is a nice gain, but more was expected from the stock, so it did not make sense to get out. At the same time, however, the author wanted to take some money off the table to reduce the total BZH exposure in his portfolio as the gain in the options made the position a larger portion of the account than desired. The author sold the 115 calls and bought the 130s, which were trading at $8.60. In doing so, he not only took nearly $9/share out of the market, he also reset his position size to even lower than it was when originally putting on the trade. When BZH hit $145 in December, the process was repeated, selling at $18 again to take another $9+/share in profits and getting into the 145 calls at $8.30. In this way the author took quite a bit of money out of the market, yet maintained the same basic risk profile and position exposure as there was at the start.

Final Words

There you have it, the author's system for trading the stock market. If it appeals to you, then explore its use in your own trading. Spend time testing it out and paper/demo trading to get comfortable with both the selection process and making the actual stock and/or options trades. Make it your own, as the author has done from the original CAN SLIM method. In fact, it would not be a bad idea to go back to the original source and start one's exploration from that point.

276

THE ESSENTIALS OF TRADING

2004 Options Trades

Table B.1 shows the actual options trades done by the author in 2004. No-tice that he actually did little trading May to July (traveling for six weeks) and August to October (busy at work).

Note: The Exit Prices listed for the last five positions are the final bid price at the close on December 31.

Notice that there was a string of losing trades at one stage. One loss was quite small. Two were very close to the 50 percent cutoff generally used. One was significantly higher. Despite the unfortunate spell, because the author maintained good risk discipline, that period did not have a ma-jor adverse impact on his portfolio. See how important good money man-agement is?

An Actual Stock Analysis and Trade Plan

As a way to help the reader better understand the trading system, following is an actual analysis done January 1, 2005. It is for a stock which made it through the screening process at the time—Hovnanian Enterprises (HOV).

Let's start with the first cut. According to the broker's screen, HOV had a relative strength of 90. This may not be exactly the same figure you

TABLE B.1 Author's 2004 Options Trades

Stock Symbol	Option	Entry Date	Entry Price	Exit Date	Exit Price	Return
LM	May '04 80C	1/7/2004	4.80	1/21/2004	10.00	108%
BD	Mar '04 40C	1/7/2004	3.00	2/2/2004	6.00	100%
AMG	Jun '04 80C	1/22/2004	5.70	2/19/2004	9.40	65%
LNC	Jul '04 45C	1/22/2004	2.10	3/3/2004	4.40	110%
CDWC	Jul '04 70C	1/22/2004	5.10	5/10/2004	0.70	−86%
LLL	Oct '04 60C	4/1/2004	4.60	5/10/2004	4.20	−9%
AET	Oct '04 90C	7/20/2004	3.80	7/27/2004	1.55	−59%
UOPX	Sep '04 95C	7/20/2004	4.70	7/28/2004	2.15	−54%
LTD	Feb '05 22.5C	10/19/2004	1.60	11/11/2004	4.00	150%
DY	Mar '04 30C	10/19/2004	4.10	11/17/2004	6.90	68%
BZH	Feb '05 115C/ 130C/145C	10/19/2004	9.10	12/27/2004	25.50	180%
LEND	Mar '04 45C	12/7/2004	5.20		6.70	29%
DVA	Apr '04 35C	12/8/2004	4.40		5.60	27%
CCRT	Apr '04 25C	12/15/2004	3.10		3.70	19%
DGX	Feb '05 95C	12/27/2004	3.00		2.75	−8%
MTLM	Apr '05 30C	12/27/2004	1.60		1.45	−9%

would find in IBD or Daily Graphs, but it is probably close enough for the purpose. As for the other filters: EPS Rank. In the case that you do not have access to IBD or Daily Graphs to get the EPS ranking, you can use the public earnings data to see the company's earnings growth. According to the broker's information screen, earnings have been rising strongly (see Figure B.4).

Nearness to a New High: HOV had just made a new high.

Current Price: HOV was trading very near $50.

Volume I: The 20-day average volume for HOV was about 75 percent higher than the 6-month average.

Volume II: HOV was trading several hundred thousand shares per day.

So now it's on to the next step—earnings growth prospects. As you can see from Figure B.4, the expectation for earnings in the next fiscal year were good. On a per share basis, they were forecast to rise in excess of 20 percent. That's just what we're after! What's more, HOV had a P/E ratio below 10. Even better!

We liked the fundamental situation. That meant we had to take a look at the technical view. Figure B.5 is a chart from Big Charts (www.bigcharts.com).

This chart covers three years of price history. Remember that the longer the time frame of the high being broken, the more significant the breakout. HOV broke its high from approximately a year back, which is the highest high recorded. That's the kind of break we like to see. It means there is no overhead resistance to hinder further price advance. The technicals were positive, too.

Having gotten good reads from both the fundamental and technical views, we were left to do some more detailed research. The stories were good. Hovnanian is in the home building sector. It's a group that had been

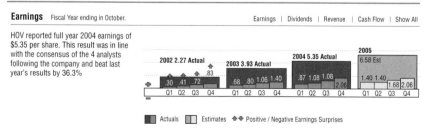

FIGURE B.4 Hovnanian (HOV) Earnings Growth
Source: Charles Schwab & Co.

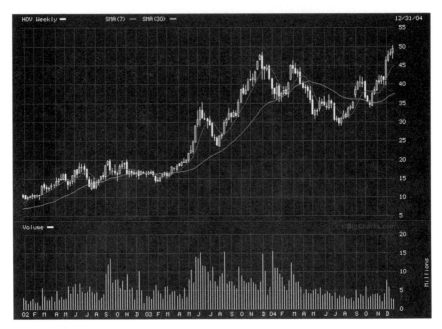

FIGURE B.5 Hovnanian (HOV) 2002–2004
Source: www.bigcharts.com.

catching a lot of heat from the investing public because of the so-called "housing bubble," which many folks believe was developing. Regardless of that, J.P. Morgan had recently initiated coverage of HOV with an "overweight" rating. Earnings reports from other home builders had been strong, and HOV not only had announced a very good fourth quarter a few weeks prior, but had upped guidance for 2005 to $6.50/share. That certainly constitutes good, positive news.

Now that the buy decision had been made, it was time to think of risk.

As mentioned previously, the author likes to use the stock chart to determine risk. By that, we mean defining an exit point (stop), done by looking to find a point at which the expectation for further upside action is proved wrong.

In the case of HOV, you will notice in Figure B.6 that the stock, after its strong runup on the $42 break (it would have been great to get into this stock at $43!), had a couple of pull-backs toward the $47 level before the move at $50.

That $47 point on the chart represents a very good exit point for stops. More specifically, we could use a point just below that, in this case $46. That's a risk of less than $4/share. We can then take that and use it to calculate the number of shares to purchase based on a 10 percent risk.

FIGURE B.6 Hovnanian (HOV) Daily, August to December 2004
Source: www.bigcharts.com.

With the purchase sorted out, and risk defined, we now need a good exit strategy. Let's go through the list:

Stopped Out: We set the stop at $46. If that gets hit, we are out.

Inactivity Exit: Eight weeks from entry is the beginning of March. If the market has not gained at least 10 percent, exit.

Divergence: Similar to the inactivity exit, we also watch to see how the stock is doing compared to the overall market.

Negative News: The next earnings announcement was not until March, so there should not be a problem there for a while, unless there is some kind of surprise release. If so, though, we would evaluate the potential impact.

Trailing Stop: Once a stock starts moving in the right direction, we will raise the stop using chart points as done with the original stop.

Target Reached: Since HOV was a low P/E stock, we could make a rough earnings-based target. Management expected earnings in the next fiscal year at $6.50. The industry average P/E is 10 to 11. For simplicity we will stick with 10. That projects out to a stock price of $65. Of course, this is a rough estimate. We would not use that as a hard exit, but rather a point to possibly start getting a bit more cautious about the position.

So there it is. We would buy HOV to start 2005, with a stop of $46 and a rough initial target estimate of $65.

But wait! The real money's in the options. That's where we want to be.

The basic rule is to make sure to buy an option with at least two months left until expiration, and preferably three for a trade expected to go at least eight weeks. In HOV, there are January and February options, but the next one isn't until May. February is too short (only about six weeks), so we have to go out to May.

The other basic rule is to trade the at-the-money options. In the case of HOV, that means the calls options with the $50 strike. Remember, we do not want to trade the cheap well out-of-the-money options (lottery tickets), and we do not want to tie up huge chunks of trading capital by buying well in-the-money options.

As you can see in Figure B.7, the May 50 calls finished up on 12/31/2004 at 4.70 bid—4.90 offered. That means it would probably cost close to $500 per contract to buy them.

Recall that we use a 50 percent cutoff for options trades. This is in ad-

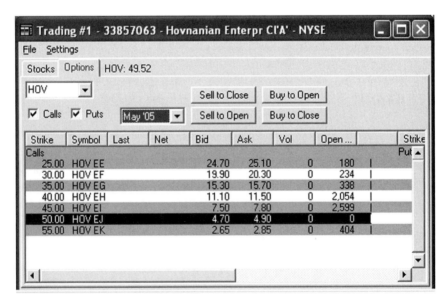

FIGURE B.7 May HOV Calls
Source: Charles Schwab & Co.

dition to the exit strategy previously discussed. In most cases, if an ATM option falls 50 percent, the stock is not going to perform as expected.

Before finishing, it is worth discussing a possible strategy adjustment. It was mentioned before that most of the stocks selected through this strategy will rise 10 percent or more within a couple of weeks. The strategy to take advantage of that is to use short-term options and exit when the stock makes that gain. For HOV, we could buy February 50 calls for about $270 per contract. This is not to say that in this particular case the best option would be to go with the 10 percent strategy, especially since HOV is a low P/E stock, but it is a possible path one could take. The February options should be sufficiently long to serve the purpose (See Figure B.8). In the 10 percent strategy, one is looking for a relatively quick move, especially when trading shorter duration options. It means being quicker to exit a trade. Instead of waiting eight weeks, one would probably look to get out in two to three if things are not moving as anticipated.

HOV Result

The initial purchase of HOV, as just outlined, actually resulted in a loss when the stop of 45 was hit shortly after entering the trade. As can be the case with this system, however, there were other buy signals (breaks to new highs) later in the year that would have proved quite profitable.

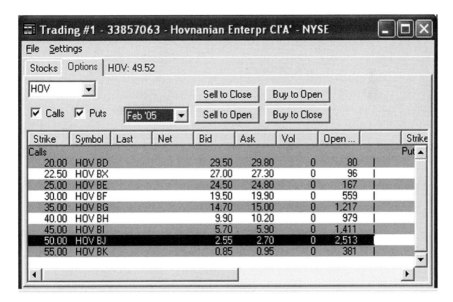

FIGURE B.8 February HOV Calls
Source: Charles Schwab & Co.

Index